True Tales
of College Golf

Meet Me at the Chain

To: Joyce   *12-19-05*

By

Frank E. Landrey

For ALL You DID
To MAKE THIS
BOOK BETTER !
"Thanks"

Foreword by Dr. Jerry Falwell

Frank Landrey
"Coach"

True Tales
of College Golf

Meet Me at the Chain

ISBN 1890306894

Library of Congress Control Number 2005936246

UNLESS OTHERWISE NOTED, SCRIPTURE QUOTATIONS ARE FROM THE KING JAMES VERSION TRANSLATED OUT OF THE ORIGINAL TONGUES AND WITH PREVIOUS TRANSLATIONS DILIGENTLY COMPARED

Disclaimers: Information provided is intended as a broad general overview of college golf, my own experiences, and personal opinions that are not a guarantee for results.

Cover design by: Prototype Advertising.

Warwick House Publishers
720 Court Street
Lynchburg, VA 24504

DEDICATION

I dedicate this book: First, to the Lord, who led me into the exciting position of Liberty Golf Coach, then to my wife Carol for her belief that I could do it and lived it with me.

I dedicate it to my father and older brother, who taught me the game of golf and to Dr. Jerry Falwell, my friend and pastor. God used his Christian schools to bring us here.

I dedicate the book to high school coaches who serve others with very little thanks or pay and to college coaches who "chase the dream," an NCAA Championship. May this book encourage them to press on!

Special Dedication to the "Gift Givers"...

To the 50+ percent of the people who buy books to give as gifts, may I say, "Please, Give them the Gift of Golf this year *True Tales of College Golf* to be more specific.

Why should "Givers Give" *True Tales of College Golf?* Because it has been written to uplift, and most who read it will eagerly apply its suggestions and life-changing ideas.

Special $2.00 Dedication of Book Royalties...

One dollar of book royalties will help Liberty's golf team have a freestanding, self-contained practice range. Fifty cents will go to the Fellowship of Christian Athletes and fifty cents to College Golf Fellowship. These funds will come from after expense profits and out of the first year's sales.

Division I - Mid-Atlantic Region

Newsletter

Vol. 3 No. 6   The George Washington University ♦ 600 22nd St. NW ♦ Washington, DC   June 2003

PLAYER OF THE MONTH

The toughest part of selecting a player of the month is that we have players playing a wide range of events who don't get head-to-heads against each other while others see each other every week. This week is a perfect example. We have one player with 3 wins in the month of April, but doesn't have a lot of head to heads with the top 100. We also have teammates that both played great golf.. So I am going to cop out this month and name tri-Players of the Month. If you don't like it, blame the other Scott Allen at Seton Hall (see bottom of page).

There were several other noteworthy performances this month including Tim Kane who won the Wofford Invitational and was 5th at the Rutherford, Chad Perman (Penn) who won at Towson and finished 5th at The Ivy's and Jay Lindell (SBU) who was 4th at the Rutherford and 5th at A-10s.

However the first of our Player's of the Month is Eric Couture from St. Francis who won three events in April. The Robert Morris-Duquesne and Canisius Invites (both with 149) and the Northeast Conference with 67-68.

Not to be outdone, teammates Billy Hurley and Brian Crum from Navy were quite the 1-2 punch. Crum won at Navy with 139, won again at the Patriot League with 212 and shot 146 to finish 2nd at the Rehoboth Beach Invit., where he tied teammate Hurley who was 2nd at both Navy and the Patriot League with 140 and 215, respectively. To cap it all off, the two tied for 27th at the West Regional with 220.

THE RANKINGS ARE IN

The Mid-Atlantic Regional Advisory Committee has come up with it's final ranking of the spring. As it's been all year, things were very close again and we had some tough calls to make to break ties, but we hope we've done our best.

1) Penn State
2) University of Maryland
3) James Madison
4) Liberty University
5) Georgetown University
6) Princeton University
7) University of Richmond
8) William & Mary
9) US Naval Academy
10) Towson University
11) Rutgers University
12) St. John's University
13) George Mason University
14) University of Pennsylvania
15) Temple University
     Saint Joseph's University
     George Washington University
18) Iona College
19) Lehigh University
20) Seton Hall University
21) St. Bonaventure University
22) American University
23) Loyola College
24) Villanova University
25) Colgate University

ALL-REGION HONORS

Each year your MAR Committee is responsible for selecting the 15-person All-Region team. Those players will also be considered for All-American status. Below are those players as well as several other MAR award winners.

Player of the Year
Jim Fuller - Penn State

All Region Team
Nick Cook - Georgetown
Brian Crum - Navy
James Farrah - Georgetown
Jim Fuller - Penn St.
Billy Hurley - Navy
Tim Kane - Maryland
Mark Leon - Penn State
Jay Lindell - St. Bonaventure
Craig Mason - George Mason
John Moheyer - Maryland
Chad Perman - Penn
Craig Pieczynski - Penn St.
Andrew Svoboda - St. John's
Billy Wingerd - Towson
Jay Woodson - James Madison

Coach of the Year
Frank Landrey   Liberty University

All American Scholar

Brian Crum	Navy
Billy Hurley	Navy
Mark Le Veck	Iona
Chad Perman	Penn
Andrew Svoboda	St. John's
Jeff Tracy	St. Bonaventure
Cassidy Traub	Princeton
Justin Van Hyning	Seton Hall

CONTENTS

FOREWORD

Frank Landrey is a great man, a wonderful husband and an incredible coach. His new book, *True Tales of College Golf* will thrill your soul, bless your heart and challenge your mind. Frank weaves a delightful tale of real life experiences that teach life-changing lessons. He sees the principles that can make a difference in our lives and applies them to everyday situations on the golf course to help us all live life to the fullest. Each story unlocks a truth that can change your life. Don't miss this exciting, humorous and helpful look at life from the tee to the green.

Dr. Jerry Falwell
Founder and Chancellor
Liberty University, Lynchburg, Virginia

What Others Say About the Author and Book

"A great read for golfers of all ages, its many humorous, human interest stories will catch the eye of all. This book would certainly be a wonderful gift, especially to a junior age golfer." —*John C. Maxwell, NYT best selling author of* The 21 Irrefutable Laws of Leadership *and Founder of INJOY Stewardship Services and EQUIP*

"Congratulations on the great season. You deserve the reward for your efforts!! Best wishes with the book. I still owe you one for enlisting God's help to beat us in 1993 at Hawthorne Valley. Or, was that just great coaching?" —*Your friend, Coach Bud Hall, UNC Greensboro*

"Having known Frank as a member of the Golf Coaches Association of America and as a Christian brother, it was special to be able to compete against his team at the NCAA Regional.

His passion for collegiate golf and a Christian walk were always vitally and positively evident." —*John A. Affleck, Golf Coach and Professor, Binghamton University*

"Frank Landrey inspired and challenged my son and his teammates not just to excel in golf but to excel as a Bible believing Christian after golf. I am deeply grateful for his impact on my son and thankful for Liberty University who made it possible." —*Mark Humrichouser, Todd's Dad*

"Frank Landrey is one of a very few men I know who never got over being saved. He truly has had a vision for lost souls." —*Pastor Daniel L. DeHass, Community Bible Church*

"Frank is a dear friend who I owe my deepest gratitude for him showing me his personal relationship with the Lord: God Bless." —*Jon H. Leonard, Sr., PGA Professional*

"We enjoyed hosting you and your fine team for the 2003 NCAA East Regional. Good luck to your future teams." —*Mike Griffin, Men's Golf Coach, Auburn University*

"It was great to have a fellow believer as coach and friend and as someone who could be relied upon for advice and counsel. As Frank conveys in his writings, it is not always an easy job trying to be Coach, Mentor, and Role Model to these young "Men." —*E. Murray Rudisill, Old Dominion*

"Frank Landrey's *True Tales of College Golf* is more than worth your time. How should believers actually apply convictions, day in and day out? Frank shares his own answer to this most practical question with warmth and humor, while he shares how, as a college coach, he honored his Biblical convictions, sacrificially investing in several generations of player/students." —*Ronald S. Godwin Ph.D., Dean of the Helms School of Government, Liberty University*

"Frank was the most competitive person I had ever met; he would do anything to win. When he found the Lord he still carried that desire to win, but wanted the Lord's blessing. I hope your junior golfer learns from the lessons Frank shares." —*Thomas J. Meeks, USGA Staff Retired*

ACKNOWLEDGMENTS

For their assistance, I would like to acknowledge the following people: Joyce Maddox's editing of the book, Jane Kreger plus Jim Whitaker for valuable publishing advice, Josh Oppenheimer and Isaac Harrell for their part in the front and back cover as well as Bryan Beman for his many Liberty Print Shop "rough drafts" and his help in the process.

I extend thanks to James Shaner, John Hunton, and Ken Linthicum for their "persistent" prayers and editing suggestions. More thanks go to the Liberty Flames Booster Club members who listened to my many sad stories and added their support to Liberty golf.

I acknowledge Mark Humrichouser who encouraged me and supported the program in a special way with his prayers, time, and money during the last five years of my career. To him and the many other helpful parents, I am grateful.

Finally, I need to thank all of my golfers who allowed me to hang out with them. Guys, it was a blast. All the best!

Special Acknowledgment...

"You will find places in *True Tales of College Golf* where God intervened not only in my life but in the lives of my players. While unexplainable at the time, often looking back, after a faithful, persistent journey, a seeker sees how God did intervene for the better. I certainly believe He did."

—Frank E. Landrey, Liberty Golf Coach, 1992-2004

INTRODUCTION

Golfers walked up a narrow paved path behind their dorms. It led to a chain that hung between two posts across the maintenance road. The night before leaving for golf trips, Coach Landrey said five words.

NOW HE SAYS THEM TO YOU!

MEET ME AT THE CHAIN

Coach Landrey details twelve years of experiences at Liberty University under the leadership of Dr. Jerry Falwell. His many personal experiences with Dr. Falwell, Chancellor of the fastest growing Christian university in the world, are found throughout. In Chapter One Coach Landrey describes the ever-expanding Liberty campus in vivid detail as he suggests other possible sites for an upcoming announcement.

True tales start on Liberty Mountain at a unique location where a long awaited announcement will soon come. The last chapter describes the team's "dream trip." Sandwiched between the first and last chapters, Frank relates different experiences with Divine Intervention. Divine Intervention becomes a negative factor in the 2003 Big South Championship but is "all good" when Liberty makes it to the "Big Dance," which is the East Regional.

Learn how Frank became a Division-1 golf coach at a Christian university. Landrey's acceptance of this position involves him in a special ministry and embarks him on an athletic mission "to chase a dream."

He describes the many pranks played on him by his players. Right from the first golf trip he is heard to say, "That is going in the book." But it is not just about golf. In fact, it has been said that Frank made a hole-in-one for everyone on your gift list with his many real-life stories like: the discouraged player who makes a successful comeback after a "heart to heart" talk with Coach Landrey, another player finds success when he is emboldened with confidence, a mother shares her way to deal with a son's anger problem, and a father shares his son's fight for life and how an encounter with Liberty players years before helped him. Frank does not just tell stories. In fact, at the end of most chapters he shares thoughts that he hopes will help you.

Meet strangers along the way. One is holding a sign "work for food" alongside a California roadway. Learn how he finds eternal life. A family is stranded on a winding road in the dark. They need just what Coach Landrey has with him. A Virginia highway 29 "road warrior" and two beggars at Atlanta's famous *Varsity* get much more than just a handout.

Relive real life dramas like: a United Airlines flight to Chicago when Coach Landrey thinks he is going to die. You will laugh a lot during this tense situation with "spontaneous comedy" coming when you least expect it. Enjoy romance when two Liberty students get back together by way of a prayer at thirty-thousand feet and how another player finds his Tear Drop Tour caddie at Liberty.

A serious side of the book comes when an intimidated Coach Landrey speaks out in behalf of his peers. After several years of lobbying for his cause, a change allows 284 teams an opportunity to enter college golf's NCAA Regional as their Conference Champion. Frank's dream did come true.

Find out how the team came to adopt "SITTAWAGA" as their motivational 2003 spring push "rally word" and when it became known as the "SITTAWAGA" S-i-z-z-l-e. The book concludes with a happy ending and Liberty's first NCAA trip shared in vivid detail. It is like you make the trip yourself.

CHAPTER ONE

NCAA 2003 Announcement

The day broke with a half-risen sun outside. Excitement filled our home. My determination to remind the nineteen team members and assistant coach about the place and time prompted me to make a flurry of early morning phone calls and E-mails. A special event in the lives of Liberty golfers would soon take place on the school's campus. Later that day, the NCAA National Golf Committee's announcement of schools invited to the 2003 NCAA National Finals, Regional Site, in Auburn, Alabama, would buzz along the country's phone lines. Twenty-seven teams and their coaches would have rooms set up like ours. I watched my guys as they filed into the office of Mr. Kim Graham, Liberty's Director of Athletics during this time.

Liberty's "happy go lucky" athletes had a different demeanor today. These "fun loving" guys were very quiet and reserved, coming in and sitting down almost in slow motion strides. Their eyes moved cautiously around the room to see if anyone had been left out. Each had come to share in every college golfer's dream, which was to be on an NCAA Regional team. It would culminate in grand excitement or be just another depressing disappointment in the life of a student athlete. I felt better about our chances when Sam Nelson and Albie Powers assured me they and others were praying. With the team praying, what more could I ask?

My thoughts drifted in and out of the present. I let my mind go back. *If only the guys from my other teams could be here today.* Past players had all been told "Coach's Dream." Often I felt we had the right team but wrong D-1 region. After making a long overdue move in the fall of 1998, we began competing against teams having similar weather patterns and budget sizes. During the first years in our new home, the Mid Atlantic Region, we came close to being an East Regional participant. Maybe this time it had happened. All here would hear the magical moment at the NCAA Press Conference "live" as it happened.

Todd Wetmore and Joey Mullins hooked up a loudspeaker. This pause is what Frank Peretti calls a "speed bump." Mr. Peretti might call the first chapter a speed bump because it is a bit slow reading, but I must mention others who made this day possible like: Sarah Baker, Bradley Damron, Chris Doyle, Theresa Dunbar, Terry Falwell, Fay Edwards, Mickey Guridy, Bill Gribbin, Renee Grooms, Jamie Hall, Mark Hind, Meredith Hollyfield, Larry Hubbard, Doug Lowe, Heather Mitchell, Mike Montoro, Joe Padron, Terry Rogers, Buck Romero, Kathy Rusk, Les Schofer, Brian and Kris Sennett, Bill Wegert, and Paul Wetmore. This was my dedicated and talented silent army. Waiting for a big moment is difficult. This was no different, and soon thoughts came to me about how this announcement could have happened at other bigger and better locations. *Hum... Liberty golf deserves a higher profile here on the campus.*

Why Not Have My Team At The Ericsson Site?

To the left of Hancock, just north of the outdoor track, soccer, football stadium, and massive new 54,000 sq. ft. LaHaye Ice Hockey Center, is the newly purchased Ericsson complex. This 800,000 sq. ft. facility was secured by an amazing $10,000,100.00 auction bid offer from Liberty's Chancellor, Dr. Jerry Falwell. It won by the 100 dollars.

This building is the newest campus improvement to attract more students. Jerry Falwell Jr. continues to lay out the campus master plan to be approved by Dr. Falwell and the Board of Directors. Dr. Ron Godwin keeps things moving. Together, they have worked miracle after miracle.

During my twenty-five years of being associated with Liberty, as a parent, a student myself, and finally as a coach, I've seen these three men combine efforts to transform a rugged rock and tree covered mountain into a World Class College Campus. In addition to a much needed Law School, the Ericsson building houses the Tim LaHaye Student Center, which includes an Olympic-size swimming pool of 25 meters, the indoor Tolsma Track of 200 meters, five regulation size gymnasiums, a cardio room with over fifty aerobic machines, satellite television sets placed above for exerciser viewing, a weight room with over 100 strength machines plus free weights, a huge snack bar with lounge area, and a social activity room. Liberty Christian Academy and the church Dr. Falwell founded are going here too.

Many thanks go to Hobby Lobby's owner who had the vision of their purchase of Ericsson and subsequent generous donation of it to Liberty in exchange for one dollar. Drs. Tim and Beverly LaHaye provided for renovations, which include the LaHaye Student Center, indoor track, and soon to arrive LaHaye Ice Hockey Arena. Liberty has truly entered the "Mega Campus" list with this state-of-the-art fitness and student activities center becoming a major hub of the mammoth North Campus. This would certainly be a great site for an NCAA golf announcement.

Why Not Announce At Remodeled DeMoss?

To the right of Hancock and about four residence dorms away sits Liberty's newly finished 580,000 sq. ft. classroom complex, *the DeMoss Learning Center.* This once one-story-building is now four stories tall and adorned in the front by eighteen beautiful, white pillars. They tower above twenty-five majestic white steps. With a Jeffersonian architectural design, the gem is home to Dr. Falwell's library museum and has an "Old South" theme inside and out. Named after Arthur DeMoss in honor of the family's gracious giving to the school, it is the campus centerpiece. This building's "magical makeover" made me think of my Alma Mater, Georgia Tech, which still has many of the old buildings but with new, modern face lifts. I could see all nineteen of my players in large, white, "Lazy Boy" lounge chairs. They had replaced oversized rocking chairs. Hundreds of Liberty students and Flames Club members were there. Even so, something was missing at this location.

Why Not Have The Announcement In The Vines?

Just to the west and a wedge shot away from the DeMoss building sits Liberty's domed basketball arena. This was my first choice for our announcement site. Every time while attending a game, I had thought how much it looks like what I played my college basketball games in at Georgia Tech. With a 10,000 seat capacity, colorful chairbacks go from the floor up where Liberty plays out the night's drama. Women's and men's basketball have combined to thrill area fans with Conference Championships and NCAA trips here.

Built in loving memory of Minnie and Odie Vines, many important announcements have originated inside this campus favorite. I could not help but think of the valuable use of the four huge overhead 20'x 30' image magnification screens, located at each of four corners in the arena, to show my guys' expressions and the crowd's cheers as Liberty's name is called off for the first time as an NCAA golf berth recipient. Ours would not be a Vines Center extravaganza.

4

Meanwhile back inside the Hancock building, we had no local press conference planned. There was no I-Mag screen showing the unfolding drama. No crowd or fan club would congregate here today. No one really knew we were in the building. Nevertheless, history was about to be made.

A Family Setting, A Fitting Finish…

The Hancock Athletic Center has an unassuming appearance. Function and "frugality" are written all over it. Still, the Hancock structure does have a soft, silent beauty in its red-brick exterior and plain, practical architecture. From the Hancock's steps, in the rather large front door's foyer, a person looks out through high, arching, glass doors, with perfect views of new, three-story student apartment housing units that dot the mountainside. On the East Campus of Liberty Mountain's 4,400 acres, there are over twenty new buildings with many more planned, along with the many student athletic and intramural fields. Situated on a knoll and dedicated February 12, 1986, the Hancock Athletic Center honors and glorifies Jesus Christ.

A plaque at the top of the foyer's stairs says "Thanks" to S. and W. Hancock. Their lives of discipline and excellence, as well as for providing a wonderful Christian home, continue to matter with this gift. Located at the top of the stairs, leading into the front of the complex, the plaque reminds all what really counts in life. At the bottom of the plaque Scripture says, *"Let your light so shine before men, that they may see your good works, and glorify your Father which is in Heaven"* (Matthew 5:16). The top floor is judiciously designed with offices and athletic staffs in mind. The bottom floor has a state of the art workout facility. Both floors make the Hancock Athletic Center appropriately named. It eagerly awaits student athletes and their coaches to build more "Champions for Christ."

The fact that the Hancock building housed the golf program's office as a Club Sport in 1984 and became an official

Liberty athletic sport in 1985 made this building appropriate for our announcement site. Thanks to Mike Hall's solo efforts as the golf program's founder, I now was about to realize my dream for the program. It, too, was going to occur here if in fact we did get our NCAA berth.

I looked out the Athletic Director's office window located at the south end. There in front of me and across the parking lot stood the little white chapel. A tall steeple adorned by a cross reminds every student of the "heart beat" of Liberty's campus. Many times I had used its front steps and grassy area for our media guide's team picture. We had also used the chapel for team prayer time. My family's name is inside on a brick alongside hundreds of other bricks and names of those who have given during one of Dr. Falwell's many fundraising campaigns. Just to the right of the chapel is the home office of WRVL. It sends music and preaching out in a 100-mile radius. WRVL is home to the "Voice of the Flames," Jerry Edwards. Now, in his twenty-fourth year, he still announces all of the men's basketball and football play by play action. Jerry is also a familiar wake-up voice for listeners every morning. Just to the left of the chapel, I noticed the chain hanging from two poles, situated at each side of the narrow, paved path that winds down and behind a row of dorms. In my mind's eye I could see my five players trudging up the hill with bags in hand. At the end of that chain I could see me. I was waiting for them beside the ever-changing mode of travel. The majority of my guys lived in those four dorms. We always met at that very chain to leave for our golf trips. One-hundred-and-fifty-five adventure trips began not more than 100 yards away from where I was standing.

The Perfect Place…

It was only natural that I would consider having our meeting at the newly renovated DeMoss building or at the majestic Vines Coliseum or possibly on the recently acquired massive Ericsson properties. Any one of the three would certainly have been a fitting place for a media gathering to recognize and honor my guys. One conclusion rang out in my mind. *The Hancock building is the perfect place for our announcement and those here are the right ones to hear it.*

The Perfect Announcement...

Finally, the time came. The toll-free number had been called at the precise time that we were told to make it. An operator requested that our previously assigned code number be given. Hooked into the system, finally the time had come. In a clear and resonate voice, the NCAA Golf Committee member began.

"Now, what all of you have been waiting for, the twenty-seven schools invited to the East Regional.
Site: University Club at Yarbrough Farms Golf Course
Host: Auburn University located in Auburn, Alabama
Dates: May 15-17, 2003."

Names of the year's college golf elite began to float out of the phone box: "Clemson, Augusta State, Wake Forest, Florida, Auburn, Georgia Tech, Tennessee, South Carolina, College of Charleston, and Vanderbilt..." I looked around the room, seeing heads down in hands, which were held high, with elbows down on top of the huge mahogany conference table. Other heads, while resting directly on the surface, had hands folded on top. It all made for a curious sight. Our team captain, Nick Heyland, had his hands clasped together, obviously praying. Of course, we wanted God to move on the hearts of those making this huge decision. In this case, it seemed right to ask that we be given the season-earned berth. I knew that Liberty had the majority of wins needed and had beaten all other teams by more strokes, except the top three teams. But, there were others who hoped that somehow their team would go instead of ours, like Georgetown's Tommy Hunter and Princeton's Will Green. Both were ranked just behind us in our Mid Atlantic Region. I had heard that Georgetown, being ranked higher nationally than Liberty, might get the committee's nod instead of us, even though we had them by twenty-one strokes in our four encounters with a split of two wins each.

The eleventh, twelfth, through to the twenty-first were read off. To my dismay, Liberty's name was not called. *Could it be that we might somehow be passed over? What if the National Golf Committee overruled our Region's Advisory Committee and replaced us with Georgetown or the sixth ranked team, Princeton?* My mind raced ahead farther and faster. I knew that six school's names were turned in to the National Golf Committee, having been a past Chair of our Region's Advisory Committee. National picks four from the six to represent the Mid Atlantic Region. Those teams could be any four, in any sequence, from the list of six. I muttered out loud so the guys could hear me, "In past years, the top four ranked teams have always been confirmed and accepted by the National Golf Committee."

Then, a sick feeling came over me. I realized that it could actually be yet another Mid Atlantic Region team not on the list of six, remembering that in 1999 the Mid Atlantic Region's four picks did get changed when my long-time "hot" rival, Coach Nat Withers and his Richmond Spiders, jumped from obscurity into the list of four and made their first trip. Could something like this happen, eliminating us?

Over the loud speaker, the selection committee's final picks rang out: "The twenty-second team, twenty-third, twenty-fourth, and twenty-fifth." Finally the announcer said, *"And, the twenty-sixth school invited is Liberty University."*

Liberty Golf had taken the road to the top of this mountain in utter obscurity. Soon newspapers and television sportscasters would report it had happened, but none reported that it might happen. I had kept its possibility somewhat quiet because of my fears that we would somehow be overlooked by the national committee. Enjoying the fruits of our labor in this family setting and in near obscurity seemed like the appropriate thing to me. Besides, I pondered, *If Liberty's name had not been called, I wanted obscurity.*

Rejoicing Floods Our Hearts...

Shouts rang out with rushing echoes "of ecstatic joy" flowing from Mr. Graham's office through to his secretary, Kris Sennett's smaller office, and down the narrow hallway in both directions. The golfers sent forth reactionary sounds. They were both spontaneous and loud. A small, insignificant group of guys, in the scheme of college sports, had their collegiate dream come true and they reacted in a sense of utter fulfillment. Players leaped to their feet with hoots and hollers. They reached over tables and chairs to hug each other. With vibrant handshakes and high fives, the joyous occasion was celebrated with unbridled enthusiasm. Greatly elated myself at the outcome, I managed to hold my distance from the guys. This would become their magic moment to remember. They would think about this day over and over in the coming years. It would not become the defining moment in their life, but it would stand tall as a fond memory. It did not matter which five players would go on to participate in the East Regional. All nineteen players on the 2002-2003 Roster had had a part in this Liberty team sport record-breaking achievement. It was everyone's win. One of my "Big" dreams had come true. "Thank You, Lord."

Looking around the room and seeing most team members with tears in their eyes, I felt that my time had come for the same. Coaches are supposed to be tough and hardhearted. I tried to hold up the image. But, I am who I am. It took eleven years of coaching, many hours of planning, and more persistence than I thought possible for this to hatch. We had come very close, even to the door, in previous years. This would become a first for Liberty University sports. Golf's award of a season-earned invitation to an NCAA national event had never happened before in our school's Division-1 history. Golf would forever be part of Liberty's athletic history. Being honored with "Region Coach of the Year" capped a memorable season with blessings galore!

Those Who Rejoice With You Are Special...

As soon as it became official, I received congratulatory phone calls from Coach John Crooks of Campbell University, Coach Paul Gooden of James Madison University and from Elon's Coach, Bill Morningstar. They all expressed excitement for us, proving once again that they are truly interested in the sport wanting college student athletes to experience the excitement of NCAA competition.

Having been blessed by them, I determined in my heart to try to congratulate other golf coaches who make their first trip, even if they go instead of my guys. This time, however, I felt that we were going for all D-1 coaches who had never gotten to experience this trip for themselves. In some mysterious way, it has happened, having written this book about the year that produced our magical come-from-behind season, which earned us an NCAA Regional trip. May others follow us! Only time will tell if one coach's dream come true being told in a book could encourage other coaches and team members to hold onto their dreams of reaching an NCAA Regional. My prayer is that it will change lives for the better spiritually but having someone reach a golf goal along the way would be nice. SITTAWAGA, to all of you who are listening! Maybe my ears will hear your team's SITTAWAGA yell. Tell your NCAA true tale for all to hear.

Seven Things I Found Out About My Calling To Coach…

1) Others can see each of us doing something special.

2) Others will offer us "servitude" suggestions.

3) It is important to get good counsel on a decision.

4) A spouse and or friends know you best.

5) A spouse should be on board with a career move.

6) Prayer is important in any change.

7) If God is in it, you will last longer.

CHAPTER TWO

Once Upon A Time

I suppose an explanation is in order here. The process needs to be shared as to how an NCAA golf trip became possible. Let me begin by explaining how it came to be that I was hired as Liberty's Head Men's Golf Coach.

One peaceful December night in 1991, I had settled down. This is not a Christmas story. But, I did get a lot of unexpected packages. It all started on an evening with my favorite team and sport. Carol could not make it this particular night, although she was a staunch fan, too. With her staying home, busy with something the girls had going, I sat alone in my well-padded stadium seat. Tranquil and "at peace with the world," I was. Watching Liberty compete against a Big South Conference rival had given me something to cheer about. Basketball, my favorite sport in high school and college, usually gives me an adrenalin surge.

My Life, Finally Coming Together...

I had been busy during the first ten years in Lynchburg. The first person I met in our newly adopted community was an aspiring young preacher. He soon wanted me to set up revival meetings. Dan DeHass had formed DeHass Ministries and asked me to help him get it off the ground. We planned a Revival Campaign across America.

Soon I was selling my family's barbecue to food distributors by day and doing congregational soul winning workshops using "live" telephone evangelism calls from church pulpits at night, following Dan's preaching. When people said their own salvation prayer over the loud speaker, unbridled spontaneous cheers rang out. We had great success together. However, Dan and I went our separate ways in our own "over the road" ministries, him driving and me flying. God had blessed, but I needed to cover more territory quicker. I shared Christian testimonials, continued Gospel church telephone evangelism, and sold barbecue as a means of financial support.

Within a few short years, time had become a valued commodity. My life had gotten too complicated, having gone back to school for two Master of Arts degrees and taking several overseas missionary trips. I had picked up another goal, after turning fifty, trying to make the PGA Senior Tour. Monday Qualifiers plus Senior Tour Qualifying Schools had also taken a toll on my time. After a closing thesis on the subject of "Stress" for a Master's Degree, I gave seminars, too. As you can see, I had become a busy boy during the first ten years after our move to Lynchburg. Carol had endured a lot. She and I had had more than one "heart to heart" on why a man and woman get married.

Finally, my life had changed. I had committed myself to more home time with my dear wife and family. Carol and I had both agreed that the time had come for me to settle into a more reasonable schedule. With reorganizing the family business in 1977 and fighting banknote deadlines for years due to business failures and financial struggles, I had just made the most money ever for any one year in business. Yes, 1991 had been a great year. I had settled down, letting life catch up with me for a change. This night I had taken time to relax at one of my favorite pastimes, a basketball game. Little did I know that my life would soon change!

Enter Mike Hall, A Stranger of Sorts…

Then a very unusual thing happened. Mike Hall came and sat down beside me. We had only talked once before. After a few casual verbal exchanges about the basketball game, he began to talk about his Liberty University golf team. He told me a little about how golf started at Liberty. Mike explained that he had served eight years in his present position. "Frank, I wear several other hats like academic advisor and assistant director for athletics." With a slight smile he went on, "We now have several young children in our family and I want to be home more. My responsibilities at Liberty and home are such that I feel it's the right time to leave coaching." I had only played golf with him on one occasion during my ten years in town. However, I knew we both liked Dr. Falwell. Mike knew I agreed with Liberty's philosophy and ideals.

All of a sudden, Coach Mike Hall dropped a bombshell. "Frank, God has laid your name on my heart to be the next Liberty University golf coach." My first thought seemed harmless. *It is a huge honor to be considered for the position. Being involved with competition does have an appeal to me.* My second thought was much more serious. *I would not be able to take golf coaching on unless I stopped traveling for the family business. I have way too much to do. Covering thirty states, selling barbecue and preaching, plus stress seminars, I have very little time to spare.* I laughed under my breath when he told me about the small amount of income paid to coach golf at Liberty. I don't know how you describe that kind of laughter, but we have all done it.

I explained that I could not leave my present job. Looking at him, I began thinking. *With us finally making serious money and almost out of debt after fifteen years of financial struggles, why accept a setback? Besides, is this guy serious? Who would take this job, especially considering the little amount of income earned for doing it?*

When Coach Hall explained his ideas for the program and a bit more about the year's activity, I soon became overwhelmed. I began my mental rebuttal. *Who would want to take a team to four or five tournaments in the fall and seven or eight in the spring, plus hold practice and qualifying, all for $3,000.00 a year?* I believe it was half time in the basketball game when Coach Hall asked, "Well, Frank, what do you think so far?" I looked at him and shrugged my shoulders, as if I needed more information. To tell you the truth, I was a bit horrified to find out more.

I could not believe what I was hearing. Coach Hall then told me that I would need to think of it as a ministry. He had answered my question before I could ask. That bothered me, too. How did he know? I asked, "Is there much paperwork to this job?" Before he could answer, I went on, "I have never been one for homework." He said, "No. Not much at all." Then I asked a big question, "How much time does it take?" Mike answered, "There is not really a lot of time involved." Finally, he had said all he could think of and I had heard all I needed to know. I looked at him with a glassy stare, "Mike, I just don't think I want your job at this time in my life." I explained that my wife and I had decided recently that it would be good for me to spend more time at home. "Besides, I have had no real experience in coaching." *Maybe this fact would discourage him.* I continued, "How would I begin to learn it all?" Mike, getting up to leave, said, "Go with me this spring on a few of our golf trips. You will learn a lot. But, if you don't want the offer, Frank, I'll ask someone else. Please, go home and ask your wife what she thinks. Pray about it and let me know in a couple of days." As he walked away, Mike turned back, "It is yours if you can work it out."

Eight years after my 1991 meeting with Coach Hall, I asked him about the three statements made to me that night in the Vines Center. I listed them.

(1) God put your name on my heart…

(2) Not much paperwork to it…

(3) Not much time involved…

Now several years later and his hair graying at the temples, Mike looked at me with his eyes wide open. Astounded, he said, "I cannot remember any of your questions or any of my answers." *Hum… Maybe I heard wrong or had Mike truly forgotten our conversation that changed my life forever.*

Women, Who Can Know Them?

I remember thinking several things on the way home. *What is the best way for me to turn down this offer? Actually, it does not need to be my decision.* Calmly assuring myself, in a muffled voice, I said, "This will be the quickest 'No' answer from my wife's lips in the nearly thirty-year history of our marriage." I absolutely had no question about that fact. I mean, I knew what she would say. How many of you male readers know what I mean? In fact, I kind of did not want to bring it up, it was so absurd. As a matter of fact, I did not want my life complicated by it.

Walking into the house, I said, "Carol, you will never guess what happened tonight. While at Liberty's game the golf coach came up and offered me his position, Liberty Head Golf Coach." I absolutely, unequivocally knew that her answer would be a "big" flat "No!" Go Figure! You guessed. My wife said, "Why, honey, I think coaching college golf is exactly what God has prepared you to do." More than slightly disappointed, I interrupted. "What do you mean?"

She began her intuitive in-depth logic, "Well, you played college golf yourself, didn't you?" "Yes," I replied. She put legs to her madness, "You played small local Indiana and Florida professional golf events and tried the Senior Tour, right?" I agreed. "Growing up around golf like you have makes a good foundation for coaching, I think. Don't you?" Stumbling for an answer, I replied, "Maybe." *Dear Lord, are you trying to tell me something through my wife? If this is the case, please help me to listen.*

I could see that God had prepared her heart for my negative attitude. She went on, "After all, you went back to school for a Masters in Ministry degree and you are about to graduate from Liberty in a Counseling Masters Degree program. Did you do all of this just to continue selling food products?" I responded, "Gulp, Gulp…I will consider it, dear."

I had started my MM Degree at conservative Luther Rice Seminary in late 1982. That happened because I felt uneasy about assisting Evangelist Dan DeHass in his first National Evangelistic Tour, which began in January of 1982. Determined to be more qualified for evangelism, I felt that I had to get more "ministry tools."

My entering Liberty's distance learning program for a Master of Arts Degree came from a mildly guilty conscience. That all started when my daughter Lisa needed a "fast-take" on a TV promo spot for Liberty's School of Life Long Learning. Having graduated from LU and now working for Jerry Falwell Ministries in his TV Communications Department, setting up television promo spots became part of her responsibility. Every time the advertisement aired, I told my wife of my guilt, my acting like a student. Eventually, she said, "Frank, PLEASE, go get the degree."

One thing I have learned over the years is that when my wife is for something, I think twice before I say "NO" to it. God has used her insight more than a few times to give me direction. God's Divine Intervention seems to work through her brain. When I refuse it, my success rate becomes far smaller. I began to ask myself questions and then give answers, too. *Could becoming Liberty's golf coach be the real reason behind a lot of these things that happened in my life? Maybe Carol is right on this one. I do not want to pass up God's calling. If He wants me to be a coach, I must obey.* Consequently, I began to consider how it happened that we ended up here in Lynchburg, Virginia.

How I Became Motivated About Liberty...

My first time to see Brother Falwell in person came in 1978. Little did I know then that I would call him "pastor" and, even more of a surprise, my "boss" one day. It all began with a Pastors' Conference "morality issues" rally at the Indianapolis Baptist Temple. A very unique group of pastors and lay people gathered there for an inspiring Christian "Call to Arms." Thousands of church members and pastors from hundreds of miles around came to hear how they could become a part of America's solution. They all wanted to help stop our country's moral "free fall." Much like it must have seemed in November of 1620 for the Mayflower Compact signing, it was an electrifying sanctuary.

Many Christians with political aspirations came to hear the speakers that night. God knew every *seeker* who would attend. Already inspired through speeches and writings by a rising star in the Republican Party, I could not wait for the evening to begin. My two-and-a-half hour drive from Vincennes, Indiana, became a revival in itself during my spiritual "car talk" with God. My conservative and political hero, Ronald Reagan, had become a "bright hope" for me. Republicans and Southern Democrats alike had begun to support him. We wanted him to become our next president. The only other conservative voice heard was Paul Harvey.

Ready to charge hell with water pistols, many of us lacked direction. All we knew for sure was that the mainstream media types never gave a "fair and balanced" view of the nightly news. Of course, we had much more on our side than just politics. God had emboldened us through His Scriptures. My political enthusiasm came from statesmen like (R) Ronald Reagan and (D) Larry McDonald. But, pastors played a big part, too. Ron Kerr, David Beaty, Greg Dixon, and Jack Hyles were the most influential pastoral leaders in my early thirties. All had congregations in Indiana. Publications like "The Sword of the Lord" and published sermons in it made a huge impact, too. Men of God, from the past and the present, were published there like: D. L. Moody, R. A. Torrey, John R. Rice, Curtis Hutson, and Jerry Falwell. They all helped to prepare my heart with a *Patriotic Passion*. We are molded by the people we meet and what we read.

The messages that night ranged from personal examination of our own lives to how we could be a part of the future rescue effort. Our country's political parties were on a slide into liberalism. That night, Dr. Falwell told us about a college he had founded back in 1971. Although I had been aware of the school from articles and area pastors, it sounded even more exciting when proclaimed by the master storyteller himself. Dr. Falwell's belief in the "Mission of the College" captivated my mind. Although I did not actually meet him in person, Dr. Jerry Falwell explained his vision of preparing students to become "Champions for Christ."

Brother Jerry wanted America to return to a social morality that included a lifestyle with what he described as Judeo-Christian values. He told how he thought Liberty would become a part of the solution in changing our world for Christ. Dr. Falwell wanted to one day have a "World-Class" Christian college. Right then and there, I wanted our oldest daughter to go to Liberty for her post high school education. Having no idea or inkling that I would become a part of his staff, I made plans for a trip with my wife and four daughters to visit Liberty in the spring of 1981.

While there, we attended Thomas Road Baptist Church and found out about Lynchburg Christian Academy (later changed to Liberty Christian Academy). Carol and I decided to move to Virginia with our daughter Lisa, who became a Liberty student, and put our other three daughters in Pastor Falwell's Christian grade school and high school. Many of our friends and community leaders warned me against moving. I heard things like "cult worshiping," "fanatical fool," and "political puritanical pastor" to describe Dr. Falwell. Risk little, gain little. The opposite is true as well. I thank God for His strength given to us at the time.

To be fair to those who tried to warn me, none of us knew a lot about Dr. Falwell at the time. I must say that I am glad those dissenters in my hometown were wrong about him. I am grateful to those who cared enough to speak their minds. Tony Riley gave me the best input "friend to friend." George Dooms had good words about Liberty and Dr. Falwell.

In reality, our move to Virginia was the result of a heartfelt need to get a Christian education for our daughters, one that would at least give a balanced view of creation and evolution. This reasoning became our main incentive in making such a drastic move that took us 640 miles eastward. I had discussed starting a Baptist school in Vincennes with a local pastor, but could not get it off the ground. A disagreement with a local high school science teacher involving one of our daughters and a biology paper led me to start a local organization to explain special design/creation better. The name of it was ASKS, Americans for Scientific Knowledge in Schools. ASKS brought Dwayne Gish to town for a debate held at Vincennes University to present a balanced view of evolution vs creation; neither fit science. While on the way to the Evansville airport we stopped and prayed for Dwayne to have a nationally televised debate on Liberty's campus in Virginia. Not having any idea that we would move there at the time of our prayer request, I was amazed to find myself in the audience. God had answered our prayer in Indiana five years earlier. The rest is His story.

Three reasons for accepting came to mind while considering the offer to coach golf at Liberty University.

(1) Mentoring of soul winners builds future husbands and fathers into better family men.

(2) Problem solving, from a Christian perspective in a real life setting, builds next generation leaders.

(3) Being back in competition had that natural draw. "I wanted to see if I could make a difference."

CHAPTER THREE

Internship To My Frying Pan

I contacted Coach Mike Hall a few days after our *Divine Meeting*, telling him to figure me into some 1992 spring season trips. I explained that I wanted to better understand the responsibilities. Actually traveling with him would serve to help me know if I could balance the four big projects: Barbecue Sales, Stress Seminars, Testimonial Preaching and now Golf Coach. Of course, I had to be a dutiful father and husband before all the rest could happen with any success.

My Ongoing Battle: "Doleful Doldrums"…

Two of Mike's key players, Daniel Owen and Troy Dickson, graduated in 1989. They helped drive the success for Coach Hall's years as Liberty's Head Golf Coach. Another key player for Liberty's 1988 success in D-2 golf had been Chris Turner. All three players averaged 76 for four rounds in their 1988 NCAA D-2 Championship fifth place finish. Daniel and Troy were honored nationally. It was a great accomplishment. Liberty had made a mark in D-2 golf.

Since then Liberty had gone up a notch, becoming D-1. Things became even more intense and competitive. There were more rules and regulations to account for at this level. Under Coach Hall, Liberty had never gone to a Division-1 Regional. It looked remote and far off to me.

My intern semester became a real eye opener, even with Coach Hall doing his best to get me grounded. I remember Chris Turner had a bad shoulder. I recall, as a volunteer coach, taking him to the Liberty trainer. I asked him if he had considered redshirting. He replied in the negative and wanted to graduate in May. I thought, *I wish Chris Turner would redshirt for the year. Having him back and healthy in my first official year would be comforting.* Those words came from a coach wanting immediate help. During that spring internship season of 1992, I kept up my thirty weeks on the road (and in the air) selling Landrey's Barbecue. I also traveled fifteen nights with Coach Hall's team.

Coach Hall's nightly devotionals and golf strategy sessions seemed overwhelming to me at the time. Going with the golf team as a volunteer did help me get a picture. In fact, I realized that to compete at this new D-1 level would require me doing a lot more than what I had originally thought. I wondered how I could keep my business going while coaching. I had fought "Doldrums" and "Doubts" often. Finally, I moved on to the stage of saying, "I can do this with the Lord's help." My prayers for guidance began in earnest.

I Had Coached One Basketball Game...

I did coach one time in my senior year of high school. While watching youth basketball at the local hometown YMCA, Robert Thacker came up to me and asked if my teammate and I would coach him and his team of grade school friends. He knew Norm Starks and I played for the Vincennes Lincoln High School basketball team. Reluctantly, we agreed, after being told the boys would be disqualified without a coach. I did not realize it at the time but winning that championship was a big thing in the lives of those kids. Years later, Mr. Thacker came up to me while my wife and I were eating in his co-owned restaurant, *The Pier.* Striking up a conversation, he said, "Mr. Landrey, do you remember the night you and Norm coached our team?" "Well,

I'm not real sure that I do," I replied. Handing me a forty-year-old picture, he said, "Maybe this will refresh your memory." That picture of Mr. Thacker and his teammates with Norm and me brought back lots of fond memories indeed. Many were of my friend, Norm Starks, who had since passed away. I now cherish that picture.

Top Far Left Norm Starks and Far Right Frank Landrey
My First and Only Coaching Experience Came in 1959

Coach Blackman Helped Me The Most…

Soon after my 1992 spring internship semester, I accepted the job. But, not ever coaching golf, I realized I needed help. Knowing that you go to the best source possible, I decided to get advice from one of the country's top D-1 coaches. Having returned to my own college alumni golf outings, there came to my mind one person who filled that bill. I called my Alma Mater's head golf coach. Georgia Tech's Puggy Blackman, an accomplished and successful coach, took the time to talk with me. We had met a few times in and near Atlanta for alumni outings, but who was I to him? With NCAA Championship success and many tournament wins, he knew how to get the job done. Amazingly, Coach Blackman agreed to meet with me. My wife and I drove to Atlanta for this meeting of the minds. I must admit meeting coach Blackman as a new head coach was "big-time" scary.

While we walked down a set of concrete stairs inside the huge football stadium, my mind raced back to my own college days at Georgia Tech. First, we passed by what used to be the Athlete's Dining Hall in my "heyday" on campus. When he showed me his office, I stood in the doorway quite astounded. What Coach Blackman did not know was that his office had been the 1959 T-Club site, if I had my mental notes correct. Later in my sophomore or junior year the coaches moved it to a free-standing building. That building, still in the stadium complex, stood about a 60 degree wedge shot away from where we stood. I looked around his office. Gone were the ping pong table, lounge chairs and television. In their place sat his desk and a few chairs. Renovators had left his office about the size of our T-Club Athlete's Lounge. Except, now, it was cut into two rooms.

Coach Blackman immediately cautioned me, "Frank, you need to host a good college tournament of your own. This is a business that requires an invitation." He went on, "What I mean is this. You need to do something to help other coaches, which will prompt them to reciprocate." Puggy explained to me that I needed to develop a schedule that would attract recruits which would also help me hold my existing players. He explained that good junior players look at a school's schedule to see where they can travel and play golf in college. With a friendly warning, he said, "Everyone competes for the best players in the junior circuit. Liberty will be one of 284 Division-1 schools. All of these coaches will be searching for quality players, too." I got the picture and told him I would take care of that item.

As we entered the first room, which was located just outside and in front of his private office door, I noticed five *GT* golf bags. Each one stood alone and upright near the three walls. Five different manufacturer's clubs rose out of their tops. Along one wall stood a table, which had eight sharp-looking *GT* logo golf shirts, neatly half-folded. I asked why he had so many sets of clubs and shirts. Puggy said, "Frank, when I bring a 'key' recruit in for an official visit, I tell them they will be allowed to pick a set of shirts and clubs as soon as they are admitted into Georgia Tech." I told him that this seemed like a "Big Time" sports presentation and that my school's budget would start small. Again, his advice gave me a lot to think about. He said, "Still, you should develop some kind of golf package and present it to prospects. This will help in your recruiting." Then, Coach Blackman told me to begin building a standing list of potential contributors. He explained, "Have golf outings and raise funds. Invite friends and alumni. Keep their names."

After this good advice, he took me to the new Athletic Dining Hall. I remembered the amount of food I had consumed in a room not as nice, but it was filled with the same great smells. While sitting at a table recalling my own *GT* "albeit" glory days, a young man walked up and introduced himself. Georgia Tech's All-American golfer, David Duval, revealed his character and class in that brief exchange. It was his senior year and I was impressed by him.

Soon, my wife and I were on our way home. I had a lot to think about. One thing I knew for certain, Coach Blackman had opened my eyes. He had given me a lot of ideas. Determined to meet him again one day in an NCAA Regional, I knew the road there would not be easy.

Returning Encouragement...

A few years later, I met David Duval again. This time it would be at Reynolds' Plantation Golf Course during a College Golf Fellowship outing. David had been on the Mini Tour, having missed making the PGA Tour his first attempt. Wanting to support him, I made my way onto the practice green where he was working on his putting. While getting ourselves ready for the outing, I dropped golf balls next to his. "How are things, David?" He rose up out of his putting stance and said, "Coach, if I don't make it to the PGA Tour next year, I'm not sure I will continue to try." His countenance revealed deep disappointment. I told him to trust his swing, believe in his talent and not give up. This was how I recalled the exchange. I'm not trying to take any credit for his eventual success, but David did go on that year to earn his PGA Tour card. Thanks to his great skill, determination and faith, it happened. David won numerous PGA tournaments and came in second twice at Augusta.

Bob Duval, a proficient player in his own right, encouraged his son. His book about the two of them is great reading, *Bob Duval-Letters to a young golfer,* subtitled *The Art of Mentoring*, by Bob Duval with Carl Vigeland. I encourage you to add it to your shelf.

My Illuminating Journey Begins…

Coaching golf was a totally new adventure. I had driven trucks and vans in my business, but not with five guys in back. I had driven vans and wagons with five women in them, a wife and four girls. *Hum. Maybe, I had been prepared and did not realize it. At times, the sounds were certainly similar, now that I think about it.*

Coach Hall did not know for sure that I would take the position until I signed the dotted line in the summer of 1992. As an observer, I remember thinking that I was not cut out for this kind of servitude. Yes, I had served others in church revivals. While it was quickly evident that this was no church setting, it was a ministry to be sure. Mike's golf trip duties more closely represented a "tour guide" with their many responsibilities.

These five college guys demanded attention like any group of sightseeing travelers. Coach Hall was a personal caddie to each player. He served as mom, dad, friend, and coach, all rolled into one kind of like a "Caddy-Daddy." Many times on these "trial runs," silently I asked God, Why do you want me subjected to this?

Each time my courage grew faint, I would see or hear another coach say something about his players. Most of the time, I learned something that would help me be a better coach. Sometimes, I did not like the way a coach treated his players. I would think things would work better done differently. Walla! "Mentor's Magic" had touched my heart.

Things Did Not Go My Way…

To start off my initial year, I lost my best returning player. It turned out that Dale Tyre had changed his mind about coming back to Liberty for his junior year. He decided to transfer to Florida State University. Dale had high hopes of making their golf team. His success at Liberty had given him reason to believe that his childhood dream of playing golf at his hometown school would finally come true. He also had a girlfriend back home. Had I known sooner about Dale's decision to transfer, I would have tried to get him to stay. The last thing I understood before verbally accepting the position was that Dale would be coming back. *With me not knowing sooner that Dale was leaving, do I have a good reason to back out?* I almost decided that God had sent me a message. I was devastated by Dale leaving Liberty. The first thing that came to my mind was that he had rejected me and asked God, "How could You, Lord, let the best player leave?" God works just like this in my life. He does not want me to know too much about what might come down life's road. He knows how to keep my interest while not discouraging me too much. This helps keep me in His will.

Dale came back to Lynchburg several years later to an alumni function I had sponsored. While participating in a golf fundraiser for our team, I asked him my burning question. "Dale, are you glad that you did not come back and finish at Liberty?" His facial expression changed and the chin dropped a few degrees. "Coach, it was a big mistake." He went on, "I was out of God's will and I paid a huge price for it. I am doing fine now. You knew what was best for me all along." I felt badly for Dale but I did feel better knowing that it was not my fault.

I had five players coming back that first year, three who had played the previous year, averaging 79.3, 79.6 and 85.9. Two other players had redshirted the year before. Kelly Chamberlain had a serious shoulder injury. His career ended. The other redshirt, Gary Leeds, did play in tournaments for me and proved to be a fine addition to the program. Coach Hall helped me recruit two new players. However, I was in for several huge rebuilding years. I guess ignorance is bliss.

Sometimes We Need A Confidence Make Over...

The problem I found with most of my college players was that they often did not believe enough in their golfing talent. It occurred in my first year and every year that I coached. Players were destined to live under a cloud of doubt about their potential unless someone could help them change their self-perception. A "confidence" success story is Tom Anthony. Tom had the second lowest average for all players coming back in 1992, but a 79.6 average score did not do his talent justice. He was a rising junior the year I took over, which gave me two years to work with him. Watching Tom's swing in my volunteer semester prompted me to file away in my memory one thought about his golf game. *This guy has remarkable potential. I just know he has natural talent to be a great player.* I never considered myself a special "swing master" or golf instructor. However, I had confidence in my ability to detect good swing technique and a will to win.

I always asked prospects to mail a video of their swings. From it I made my final decision. While not the only factor, solid swings did help in a fast-paced golf season. Many things help produce consistent golf scores like: the heart of a player, his ability to cope under pressure, and an ingrained swing technique which makes a repeat swing possible. Last but not least, a golfer needs confidence in my opinion. Tom had a lot of the first three but needed more confidence. Immediately, I knew my job was to build up Tom's confidence in his many golf talents. This was not going to be hype but rather what I call my *truth serum*. Meant to act like a *mental antitoxin*, I set out to make him immune to the specific disease of *self-doubt*. First, I kept telling Tom of his natural golf ability and of his possessing potential greatness. I told Tom that I thanked God for him choosing Liberty. I told him often. My idea to inoculate his mind with good things seemed to work right from the start. Tom played much better in his junior year, averaging 77.5, and finished in the top five at the Big South Championship while leading that tournament for the first thirty-six holes. When I realized that my players could stay with the fine talent from the Big South's Carolina schools, my desire to win a Conference Championship deepened. Tom Anthony had set a high mark for future Liberty golfers and finished his senior year with a 74.8 average. A great read, *Golf Is A Game Of Confidence,* backs up my belief as it relates to the value of confidence.

A Brother's Confidence Changed It All...

How did I know about confidence being so important? Personal experience gave me insight into this immeasurable *performance enhancer*. While in my own high school junior year, I sat on the bench thinking that a basketball career and college offer had passed me by. A taller and very talented senior had taken my point guard starting position. During the end of my football season, and while he had been practicing with the basketball team's new coach, I got hurt. A football knee injury had hampered my ability to cut and jump on the basketball court. Relegated to the bench with no hope of proving myself, I had all but given up. Then my older brother cornered me at home. Rich asked when I'd be making the starting five, to which I replied that it looked to be all over. Putting his arm around my neck and pulling me close, he said, "Little brother, you have more talent on one leg than most guys have with two. I believe you can do it."

A few weeks later I had that guard position. One year later confidence allowed me to make the Indiana South All Stars and score 18 of my 24 points in the final quarter. We came from 19 down to defeat the North All Stars 99-92 for the first time and to avenge our loss to them the week before. The next year I entered Georgia Tech with a full scholarship. You see, I knew what a "good word" *fitly spoken* could do for a person's career. "Thanks," Big Brother, for your "faith and confidence" in me. I have passed your "faith and confidence" in another's talents on to others many times.

Coaches Are "Dream Chasers"...

Most college golf coaches want to have a team that makes it to what basketball calls March Madness, "The Big Dance." This "Dance" for a golf coach entails a trip to an NCAA post-season tournament. I like to call ours *May Madness*. Coaches quickly seek out the different ways to change or adapt their program for this to happen. We explore ideas and make plans for the day that "the dream" becomes a reality. We go for it with passion lived out daily. There is no turning back. Coaching gets into your blood. You live, eat, and sleep it. You get attached emotionally with the new recruit's hopes and dreams for his career. You want to see recruits fulfill their goals and dreams. Of course, you hope that when this happens you will also reach your own goals and dreams. It all gives your hard work meaningful outward evidence for the time and effort expended. This is true for coaches in any sport. Golf is competitive at any level. Drawn to the heat of the battle by personal desire for competition, we press on. Having played high school and college sports, I soon thrived and wanted to keep reliving that adrenaline surge and rush. A college golf coach can do just about everything during a tournament except hit the golf ball.

Watching my players, I lived and died with three putts. Missed opportunities sent stress shocks through my aging bones. Any and all of these things happening to any one of my five players touched me deeply. If you have a son or daughter who plays competitive golf, you know what I mean. Multiply that feeling by five. Now you are on the ground floor of coaching college golf. It is very stressful. I like to call a golf coach "Caddy-Daddy." A good coach is both.

While watching my guys, I often became so stressed out that I decided I would quit. How many fathers can identify? Then something would happen. My desire to see the thing through, a word someone would say good about my guys, or a sun bursting through the clouds, something would make me look up and thank God for this privilege. Every time that I wanted to quit, and there were many over the twelve years I coached, I reminded myself that I could not quit on God's calling. At times I actually got mad at God for not stepping in and changing things to my golf program's benefit. I often had to come to the place where I asked the Lord to forgive me for believing that someone else had caused my pain. Reluctantly, I finally admitted to myself that this team belonged to God, not to me. Rather, God had allowed everything for a reason. I was finally beginning to understand that I was His assistant. After all, God had led me into this ministry. Now, I would need to continue my search for the reason I was a college golf coach in Virginia.

Seven Things We Need To Know About Doubts…

1) Doubts are common to us all.

2) One remedy for doubt is confidence.

3) Someone believing in you builds confidence.

4) Gather the facts and decide how to apply them.

5) "Action Application" means to put it into practice.

6) Progress comes by "trial and error." Expect failures.

7) Persistence means to never give up.

CHAPTER FOUR

Honey, I think I'm Gonna Die!

No worthwhile journey happens without some setbacks. You may just learn a valuable thing or two for your own good health in this part of the book. First of all, let me tell you that doing two jobs and several big projects all at the same time can become too much for the best type "A." Many Americans can attest to that without me telling them. Bob explained it in the movie, *What About Bob.* He said, "I'm doing the work." In fact, I had overloaded myself with a lot of good things to do, along with my two jobs. I lived like I did not need sleep. I managed to get very little rest. *Say. That sounds like the life of an aspiring author.*

This chapter is about my August 7-9, 1992, hospital stay. It occurred during the very first month of my initial and official first year as Liberty's Fairway Flames Golf Coach. I was looking forward to the new challenge with five tournaments from September through November. On the other hand, with many other things on my plate, loose ends needed a knot. I needed to clear my calendar for the upcoming golf season.

A couple of months before this happened I diagnosed my health situation in a church "Stress/*less* Seminar." Telling the crowd of eighty *health seekers* about my own stress problems in a light-hearted manner, I exclaimed, "Folks, my stress levels are so high that I should not be leading this meeting. I've studied my material and know my subject."

"The Good," "The Bad," And "The Awful"...

Usually, some good comes with every sad story. Let me tell you The Good, first. What happens in this story did lay the groundwork for my decision to sell the family food business. In fact, a deal was consummated in February of 1996, four years after this incident. That was "the good."

Anyway, back to my story, The Bad. Rushing around the day before my business trip trying to get all of my sales materials together, I raised my stress level dramatically. Knowing that I had several upcoming food demo presentations in Iowa, my mind would not rest. Things had to be done before the upcoming fall golf season. August had rushed up behind me, with players beginning to arrive. However, I still had "Barbecue Business" sales details to finalize. My younger brother, Larry, and sister, Margie, expected me to sell. I just had to get this last trip to Iowa in the books and out of the way.

The night before my flight out, Carol listened to my heart and told me of her concern. "Frank, your heart sounds very irregular. Maybe you should stay home and go see a doctor tomorrow." "Carol, my schedule would not allow such a drastic change," I rebutted, assuring her that my heart would be just fine. After several hours of half-in, half-out blurred rest, I fell limp in the bed. Finally, I stopped thinking and planning. Sleep reluctantly came. After a couple of hours, at four in the morning, alarms rang out. My getting ready in a rush to make the flight did not help. With necessaries completed at the airport and my goodbyes made to Carol, I boarded the plane. The schedule called for three planes with a final destination of Des Moines, Iowa. My plans were to arrive late that afternoon on August 7, 1992.

My flight left Lynchburg, Virginia, at 6:00 A.M. and much to my dismay, it turned out to be a "Puddle Jumper." Regular business travelers dubbed them "Flying Coffins" or "Cigars" masquerading as airplanes. Correct me if I'm wrong, but I believe this "Cigar" held eleven humans, and one open seat.

The trip started fairly normal. Our plane arrived at Washington Dulles International Airport a little late. After a long hurried half-jog out and down the airplane steps onto the tarmac, over to a set of stairs, up and through the airport, I pulled, carried, pulled, carried and finished pulling my two-wheeler, which was stacked with a brief case and BBQ skillet. Somehow, I did get to my gate just in time. I had boarded many planes this way over the years. But, combined with other stress in my life, it probably helped precipitate The Awful, which happened next.

After a short wait on the runway, we headed to Chicago's O'Hare Airport with about 100 passengers on board flight 199 at 7:50 A.M. I settled back for what I thought would become a quiet, restful, trip. My deep sleep came to an end with an airline breakfast. Not long after it, my heart started pounding hard. I got real clammy. Excruciating pain came next. It seemed to start in my right arm area and worked into my chest. Sweat broke out on me like hives and a weakness engulfed my entire body. *Could this be a heart attack?* I wondered, having read about symptoms. After all, I had been giving my own stress seminars.

While fighting off human fear and worry, without doubting my faith, I knew the situation was serious. God had my attention. I began to think a lot. *I'm just fifty-two. Could this be the end, so soon? My dad died at forty-eight. But, I stopped smoking and drinking long ago. My stressful gambling days had ceased in 1970.*

In case He had missed it, I reminded the Lord, "How about my twenty-two years of faithful service?" Well, you know how we tend to exaggerate our importance when a request is about to be made. "It is just before my first golf season. Besides, I want to see my wife and family again. You called me into this ministry and I can't sell the business right now because I need the money. What am I to do?"

I had been recruiting players, trying to learn all of the details needed to take over the coaching position and doubling up on the family business in the summer. This trip was the culmination of those efforts to catch things up. *Had I pushed myself to the edge of death?*

Just then I noticed a phone in front of me. This was a first. I know phones in planes are normal now. But, I had traveled a lot without noticing one on seat backs. I could not help but think positive about it. *God is so good. He is letting me say good-bye to Carol before He takes me home.* Believing God had intended for me to call home, I overcame the pain without fear of dying. Just to get my wallet out of my back pocket created excruciating pain. I struggled to move my arm above my head to swipe the credit card. While dialing the number, one thought kept running through my mind. *Your end is near. Time is short. Tell Carol good-bye.*

Finally, I dialed our complete home phone number. Anticipation grew with every ring. When she answered, I spoke hurriedly and in a very low, soft voice. Because of the pain caused by talking, my grimacing became evident to those around me. They began to monitor my call. This was no private phone booth.

I began unashamedly speaking rather loudly, "Honey I love you," I took a deep breath. I spoke again, "I think I might die on this plane." Looking around like in E. F. Hutton television ads of old, passengers gazed back with sympathetic half-smiles. I went on, "My *will* is in the *lock box* at the bank. The insurance policy is there, too. Tell the girls I love them." About that time, I could hear the voice on the other end say, "I'm not here right now, leave me a message. I'll get right back to you." I told Carol's voice recording that I would call back. Snickers came from my *Reality-Real-Life and Death-Call* crowd. I could tell that they felt bad for laughing by the hands that went up covering their face as my eyes scanned them. I could barely bring myself to force out a half-hearted smile.

Soon, a stewardess came up to offer her assistance. Excitedly, she said, "Sir, you look really sick. Do you need a doctor?" I nodded my head Yes! She turned and hurried shuffling faster than normal to the front of the plane. My fleshly side, "the old self," wanted to go Daaaaaaa. What does it look like to you? But God had me very spiritual now.

Later, the nice lady reported back. "Sir, I am still looking for a doctor." Soon, she was gone again assisting other passengers. I fought the good fight and spoke the truth to God like never before. *Lord, take me, if You want me. I know I will be with You when it happens. But I would like to go home, too. However, Your will be done.*

I'll admit that I did offer God reasons why He might need me here for a while longer. My mind searched the Scriptures for others who had faced death. I wanted to remember how they had handled it. Lots of things ran through my mind. I told God that I would make a list of those I needed to thank or deserved an apology. Time crawled for me for the rest of that flight. My list got kind of long and revealing, if you know what I mean. In fact, this book is part of my promise to God that I would be more thankful to Him and to others.

The stewardess interrupted my pithy personal pity party. Having become her emergency situation, I said, "Thank God for caring stewardesses." Handing me cold towels, she said, "Sir, there are no doctors on board. I've notified Chicago."

My Ride Arrives, For A Chicago Tour…

When the plane landed, an ambulance team came on board before any passengers were allowed to get off. A sedative administered helped to calm me a bit and the sweat slowed. Three men in white began to speak. One loosened my collar and said, "Sir, try to relax." Another said, "We will get the help you need." My *new* friends seated in the plane wished me well, too. At that moment my *newest* friends, lifting me onto a stretcher, carried me off.

Please, Take One Of These...

I remember handing out several of my tracts as we were leaving the plane. It probably got a lot of passengers thinking. The tract's outside cover is all black, except for the white tombstone etched on the front. The words, **But A Memory,** are prominently displayed. At the top, on the inside, is this question: **If you died today, would you know for sure that you would go to Heaven?** That question is followed by a number of Scripture verses which say that Jesus Christ is the answer to our sin problem. It maintains that He can save us from the penalty of our sin. A key verse on the tract, Hebrews 9:27, may have alarmed the eager-to-deplane passengers. It says, *"And it is appointed unto men once to die, but after this the judgment."* Only Heaven's records and the "Book of Life" will reveal the benefit of giving out those tracts. When your health fails, all of a sudden the sale of another tub of barbecue or who wins a golf tournament has little value. Getting back home to loved ones and telling others how to be saved becomes most important. I ask you, what is important to you today?

Resurrection What, You Say?

When I woke up, I had a mask on my face and a drip bottle hanging above my arm. I looked up and inquired, "Guys, where am I being taken?" The fellow standing over me looked down and calmly said, "Sir, you are going to Resurrection Hospital." After the shock of hearing resurrection, I put myself in God's care all over again. I have learned to sing my favorite Christian songs when faced with scary situations. My three favorites are: "Thank You Lord, For Saving My Soul" and "Amazing Grace How Sweet The Sound, That Saved A Wretch Like Me." I finish with "Sweet Hour Of Prayer, Sweet Hour Of Prayer, That Calls Me From A World Of Care."

My heart's pounding slowed. I settled in for whatever the Lord had for me. Finally, I said a prayer of thanks for my first aid crew and my stewardess on the flight. We were going someplace fast with sirens blaring. I had never tried this vehicle before and it did not appeal to me. You are talking here about feeling out of control for sure. Under the circumstances, I had no choice about the matter. I learned later that the Catholic hospital's actual name was Resurrection Medical Center. The Bible says there will come a time when you will be taken places and have no choice in the matter.

Upon arriving at the hospital, they put me into a holding area to wait for my room assignment. I called Carol again only to get her message once more. Her voice certainly encouraged me. Eventually, we did speak. As I had feared, she became very much alarmed. In spite of my request not to do it, Carol caught the next schedule of flights out to Chicago. I'd like to thank her cab driver. Although his appearance and driving skills were scary, he did do a good thing getting her to the hospital safely.

Thanks to a lot of nice hospital people, room 371 soon became ready. Carol was allowed to stay overnight. She slept on a mat on the floor. I know you think a good man would have given up his bed. But I was very sick. I had taken several tests and there were more on the way every couple of hours. Besides, what would I do with the drip bottle? She could have slept with me. Anyway, we waited and prayed for good results. They ran me through every conceivable test. I know that they did. The bill ended up being $6,000.00.

Do I Know You? "Thanks" Dr. Capobianco...

Eventually, Doctor Frank Capobianco came around to tell me that I might have had some kind of stress attack. Someone suggested that the airline breakfast caused it. If so, I had just spent the most money ever for my breakfast.

I guess United Airlines could read this book and give me free tickets until I am reimbursed for my hospital stay. Just in case, let me identify my seat number, which was 27G. However, they may be having a stress attack themselves due to high fuel costs. It never crossed my mind to sue for damages to pay bills. Christian Republicans should not think like that. The good news was that it did not appear that I had incurred a heart attack. Carol and I were both very grateful.

Having given out tracts to plane passengers, my ambulance driver, doctor, and nurse, I was glad to know that the gentleman in the bed next to mine, with only a curtain divider, actually had prayer at 11:30 A.M. on August 9th and put his trust in Jesus Christ right there in the South Wing before we left the hospital. I know that God's Holy Scriptures will not come back void for the others, too. According to Isaiah 55:11, souls will be in Heaven because of my change of plans. What is a soul worth? I guess I have a slight idea. Was my side trip Divine Intervention for Carl?

We made our way back to Lynchburg. Carol and I were both so happy just to hold each other. I know, if only we could have stayed in a warm embrace. Life goes on, doesn't it! *I must make myself remember to be less demanding and more loving. My time with her is precious.*

Be Careful What You Ask For From God...

On the way home, I realized that I now had one big problem. Sitting in my plane seat, I retraced my thoughts during the whole sickness episode. When it looked like I would die on the flight out, I had cried out to God for help. You remember that part, I'm sure. A terrible thought jumped into my head. You guessed it. I had asked God to please give me fifteen more years. He did it for King Hezekiah. A good Christian always remembers this story. When the chips are down and life is hanging in the balance, our Bible stories come back to us. You just never know when you might want God's miracle reprieve. I had evoked the Hezekiah "extended life" plea. Immediately, my new prayer became, "Lord, I humbly seek a retraction of my Hezekiah request."

On the other hand, I may be living in the midst of my fifteen years of extended life. God could have performed His own surgery in the plane or in the ambulance before the doctors got to me. This possibility exists. I might only have until 2007 to finish this book. Of course, a person must keep in mind that God could take any of us at any moment. Nevertheless, I now have had time back home with my dear wife and family, plus an extra blessing or two with the team since that weekend. Therefore, I've had far more than any one man could or should ask for, in case God would hold me to a shorter timetable. So, I stay busy getting my entire life story written into my computer and to finish this golf book.

Knowing my family really does love me blessed my soul. At least, they did hug me a lot more after all that Chicago stuff happened. Even my son-in-law Troy, *Mr. Hand Shaker Only*, gave me a warm embrace. I recall his chalky, white-faced look. It gave me a much needed chuckle to see it.

I felt bad about not wanting to die, until a dear gray-haired lady heard me say it. Giving me good advice, she said, "Frank, God will give you 'dying grace' when the time comes." I thought, *John "The Baptist" did send a request to Jesus, asking if He was the one foretold to come. Could it be that John, while sitting in prison waiting for a beheading, had not yet received his own "dying grace?"* If he had not received "dying grace" yet, I'm sure it came. Then, I thought, *The Apostle Paul slept soundly the night before his beheading at the hands of evil doers. He must have had "dying grace."* In Philippians 4:12, Paul said, "*I know both how to be abased, and I know how to abound...*" In verse 13, he said, "*I can do all things through Christ which strengtheneth me.*" He also said in verse 11, "*Not that I speak in respect to want: for I have learned, in whatsoever state I am, therewith to be content.*" I will trust God for it.

Memories "or" Money, Which Will It Be?

We now had to decide which of my two jobs I would continue doing. The "money" was in the barbecue business. But the "memories" would come from my being "Coach." Carol and I had long talks and came to the same conclusion. After consultation with my younger brother and sister, we all agreed. My added job description now included looking for the right buyer. It took three years to get ready to sell the family business. Shortly after Jeff Thomas graduated, I hired him. The fact that he had played golf for me, I knew I could get along with him on trips. Jeff became our employee in June of 1995. Hiring him took some of the sales work off me, while I searched for a buyer. A wonderful family owned business from Westfield, Wisconsin, Brakebush Brothers bought our plant in Vincennes, Indiana. They hired Jeff and all of our other employees. These were two of my prayer requests at the time to know the right company to let buy the family jewel. We would retain the memories and its over sixty years of financial provision to three generations. Thanks to Bill and Carl Brakebush my prayers were answered! I now had time to focus on being Coach Landrey.

Seven Type "A" Principles For Victory Over Stress…

1) Know your body's physical signals.

2) Listen to warnings from your spouse and friends.

3) Be willing to follow good advice.

4) Listen to medical professionals.

5) Believe you can change your lifestyle.

6) Confess your sin and health failures.

7) Never give up on yourself. You can change.

Note: God cares about our stress. Let us give our anxiety to Him before it becomes stress. I know it is easier said than done. What I am saying is, let us try harder to do it.

CHAPTER FIVE

Holy Servitude: I'm My "Old" Coach

What I remember most about playing golf for Georgia Tech are the spring break trips to Florida. One trip stands out more than the rest for a good reason. His balding "top-spot" would shine back at me. With a wax on it, when the sun hit it just right, the result was a glare. His special version of a crew cut stood about one inch high. Irregardless of a serious thinning problem, what hair he did have sat up tall on top and in front. A "crew cut" was the preferred style with most college guys in 1963. Coach "Plax" had his own version. Think of a diamond-shaped hair cut, with an oval out of the back wedge. He must have used some kind of hair jell, like I use now. Something gave his hair body. The front came to a point like an arrow, always leaning toward his destination.

My hair was long on off seasons which required a "slick back" cream. I cut it short in season, like Coach Plaxico, which helped with heat and kept it out of my eyes. These days, I fight the balding thing, too. I did not think it could happen to me! Maybe I was too naive while in college. Little did I know that I'd have guys in back of my van looking at my "balding top-spot!" I now leave my hair longer in front and comb it back. My A-Plus Barber & Style Shop is even more important at my age. After wearing a hat all day, the spray and its mystery mist would lose its holding power. What was left to see was my very own balding reality. God does have a sense of humor. *Hum…We do reap what we sow.*

Plax was my short version of Plaxico, although I never told him. Him being a Marine "sergeant type," I marched to his drum. He kept his golf shirt collar standing up, like at attention. I never asked him why. I began doing the same thing when I started coaching in the hot sun or cold wind. Coach Plaxico was right more times than wrong.

I never appreciated those trips with Coach Plax as much as in my senior year, needing to feel a part of something again. My heart broke when basketball was taken away after the seventeenth game of my junior year. I was falsely accused of something. Without golf I just might have jumped off the end of life's train. That is a true tale for another time.

It never crossed my mind that one day college guys would be making fun of me and possibly thinking some of the same things that I thought about my coach. I remember thinking bad thoughts about Coach Plaxico. Some things had truth and some did not. All of it came back to haunt me when I became a coach, and "in the Plax" myself. Here are some of the things that went through my mind while in the back of his van. *What a loser. He drives a bunch of college guys around the country to play golf. He should get a "real" life. All he does is play golf all day. What a great life.* It never crossed my pinhead mind how little he was paid, the amount of planning required, or the hassles he lived with.

Coach Plaxico did play golf with opposing coaches, while we played matches. I left my team during practice rounds but only a few times in twelve years. Playing golf with my old college roommates Richard Faulkner, John Cook, and J. B. Dickinson or with an opposing coach ranked high enough for me to miss my team's practice round, which we played before every collegiate tournament.

Coach Gutshall's Golf Impact...

I recall one such occasion Coach Kelly Gutshall requested a game of golf with a few coaches. This "kind and gentle" man coached Lehigh University's golf team located in Bethlehem, Pennsylvania. Liberty placed third in his event that year. What a nice tournament Coach Gutshall put on for the eighteen teams. Leaving my team during our practice round, I met up with Coach Gutshall at nearby Saucon Valley Country Club. I'm sure Hale Irwin enjoyed his 2000 Senior Tour Championship stroll on the beautiful, lush green *Irish Gleann* golfing gem a bit more, but not much. That day of golf will be remembered as a "blessed day," riding with a "giant" in college golf granted not in NCAA Championships but rather in the arena of loving the game.

For several years after that outing, my wife and I sat with him and his lovely spouse at GCAA National Conventions. I marveled at his golf stories. Thirty-four years worth of calendars are still in his possession which account for rounds and total monthly scores. He has records on playing over 7,500 rounds since 1971. Eighty years old in 2005, Coach Gutshall has coached sixteen years, plays golf often still, and has shot his age 234 times. He has a volunteer driver to take him on team golf trips. Coach Gutshall always spoke highly of everyone. Lehigh has about 4,500 students and gives no athletic scholarships. Coach Gutshall thrives on helping great junior golfers who are in need of financial assistance with an abundance of money available to low income families. I know my coaching skills improved by associating with this *Gentleman of Golf*. "Thanks," Coach Gutshall for your faithfulness to the game and to the players you have coached. Much SITTAWAGA on Lehigh golfers for *Coach Gutshall*!

Thinking Back About Coach Plaxico...

Let me return to my college days. I remember thinking, *Coach can't play as good as I, what can he possibly know?* I'm not sure we ever played together, but I just thought it. Up until I hit sixty, I could hold my own from the back tees with a lot of my Liberty players. Most coaches wanted players that could beat them. I had a lot who I could not outplay. This was a good

46

thing. However, I might win once in awhile in scores but throw off on wedge games during pre-tournament practice. I often had games with the guys where it was my flip-wedge against theirs. If anyone beat me, they all won. My trusty sixty-four degree wedge would win most times from where I took them like behind bunkers and bushes for difficult shots. The stakes were a dessert or extra balls. Some got to win because I had concerns. I felt we had better tournament results with players who had confidence in their short games. Having an "Old Coach" hit wedge shots closer than all five on the team might not build confidence. Besides, I got to share their desserts.

When I played college golf, a thought came to me: *Georgia Tech doesn't spend enough money on us golfers.* This certainly proved to be true back in my day when it came to extras like clothes and clubs. My Liberty guys never got enough of these types of benefits when I coached. This did improve some during my last few years. More financial help is on the way and all donations will be appreciated.

Other thoughts went through my head while a *GT* golfer. *They expect me to practice a lot. But, I have to pay for my own gas driving my car to East Lake Country Club. And, how about the time it takes to drive there.* It never crossed my mind that we were practicing on the same golf course that Bobby Jones grew up playing. Now I watch TV programs praising East Lake as every golfer's *dream course* because of Bobby Jones and its history. Of course, I also had no idea that it was against the NCAA rules to pay players for driving to a practice site. My guys wondered why they used they drove to practice at their won expense so I often explained the reason why it had to be, showing my empathy.

London Downs Golf Club took my guys ten minutes to drive. Poplar Forest Golf Club, for range work, is fifteen minutes away as is Ivy Hill Golf Club. Poplar Grove's new, beautiful course is only twenty minutes and classy Winton Country Club is thirty minutes. We drove an hour to plush Water's Edge Country Club, Water Front Country Club, and West Lake Golf Club. Beautiful courses like Wintergreen's Stony Creek and the famous Homestead Resort took one and two hours, respectively. I often said, "You Liberty golfers are blessed with great places to play golf. Every college player pays his or her gasoline expense to practice. Complain to the NCAA not me." I told my guys to share rides to cut down on the cost. "Don't ride with anyone who does not obey speed limits. Remember, it is a privilege to play these great courses and pay no green fees." *All we need is our own driving range on campus. I'm praying for one to come soon.*

My final *GT* "poor thinking" flaw came in my senior year. *I don't have time to practice. After all, don't they know or care that I've got tests? Besides, I don't like to hit balls or chip and putt. I can shoot 75 without that stuff.* This will be said to the end of time by almost all, if not every college golfer. Here is a good place to talk about the importance of practice and competition. Either you keep your game sharp in the twenty hours a week allotted to teams by NCAA rules today, or you do it on your own time after required hours. Players know that the trips will always be taken by those golfers who can play the best. It is especially true these days with all the talented players. This is why I always tried to get the smartest student athletes recruited, who could also play the best golf. I required them to put in the twenty hours of practice, but results in qualifying and tournaments showed me who played best under pressure, which usually proved that "preparation meets opportunity." Those players with the least practice made the fewest trips. This formula held true "best" with twelve highly competitive and talented college golfers trying to earn one of five seats in the van.

Coach Tommy Plaxico, My Hero…

I'm ashamed of myself for all I said and thought while in college. Of course, I had no faith and no Bible to look to for answers. My chosen trinity, "me-me-me," became all I cared about. Under no circumstances would I look to Jesus for help. Those that were "looking unto Jesus" knew not to mention it to me. Let me apologize to You, LORD, and to those who tried to witness to me. I think of Josh Powell, a tall, lanky basketball center who sang hymns on the "hoops" team's traveling bus. I did not like it. Coach John "Whack" Hyder was a fine leader. I now appreciate that he took us to church and often had prayer with the basketball team.

How could I possibly have known the feeling of responsibility Coach Plax had during my *GT* golf years? When Coach Plaxico looked in the rearview mirror on our golf trips, there we were five or six sleeping college golfers. He knew that our lives were in his hands. He knew that moms and dads were counting on him to stay awake. My life was in his hands, especially when he was driving. Maybe the gum he chewed kept him awake. It must have given him a lot of energy. Coach Plax had a million-dollar smile that could easily represent Nite White Teeth Whitening Jells. The way Coach Plaxico bounced in and out of that van truly inspired me in my senior year. Being a tired and worn-out party boy, I needed inspiration. He made sure I had it.

When I Got "In the Plax"…

After God put me *"In the Plax"* and I became a coach myself, I found out what it took. Driving was okay most times while traveling distances of 300 miles on three-to-five-hour trips. On the other hand, five-and-a-half to eight-hour drives home took lots of coffee, tea, and Pepsi to stay awake. For example, I had trouble getting more than twelve hours sleep total in three nights during Big South Championships. I did not sleep well all stressed out and in strange beds. On these trips, I drove six hours to play a practice round, got up early the next morning for us to play thirty-six holes, followed by another early rise to get in the final eighteen holes before the long, six-hour drive home.

Trips back to campus were just not safe with me tired and sleep deprived. This was one reason for my eventual retirement.

College Golf Scoring Then...

Back in my college golf days, I don't remember that we played thirty-six holes in one day. We played eighteen holes a day and individual matches. The team won or lost the match based on points that each player won or lost against his opponent. We did play five players, as I recall, like today. Each player would be matched up with an opposing player and a hole-by-hole match would determine how many points a team earned in that match. All five matches were added up and the total points earned by each team determined the winning school. There would also be an individual winner. I do remember one stroke-play tournament at plush Peachtree Golf Club. I recall teammates coming out to the sixteenth hole. They said, "Par in so we can win." Somehow, I did manage to keep it together for a 75. We won the tournament. It became my college golf high point. Having coached, I now know better ways to say the same thing. I felt a lot of pressure with the "par in" request. Instead, saying things like: Everyone is playing well, keep playing one shot at a time, or stay in the present, or stay relaxed in the shoulders. These statements work better for most players while dealing with pressure rather than ultimatums or quantitative goals.

College Golf Scoring Today...

In my coaching years, we always played our tournaments under stroke-play format. In this format, a team scores by adding their best four out of five scores for a team total. The lowest team total determines the team winner. Thirty teams can play in a tournament. If it is a fifty-four hole event, there are four counters each round, times three rounds. This becomes a team's tournament total. Example: 70, 72, 75, 76 = team total of 293. If in the second and third rounds their best four counters total 295 and 300, their team's fifty-four-hole total is 888. This team total would be posted on the scoreboard for all participants and coaches to see. The lowest team total wins the tournament. An individual tournament goes on, too. The player with the lowest total in his three rounds wins the individual title. College golf became a feeder system for the professional tour which is stroke-play.

Junior golf is governed by stroke-play, too. It has become a feeder system for college golf. Youth tours and tournaments range from age five to eighteen and have become very serious. I played golf recently with Zachary Bauchou, who is nine years old. He shot par golf for his age bracket's assigned course yardage. Dr. Ed Bauchou taught his son to play and he caddies for Zach. Another fine nine-year-old golfer in the Lynchburg area is Cassidy England. Dad, Scott, caddies for her. Both players have won several junior titles already, and both are Reigning US Kids Virginia State Champions. Both junior golfers have very involved fathers, who have sought out a "swing coach" and are investing a lot of time and money into their golfer's future. They are doing the right things to help prepare their student athlete for college. I do hope they buy my book and read up on my recruiting tips found in chapter ten. However, all is for naught if the educational part is missing. Good grades are important and very helpful to a college coach. They secure scholarship money for his/her recruit and assure the coach that his or her money is well spent with having a player who can actually finish his or her career.

Both Cassidy and Zach participate on several junior tours. Parents can contact the one they play on most at www.nationalj uniorgolfclub.com. Become more informed.

Bad Decisions Hurt Us And Others...

I must state a disclaimer here. Having not been a Christian in college, God forgives me for terrible acts of misjudgment.

Those who played for me here at Liberty were all Christians. At least, they professed the same. "Guys, may I suggest that you use 1John 1:9 if you did bad stuff." God will forgive, but fellowship with Him requires our prayers of confession.

Liberty golfers, in general, were spiritual. However, isolated incidents proved poor decisions can happen to good guys. I made bad decisions back in college, too. I remember one morning that Coach Plaxico came in to wake me up. We were to play a very good Vanderbilt University team that day. I drove myself into Nashville, Tennessee, from Vincennes, Indiana, after a school holiday. I remember thinking, *What Coach does not know won't hurt him or the team.* After staying out all night, I crawled into the bed sheets in my street clothes just in time to hear a knock on our door. My roommate let Coach Plaxico in and he came over to the bed and shook me. "Okay, Coach. I'm up. I'll be right out," I muttered. After he left, I got up and brushed my teeth. Coach Plaxico was amazed at how fast I got to the van. Of course, I slept nearly all the way to the golf course. *Hum...sounds familiar.*

One of Vanderbilt's best players had been paired with me to assure them of match play points. In college match play, each player played against the other team's player in duel matches. Players were ranked like they are today based on the skill level exhibited in qualifying and tournament competition. Each team turned in their lineup, like in college golf today. I played number 3 on Georgia Tech's golf team, as I recall. I usually went against the opponent's number 3 player. Sometimes a team would play their number 1 or number 2 against another team's number 3, 4 or 5, to lock up points. This day my opponent was their number 1 player. Soon Coach Plaxico began to follow our match. He knew that if I won against a higher ranked player of theirs, it might just turn the match our way. The little crowd of interested fans and family members seemed amazed to see the head-to-head-battle going my way. Then, it hit me like a ton of bricks. I felt like I had a thousand pounds of bricks on my back instead of fourteen clubs in a canvas bag. My shoes felt like lead boots. After leading by two holes at number thirteen, my game went south. I lost the match two and one, closed out on the seventeenth. Our team lost the match by one point. How many times did one of my teams lose to an opponent because a player made the wrong choice the night before? How fortunate we are to have a God who believes in multiple extra chances.

I do know of one time that something similar happened to me as a coach. The player told me about it near the end of our season. We had one of the best teams ever assembled at Liberty. It was our year. Still, I knew that something seemed wrong. A coach has an intuitive sense about his team, like a mother and father have about their children. But I did not pursue it. Like parents, I hoped it would take care of itself. I should have known better. Neither this young man that I'm talking about nor I back at Vanderbilt while playing for *GT*, were what we needed to be. We both now know that to be true. This beloved player made a comment to a friend and I overheard. He said, "I think Coach Landrey sees himself in me." He had made a true statement. The truth is every negative personality flaw of my players reminded me of something either God had already corrected in my life or was still in the process of correcting. Neither of us can go back and change the bad decision but we can determine to be the person God wants us to be from here on out. I once embarrassed my wife "big time" in my old drinking days. I asked my childhood buddy and lifelong friend a leading question, "Tom, tell me true, how bad was I last night?" "Geno, are you sure that you want to know?" he asked. "Yes," I replied. Tom Moore decided to tell me by making this suggestion, "Whatever Carol asks you to do for the rest of your life, just do it." For the many times that we have all failed God, may I make this suggestion, "Whenever God asks you and me to be a blessing, let us just do it!"

CHAPTER SIX

First Two Seniors Come Through

Garrick Stiles was the first player that I ever protested in behalf of to a Tournament Rules Committee. My first season to coach came in the fall of 1992. My first rules question came at my third tournament to coach, The Old Dominion/Seascape Invitational. Garrick, in the practice round, just had to hit a tee shot to try to see if he could reach the green on the par 4, sixth hole. To reach the green, you had to go over trees, over the out-of-bounds that jetted out into the 90 degree left turn section of the L-dogleg. As a newcomer at this coaching game, I thought, *Why not let the boys have some fun, it is just practice.* Just then one of my other players yelled, "Loosen up, Coach." When Garrick assured me that he would not under any circumstances hit driver in the tournament, I believed him. So, I let him try. You guessed it. He hit a beautiful, long, high, soaring shot, over the trees, over the O.B. and over the creek hazard. The ball came to rest twenty feet from the cup, Garrick was putting for an eagle. Somehow I knew I had trouble even though Garrick made a promise to me after my grilling. He said, "Coach, I will not try to drive the green. Trust me." Something akin to coaching intuition deep within me yelled, "Frank, don't trust a college golfer when it comes to a promise about laying-up after you let him experience the exhilaration that comes from reaching the green with a driver in the practice round."

Rules Question Coming Up Soon…

The green sat down in a valley, just over a creek that ran alongside. Sitting on top of a slight rising mound, this rather small sloping green was waiting for a brave soul, like our Garrick. Yes, he did try to drive the green the next day. I knew that he had done so when checking the scoreboard. I saw his name crossed out and DQ written by it. This is not an ice cream story about Dairy Queen. His score was disqualified. Garrick's golf score for the round had been a 75 and would have counted for our team. If it remained a DQ, we would use another player's 81. It was a big thing to me.

I had to get the facts. First, I found the head pro and owner of the Seascape Golf Course, Mr. Bob Sullivan. Let me put a promo in here for this 6,300 yard, feisty track with sand dunes lining all fairways. Don't let the short length mislead you. This is truly a "fun-fantasy-golf-test." Mr. Sullivan listened to my long explanation. He empathized and sent me to the tournament host. Coach of ODU, Murray Rudisill, heard my long, sad story and sent me to check it out with the tournament rules committee. I immediately went to the local team of rules officials to restate my player's situation, referring them to the site of the infraction. Holding to his original assessment, he said, "Your player should have hit another ball from the tee after his first drive went out-of-bounds. Instead, he played from the wrong place and did not correct it, thus a disqualification."

Tell Me Again, Why Did You Not Lay Up?

I decided to revisit the issue with my player. When confronted with the part about a promise made to me during the practice round, Garrick testified in his defense, saying, "After all, Coach, the wind was at my back. I had to try it. I had such a good round going. This was my chance to take it deep–For YOU!" I wanted to get into his reasoning further. But, I had bigger fish to fry right at that moment. I did the next best "coaching thing." I asked, "Did your first tee shot clear everything?" Garrick knew that I was interested in making sure that he saved every stroke possible for the team's sake. It would be easier for a player to just drop a second ball and hit away again. If that happened, the player would be forced to take that ball and two penalty strokes, even if the first ball turned out to be in the hazard which is only a one stroke penalty. Who knows, he could have hit a second ball out-of-bounds or worse. That would be the end of any good score. "Coach, I went up to see if it cleared everything like my drive did yesterday. When we could not find it, I hit my second shot (third for scoring) from the corner up there on the hill." Again, I questioned him, "Are you sure the first ball cleared the out-of-bounds?" "Yes! And, all of my playing partners will back me up."

To go for the green on the sixth hole, a player's golf ball had to cut the corner and it carried the out-of-bounds stakes which were about 280-yards out. That was the first and main objective. If the ball cleared the O.B. but not the ditch hazard, which covered about forty yards just past the O.B., you "would not" be required to hit a second ball from the tee box. Instead, the worst that could happen would be that your ball was in the hazard creek area, meaning only a one stroke penalty. In this case, you could drop the ball at the 150 marker on the top of the hill and be looking down on the green, hitting three. It saved the player a minimum of one stroke. Between the creek and the green there were about twenty-five yards of nothing but low cut Bermuda grass. If a ball cleared all of the above, it would certainly be seen easily by all. Of course, Garrick had hoped to see it on the green which was not to be the case this day.

I went back to Coach Rudisill again. He told me that my only recourse was to take it to a higher court, "You could call the USGA and ask them to overrule the local committee." That is exactly what I decided to do.

My USGA Closing Arguments...

I began my rebuttal, "Sir, my player's ball cleared the O.B. and because the grass is so short around the green, you know that if you can't find the ball, it had to be in the hazard. Both playing partners from the other two schools say that his ball cleared the out-of-bounds but not the ditch hazard area."

The USGA official on the other end ruled in my player's favor after some interoffice consultation. He explained the ruling, "We rule that the opposing players in Garrick's group had the last say on the ball clearing the out-of-bounds. Being that they concluded it cleared means that the ball had to be in the hazard, since it could not be found in the clearing beyond the creek. We concluded Garrick proceeded correctly, taking a stroke penalty, and hitting his third shot from the top of the hill." They were wonderful words of vindication. He went on, "Let me speak with the local committee's head official." The committee on site eventually changed the ruling in Garrick's favor and his score of 75 counted. Liberty finished much higher up, twelfth out of twenty-one teams. I stood up for what I knew in my heart was correct. It would not be the only time during my coaching years that I would find it difficult to take a stand for what I thought was right.

The last I heard, Garrick lives in his hometown of Athens, Georgia. His business does well and his family is growing. Friends and family alike, beware of the "prankster at large." Mr. Stiles is in business and doing great. He is married. Last time I knew, they had two sons. *Hum... Could he have pranksters in his van? Wouldn't that be lovely poetic justice!*

Rules Officials Make College Golf Better...

I worked with many fine officials over my twelve years: Dr. Lewis Blakey, Tim and Dorothy Kilty, Tim Mary, Richard Smith, Richard Wight, "Mr. Rules" Clyde Luther and Tom Meeks, who was fondly referred to by many friends as "Mr. USGA Rules." Thanks to all who make it happen!

Liberty's First Scholastic All American...

I had a short, rather thin rising senior in my first year. Chris Easley's red hair was always combed neatly to one side, and a few leftover freckles made him look younger than his age. Be not dismayed, he was smart and had a heart of gold, with courage far above his stature. Chris would tackle any challenge. Early that fall, I told him that he could become our first Scholastic All American. He made great strides in his senior year, accomplishing much in golf and academics. I remember how he and I prayed together about his potential of becoming a D-1 Scholastic All American. First, in anything, is often the most difficult. Chris wanted God's will in the matter. I think I wanted the honor for Chris more than he did for himself.

We were at our last tournament of the spring, The Wofford Intercollegiate. Wofford's Coach Dan O'Connell became a good friend of mine, right from the first year that I coached. Another great friend, my tough competitor at Old Dominion, Coach Murray Rudisill, introduced us. I recall the first Golf Coaches Association of America's National Convention in Orlando, Florida, in January of 1992. I passed out business cards along with a "Christian Challenge" card I had written. Five years later, Coach O'Connell stopped me at a golf event. He pulled out his wallet and removed that now worn and tattered card. He told me how it had been a blessing.

Coach O'Connell was gracious to invite Liberty to his 1993 spring event. His elite field made this tournament a plum on anyone's schedule. His field of teams had many top-twenty ranked golf programs represented in it. It also became Chris Easley's last tournament of his career. He had played well during the first day's eighteen holes. Immediately I tallied fall and spring totals for his twenty-nine rounds. Chris had a golf average under the required 78 and an academic accumulated GPA well above the required 3.2. It looked good for him to become a Golf Coaches Association of America prestigious 1992-1993 Scholastic All American. He would need to meet additional qualifications with reference letters from Liberty Academia and the Athletic Director. Only forty or so players from all 284 Division-1 programs make the grade in any given year.

Before the last day's eighteen-hole round started, Chris came to me with an upset stomach. It could have been caused by a flu bug or just the fact that we were playing in one of the best tournaments of his life. However, it might have been the fact that he was under the required year long average by one tenth fraction of a stroke. If he did not play, he would be an automatic candidate for Scholastic All American. On the other hand, if he played, he could miss the award. I decided to give Chris the option of not playing in the final day's round. His answer was special, saying, "Coach, I took another player's place to be here in this important tournament. That player is back at home in the dorms. He cannot take my place today to help the team. My game is yours and the teams, for better or for worse." Chris chose to compete to help the team.

I must admit; he made me proud. I wondered how he would hold up under the added pressure. It came down to the last hole. Chris hit a great shot and split the middle off the tee. From the fairway, his approach shot came off the club face ballooning high, "chunked." It landed short of the green, in the front bunker. All that had been achieved during a long season had come down to this last hole. It was all on the line. Chris stepped up to the ball, his head barely visible by me at greenside. To his credit, he hit a great sand shot. It left him about ten feet from the cup. With all the confidence possible, he stepped up, made a great stroke, and sank the last collegiate putt of his career. It meant that he would make the required golf average by a fraction of a stroke. Had he missed that putt, he would have fallen short. Congratulating Chris, I gave him a well deserved hug. It was awkward but we got through it together with extended chests and all. I tell my grandchildren to stand up and take my hug like a man.

Chris became the first of six Liberty players who would achieve this honor. He is now a lawyer in his home state of Washington. Chris recently sent me a great picture of him, his beautiful wife, and first child. Mom and dad are proudly holding junior in the photo. Junior will grow up to be a man of integrity and a team player, just like his dear old dad.

Liberty's D-1 Scholastic All Americans Are:

Chris Easley 1992-1993 * Todd Setsma 1994-1995
Chad Hall 1995-1996 * Mark Setsma 1997-1998
Rob McClellan 2001-2002 * Jonathan Dickinson 2003-2004

Seven Mental Things That Help Golfers...

1) Forget the past. Every good player has bad shots.

2) Accept bad luck and make the next shot a challenge.

3) Plan your execution while going to the next shot.

4) A great round is reached one stroke at a time.

5) Clear your mind of bad thoughts on your walk.

6) Expect victory. Gain confidence and reflect on it.

7) Face defeat. Learn from it. Ask what went wrong.

One other thing that will help golfers, especially those really successful ones, is something Dr. James Dobson said in 1993 while speaking at the graduation ceremonies. Remarking about how the great basketball player Pete Marovich died in his arms, he said, "Life will trash your trophies. Only two things really matter in the end, family and accomplishments for Jesus Christ." Finding myself in a Chicago hospital shortly before Dr. Dobson's comment, I knew it to be true.

CHAPTER SEVEN

A New Coach Must Get Control

I had three basic lines drawn in the sand bunker, so to speak. Every player learned them early.

(1) Always address me as Coach Landrey or "Coach."

(2) "Sir" is not a bad word. I will use it to address players.

(3) Never give up on yourself or the team in a round of golf.

My opening statement in the fall and spring went like this, "Rest assured. I will get after any player who has talent to do better. You may have an award coming, but I will not let you coast." The first year that I coached was difficult for me. Trying to juggle thirty weeks of travel for my business plus the thirty-five nights out with the golf team became a real challenge. Added to this task, I had four returning players who were not absolutely sure that I had the "mugwump" to coach them.

We had several "second best" efforts early on, but eventually the guys caught the vision and soon they amazed even me. We had to take baby steps when it came to goals and dreams. We got a top ten finish, a top five, and eventually a first place finish. Many of my players did a similar thing, especially the untested ones. They needed breakthroughs too, like rounds under 80, 75, and then 70. Some needed to take baby steps while others handled giant steps. We were growing together.

I often repeated these goals and dreams to my teams.

(1) A change in the NCAA Regional selection system, to allow our Big South Champ an automatic berth.

(2) Our team's first NCAA East Regional trip one day.

(3) Liberty moving into another region that would be nearer to our weather conditions and budget size.

(4) The day we would have a conversion van to travel in, just like the "Big Boys," which is what I called the Atlantic Coast Conference and Southeastern Conference.

(5) I wanted Liberty to have Scholastic All Americans.

(6) I wanted us to have "team" and "individual" victories.

(7) I wanted a driving range on campus. I still tell this one.

Things I Had To Learn The Hard Way…

I made plenty of mistakes with players in my twelve years. For example, I had to learn that in this sport you are to be calm and collected at all times. Another "no-no" is that you do not walk down a fairway with a player on his second nine of the tournament's last day and say, "Stay even with par and you won't have to qualify for the next trip." It may be true but the added pressure is a huge "no-no." Sorry about that, Justin. I wanted our team to show well in the College of Charleston Invitational which took me three years to get. Knowing we would never go again unless things turned around, I tried everything on September 12, 1995. My adding undue pressure on Justin Jennings' game was definitely a "no-no" in my coaching "learning curve." He forgave me, in time. In fact, Justin recently left me a message, which I kept for days to replay. Who says a coach's heart is stone? With the right message, the hardest heart can soften. Justin said, "Coach, this is your favorite golfing son, JJ. I keep your encouraging messages and replay them. You were the best coach I could have ever wanted."

I often struggled with the task of coaching a bunch of great guys in their first years away from mom and dad. Knowing that these young men had minds of their own, I tried to be helpful. Dr. James Dobson said on his radio program, "Focus on the Family," that between the ages of fifteen and twenty-five are the most critical years. I agree. Many times I stepped on growth patterns, their ideas and actions, and it hurt their feelings. Right or wrong, it caused anguish. *Hum…that sounds like what happened to me during my college years.*

These guys became the sons I never had. I cared about them. Anyway, JJ went on in his phone call to say, "Sorry that it has taken me so long to get back to you. I've been real busy. The check for your "True Believers" golf outing to raise funds will arrive soon." Justin and I had our times of difficulty during his four years of Liberty golf, but somehow we got past all that to see the good more than the bad. "Thanks, Justin." I've been blessed with over seventy golfing sons in these past twelve years. Like real sons, most understood me and accepted my attempt to be a good surrogate father. As their golf coach/motivator/encourager and disciplinarian, who failed miserably too many times to count, I really did try hard to do right by them. I have been blessed to have this awesome privilege. I'll admit when one of them calls me to announce a wedding or new birth, my father instincts are revived. Parents like Ron Richards who gave visible support for his son Matt made coaching easier.

As the years went by, I learned to be myself and prayed more for God to help me be what the guys needed rather than for them to be what I needed. Finally, I came to a conclusion. Liberty's golfers wanted to follow a leader, not a tyrant. I knew this truth from living in my home with five females. It just took awhile with a team. I don't mean that leading this way rendered me weak and pliable. Using what I came to believe were biblical principles just seemed to work better. However, every person must determine who they want to impress, God or man. I have learned to please God more.

As a biblical leader, I eventually fell mostly on the side of compassion. Four things that helped me are:

(1) I tried to make "just and fair" decisions with players.

(2) Showing mercy, when possible, became my motto.

(3) Staying humble before God became my daily goal.

(4) Staying humble before my players and peers, as well as toward those with whom I worked, became my ideal.

I failed many times, I know. So, please don't write me about your son's unjust coaching decision. I'm sorry if I offended a parent or player unjustly. However, every story has two sides. I searched out every situation the best I could. Matthew 7: 12 states, *"Therefore all things whatsoever ye would that men should do to you, do ye even so to them: for this is the law and the prophets."* I tried to follow this ideal.

I had a few players who were hotheads like I was in college. You will read how I attempted to help them. God knows I cared enough to try. Sometimes parents are so into the loving part that they are blind to the gravity of a problem. But, I knew that their son would grow up to be an angry husband and father unless someone cared enough to help him change. I saw myself as his last chance. If a young golfer got to college as an angry man, I figured that the parents could no longer stop it. Therefore, it was my turn to try.

I also had to protect acquired privileges for future Liberty players. If one of my guys let his personal anger problem endanger our team to the point of being kicked off a local golf course or where a host school would not invite us back, I had to put a stop to his behavior. I owed it to Liberty's future teams and coach. A bigger reason to stop players from throwing temper tantrums is that God will not "totally" bless an angry person. People who hang around angry players pick up on it and become a problem as well. Anger tends to travel like flu. The Bible is clear about the dangers of hanging out with an angry person, lest you pick up their bad habit.

Let Your Conversation Be Respectful…

Cursing in no way proves manhood, rather a lack of intelligence to express an idea in words you would use around Jesus. Some foolish men want to make Jesus out to be a good old boy who curses with the worst of them or at least He is sympathetic to it. As an unsaved teenager and young adult, I cursed up a storm. As an adult and after becoming a Christian at the age of thirty, cursing did not seem Christ-like. Thank God. He took the nasty habit away.

Colossians 3:8 rejects cursing by coaches, players, and parents. We are admonished to put it off, along with anger, wrath, malice, and blasphemy. I would get in a player's face at times but mostly to the whole team and always minus the cursing. I stopped allowing the use of the widely accepted "P" word, too. Many Christian young men thought it wasn't a curse word. I figured that it was just one in the family of body functions like the "S" word. Then, there is that other four letter word that the world likes to use to express anger. So, I stopped it all at the front door. Also, when out on the golf course, finding restrooms or hiding in big, bushy trees for the "P" word "deed" was expected.

"In the face" coaching might work but could also backfire. The player's personality makes the difference. Mine always came from a heart of righteous indignation, I hope. However, it is my conviction that here at Liberty, the players must believe a coach speaks to them "in truth" and "in love," no matter the coaching style. I believe that every player, at any school, would like to have a coach speak "truth in love." It is the biblical way to lead (Ephesians 4:14-15). However, speaking "truth in love" to someone having an anger tantrum becomes next to impossible.

An anger problem and the resulting spontaneous action-related outbursts always caused me to try some kind of behavior modification tactic. The harm it did to our testimony and the program's reputation merited some kind of action. Within the college golf circuit, a coach works for years to get invited to a big tournament. Coaches who host events want teams to come who will not harm his/her relationship with other coaches, and they want to maintain a good relationship with the golf course members and management staff. We lost the privilege to compete in tournaments because of players who had anger outbursts. It did not happen much, but when it did, I felt the loss. It also gave rise to the idea that Christian school golf teams could not be trusted.

Angry Men Need An Attitude Adjustment...

I will share some anger situations, but without names attached. First, let me say this in their behalf. Anyone I've ever coached, especially those who could not handle the disappointment of a bad shot or score, I liked. In fact, a player who cares enough to get mad reveals a person who has pride in what he or she does. However, like a very controversial president once said, "don't misunderestimate (underestimate) me." Because a player has a competitive spirit does not excuse the anger displayed. I've often wondered how much of that anger was learned at home. I know that in my case I learned some anger growing up. Seeing myself as the last person who could help college athletes control anger made me react strongly against it. Anger problems often end up behind closed doors with a wife and children. A well-respected businessman, professor, or politician who has an anger problem might put on a happy face to the public but when he or she gets inside four walls at home on a bad day, all hell breaks loose. This was something I had experienced. Like most coaches, I turned away from high school prospects if they could not control their emotions. Believe me; no fun comes from trying to reel in a really talented but angry golfer. Verses to check out are: Proverbs 22:24-25, 29:22.

I remember a very important tournament, which we had gotten into by pure chance, or should I say by God's grace. This event had "big-name" teams from the West Coast. If we did well and they wanted to invite us back, it could put Liberty on the golf map for strength of schedule purposes. In the second day, I had a player who was about to explode. I came upon him at a par 4 hole, where he had just three putted. I could literally almost see the smoke rising from his ears. As he trudged up a steep hill to the next tee box, I hurried alongside him and said, "Let's put that hole behind us. Better yet, just think about this next tee shot. You must put these bumps behind you."

I reasoned with him in a soft but firm voice. He never looked at me. Knowing we had failed to communicate, I followed him to the top of the hill. Upon arriving at the tee, he took that bag off his shoulder and threw it to the ground. Now, this guy was built like a football running back and stood six feet in altitude. He could throw something to the ground real hard. *Crash, Clang, Clink and Rattle,* went the sounds. The noise those clubs made hitting the ground would have awakened the dead had there been a cemetery in the area. What he did not know did hurt us. Players from three other teams were teeing off on another tee box just above us and to the left. When I looked up toward them the player who had stopped at the top of his swing looked back to see who had made the racket. Three coaches looked right at me as if to say, "Who invited that bunch of unruly disconnects?" Needless to say, we were never invited back. I don't know if my player's anger problem caused it. What I did know was that he had to be dealt with and soon.

Another Liberty player, in a Texas tournament, exposed his emotions in a different manner. We were attending it for the first time, too. I had tried for several years to get our team into this tournament and it had finally happened for us. While standing on a tee box talking to the host school's coach, I heard a loud yell behind me. I thought that someone had been shot by a gun. Instead, my eyes fell upon one of my guys. He had just missed a short putt. Even though he was across the fairway and two holes behind, we could all hear the shrill outburst. The disruption to everyone's game could not go unnoticed or tolerated by the host. We never received another invitation.

Another time, during one of our team's pre-tournament qualifying events, I had a first-year player take a huge chunk of turf out of one of our home courses' lush grassy fairways. He wanted to show his teammates how disappointed he was over a mishit 100-yard wedge shot. Not seeing me standing back in the trees, down went his wedge's club head back into the ground. Up came the huge chunk of turf. I drove my cart up beside him and politely demanded, "Would you please go back and repair your property damage?" He looked at me like I had no right to ask what I had of him and hesitated just a little too long. I went on to say, "That will be a one-stroke penalty." His eyebrows curled upward with disgust. I had just ensured that his opportunity to make the next trip had become one stroke more difficult. I continued, "Next time, it will be a two-stroke penalty. A third time, it will be your last swing on our team for a while." I could see myself back in my college days in his reaction. Actually, I never wanted to disappoint my coaches on purpose. Neither did this young man. Maybe immature and spoiled with a tendency to make "bad-mad" choices is all this young man had revealed. He actually came out of it with a much better attitude. I had accomplished a lot and gained a lifelong friend. I was glad that he did not retreat into bitterness.

Angry Behavior Modification Attempts...

God Is Listening! I asked one of my players, who had been very mad on the course, if he had cursed. To which he replied, "Not out loud, if that is what you are asking me." I smiled and asked him to work on the inner man. I did not proceed to dig any further into it. He seemed to understand that God can hear our very thoughts. He made his own adjustment and told me later that he had a much better grasp of his problem when he realized that God was listening to the thoughts and intents of his heart.

God Did Not Hit That Shot. Another time I had an occasion to stop an opposing player's cursing. In this case, his coach was sitting on a golf cart not twenty yards away. The young man in question used the Lord's name in vain to emphasize his golf shot displeasure. It happened after his very first tee shot in the tournament. Standing nearby, I blurted out the following, "Young man, God did not hit that shot. If you blame Him one more time, I'll call two shots on you." Controlled anger in a righteous manner can be studied in Genesis 18:30, Ephesians 4:26, and Psalm 7:8-10. He looked over at me to see if I looked serious. After he walked off and down the fairway, I went up to his coach. Before I could say anything, he raised his hand, "Coach, you have my permission to stroke him if you hear it again. I've been trying to cure him of it for a long time." Those kinds of coaches fill the positions in college golf. They care about their players and the game. Golf is a Gentleman's game. Most golf coaches see themselves as G-gate keepers. This young man's golf game actually got really good that day and his language never again became an issue.

A Two-Stroke Tantrum. Sometimes taking away a player's favorite pastime would help. It might take years for the results of "tough love" to surface in a college athlete. One time I tried to make a good player get better by giving him a two-stroke penalty during an actual tournament competition. Right in front of the host school's coach, he slammed his clubs down on the ground in disgust. After an attempt to calm him down without success, he exhibited a horrible anger tantrum. It lasted several holes. I told him that two strokes would be attached to his total score in our next pre-tournament qualifying event. The two days of qualifying ended with him going into a play-off and losing. I sadly left this very capable player and the team's rising star at home.

A Two-Tournament Tantrum. Another time a player who was unhappy at losing his seat in the van during a qualifying event made his feelings known. While talking on the driving range with another player, I heard this crashing sound behind me in the parking lot. He picked his clubs up from the pavement and threw them into his car's trunk. Outbursts like this had occurred before. That young man did not make two tournaments because of his lack of anger control.

Mother Knows Best. While at an Infinity Publisher's workshop for authors, one of the speakers told me her son's "angry golfer" story. She explained that while assisting a high school coach, her son began to act up and got violently angry. At first, she did not know what to do. Soon it came to her. She went up and whispered in his ear. I will not identify her but she said, "Son, if you don't get control of yourself, I will have to treat you like my child in front of your golfing friends. I will need to start hugging and kissing you." She explained that with a glaring look he replied, "You wouldn't, would you, Mom?" She headed toward him arms stretched and said, "Son, I would have no other choice." With a smile on her face, the lady telling the story jumped a shuttle bus to the airport. She yelled out, "Believe me. He never got angry and upset on the golf course again." I like that mother's creativity with her son. If more mothers and fathers of junior golfers used this tactic when a youngster misbehaves we could stunt that anger growth real quick before it gets too mature or goes on to college. Her tactic was never an option for me. As their coach, I had to use other means to help my guys cope with their anger.

A coach cannot allow his/her players to lose the respect of the home course staff or its members. I had to also make sure that my guys did not violate the trust of the host coach when at intercollegiate events. Nevertheless, guess who got hurt the most? Yes, the team. We needed talented guys in the van to have a great season. To recruit a good player and not use his ability because of an anger problem was disappointing for him and me. A coach must react for the player's long term benefit and his team's reputation. These were tough things for me, desiring to win like I did.

Anger "Plus" Alcohol, "Bad Combination"...

By the way, anyone with an anger problem will see it magnified if they drink alcohol. Alcohol will be discussed at length later but if a person has either of these very bad traits, anger or alcohol, people suffer and with both, it is awful. I know this from experience, not just by reading about it.

When a discipline issue came up because of anger or alcohol, the few times that it did, I tried to gather as many facts as possible. Trying to size up the long term impact of my decision on the player(s) and my team gave me many sleepless nights. Let me suggest two great books. *Anger Is A Choice*, authored by Tim LaHaye and Bob Phillips, gives a lot of advice and insight on anger management. *Sipping Saints*, by David Wilkerson, discusses alcohol in vivid detail. Being a Christian and a coach, I always tried to immerse these matters in lots of prayer. Even though the player(s) could not see any wisdom in a negative outcome, God wants the best thing for each of us. Knowing that those in authority will stand before God one day for their decisions, I always deliberated long and hard. God looks out into the future and wants to use us to change the world for the cause of Christ. Ultimately, this is more important than winning a golf tournament, going to an NCAA Regional or even making a top thirty NCAA Championship Finals trip. I'll be the first to admit, it is easier said than done. Leaving someone behind who can help your team get to the NCAA East Regional will test most coaches to the max. It did me. I must also admit that I did not always do the right thing for the team or my players. God will judge me on that failure, too.

Alcohol Is Forbidden At Liberty...

Those who drink alcohol may be great people in lots of ways. However, the Bible is clear about warnings to stay away from alcohol, because it makes a person unwise (Proverbs 4:

17, 20:1). I will not spend as much time on alcohol as I did on anger. The reason for this is that anger was a far bigger problem on my golf teams than alcohol. On the other hand, I do think that alcohol's negative impact on student athletes requires us to be honest about its dangers. I am against it, 100 percent against it. Proverbs 23:29-35 tells how wine "in the end" bites like a serpent and stings like an adder. The mind becomes open to loose women and the mouth utters perverse things. Under its influence, a person will lie down on top of a mast, "ouch." When beaten, a person feels nothing. When addicted to its spell and poison, the Bible says that you get up and seek it again. We all know of someone who has had an untimely death caused by the numbing effect of "the drink." Take heed of tragedy in your daily papers, I often told my guys. Read the Bible for yourself and take the wisdom given in these verses to heart. Stop all kinds of liquor and fermented drinks. You have your whole life ahead of you. Now is the appointed time. Again, one drink would not kill you or a friend, but can a person really stop after one? The best assurance is to not take one.

David Wilkerson shouts the dangers of alcohol in more detail in *Sipping Saints* and explains why Jesus "did not" turn the water into alcoholic wine in his first miracle at the wedding. I agree 100 percent and was certainly thrilled to hear author, Dr. Tim LaHaye, of the *Left Behind* books and movie say the same thing when he preached at Thomas Road Baptist Church in a May 2004 church service. Recently, another very famous preacher and professor at Liberty, as well as an author of many books, Dr. Elmer Towns, made the same kind of statement while standing in the same pulpit at a Wednesday night service. He added that Jesus never drank fermented wine at the last supper either. I personally heard two different fathers use the old, old story "water to wine" to justify them keeping a few beers in the refrigerator in order to teach their son how to drink responsibly. That is like saying that a parent or coach curses in order to teach a child or player how to curse responsibly. My first encounter with this misconception came right after I was saved, while teaching a senior high group. A class member told his dad that I was preaching against drinking any kind of alcohol. His father confronted me soon afterwards. What this dad did not know was that his son was known to be a binge drinker. The "water to alcoholic wine" lie has damned many Christian youth to their drunken doom. Another time the issue came up was when a player's father made the case for why drinking a beer was okay. He used the Bible story of Jesus turning water to wine as his case in point. Chapter Two of *Sipping Saints* covers this, "Drinkers Must Be Challenged." The idea is that young people want to hear a message of holiness, more self-denial, and more love for Jesus. The author goes on to say that this generation has lost respect for the church because of foggy moral standards.

In my twelve years as a golf coach, I had only seven players that I thought made mistakes with alcohol and some of them deny to this day that they did it. My prayer remains that if they used alcohol then or started drinking after college that they will find a way to give it up. The Bible says that anyone who plays around with intoxicating drinks will be deceived by it and that they are not wise. Look up Proverbs 20:1 along with 23:32 for yourself, before you lose a good friend or family member who might have stopped his or her drive or walk "into a pit." I believe that we are obligated to care enough about others to say no to liquor ourselves if for no other reason than to be a good example. Don't cause a brother to stumble. He might be looking up to you for leadership. Be the first to say "Just 'Don't' Do It!"

The Campus "Boss" Knows Best...

As a coach, humanly speaking, I answered to my *A.D.* (Athletic Director) and my *J.F.* (Jerry Falwell). Everyone else who had an opinion mattered to me and there were many. But, I had only one main *"Boss"* on campus. One time, I had five players called into the Dean's Office. Working under the radar,

I tried to deal with it in my own way, discreetly as possible meeting with players and Dean Emerick. In fact, he and I talked about writing a book together on the evils of drinking. I had only gone through this twice before with all of my previous teams and I wanted to get to the bottom of this, too. Upon arriving on campus each day, I picked up my golf mail at the Hancock Athletic Center. Mail always consisted of important things like prospect bios and profiles, along with compliance updates, rules, regulations, bills, etc. Each head coach had a file folder with his or her name on it in the Athletic Director's office. In the process of maneuvering my car into a tight parking spot, I heard a familiar honk. Turning my head, I recognized the vehicle. "Doc," as most of his good friends addressed him, flashed me one of his patented smiles. I just never could bring myself to lower my guard that much around him to call him "Doc." After all, I had revered him so highly going back to the night at the Indianapolis Baptist Temple and the first official Moral Majority meeting in 1979, when I heard him in person. How could I call someone "Doc" whom God had used to motivate me to move our whole family to a previously unknown city 640 miles away? We had literally uprooted ourselves and traveled to a far country. All four daughters had gone through Christian schools that this man was responsible for building, with God's provision. But, he had been faithful to do it. That fact alone gave me good cause to refrain from ever disagreeing with him disagreeably. God used Dr. Jerry Falwell to completely change the direction of our lives for the better.

The Plot Thickens...

So, I backed up next to his GMC/SUV truck. Leaning out his driver's side window, Dr. Falwell said, "Coach Landrey, how are you doing?" "I'm fine, Dr. Falwell. Thank you," I replied. "Your season seems to be going well and I'm glad to have that happen for you." "Thanks again, Dr. Falwell," I replied, thinking he had good news. He began his inquiry. "By the way, about that problem you have on the team. How about it, Coach?" A bit surprised, I said, "Dr. Falwell, how did you know?" "Coach Landrey, it is my business to know everything that goes on around here." Wanting to salute, I replied, "Sir, I will take care of it." "Okay, Coach, I know you will and soon, I hope. You know we don't need programs around that bring a bad name on the Lord and the school." I clicked my heels located under the steering wheel. "Yes, Dr. Falwell, I know!"

Let me tell you. Those debates about who was right and wrong were cut short from that day forth. I immediately took care of the problem. None of the five players in question made the final trip of the year. Four would have gone had nothing occurred. We placed last in a very important tournament. Parents questioned my decision. Players said they did nothing wrong, at least three of them. Coaching is not a science. But, *JF* is part of the formula here.

Seven Things To Know About Anger...

1) *Anger Is A Choice*, a helpful book by Tim LaHaye.

2) Everyone has anger problems, Chapter 1.

3) Anger = words + voice + non verbal reaction, pg. 23.

4) Anger hurts your breathing rate, blood pressure, blood sugar; muscles tighten and blood clots form, pg. 42.

5) Anger hurts others, both mentally and physically.

6) Know your anger type, Chapter 6.

7) Answers: songs/thanksgiving/submission, Ephesians 5.

CHAPTER EIGHT

Pranksters Are In My Van

Taking control of four returning guys plus a few new ones that first year did not happen. As a matter of fact, this first group of players had some real pranksters in it. I was the "new guy," a businessman, politician, evangelist, and seminar speaker who thought he was going to run roughshod over these "old timers." Ha-Ha. I'm sure that the returning players who made trips with the team in my volunteer semester realized they had a problem. During my first fall 1992 season, opposing coaches said, "Frank Landrey, you need to loosen up. If you don't, you won't last very long in this coaching business." I pushed the guys hard. They were not ready to be pushed by some upstart "new guy," who had never even coached. Pressing a round peg in a square hole would have made more sense. My trying to take control stressed them out. I would not consider them villainous, mean guys by any stretch of the imagination.

Most things my guys did, good and bad, early or late, in my career, I told them it would go in the book. They all laughed and said, "Sure, Coach, whatever." Hoping my readers will enjoy these tales, too, here goes.

Mysterious "Loose Lids"…

During my first year, lids kept falling off. All the players participated in this "Coach Crime," either as planners or silent partners to it. All I know is someone had trouble getting the tops of salt, pepper, and grated cheese shakers on tightly enough. Others had to see the culprit preparing the roguery. Believe me; they had a great way about them. You know the type of "Good-Fellows" that I mean, don't you? Their M.O. always started out by getting really friendly with me. I should have known that this extra syrupy mood change always happened right before they sprang their next "granulated gusher."

A case in point: We were on our way home from the final fall event hosted by Charleston Southern. The guys had a heated discussion going on in the back. Their hunger pangs had kicked into high gear. This first-year team loved to eat pizza. This time I had already decided to push for a pizza place. So, I spoke up and over the jubilant noise of five happy college golfers. They had just placed third out of thirteen teams in a very good Charleston Southern event. I cut to the chase and said, "You played really good today, guys. Let's go where we can get your favorite food." My diet went to pot during my twelve years of coaching. Let me tell you. No, let Carol tell you. She certainly told me about it. Nevertheless, I had decided to eat the guys' favorite food this time. I pulled into the first Pizza Hut we came to on the road.

Garrick Stiles had just fired a team low, two under par, on the last eighteen holes. Garrick spoke up and said, "Guys, Coach followed me today and I had my best college round ever. By the way, thanks, Coach, for all your help." I had walked with him most of the round and certainly took his kind words to heart. I will admit that I looked for their approval as much as they did mine. Sure enough, Garrick "hog swaddled" me, again, as we call it in "Pig Country," Knox County, Indiana. He had set me up for his next cully. I had totally forgotten the Jeff Thomas prank that left a pile of salt on my salad when eating out on the previous trip.

My biggest mistake came when I left to wash my hands. My thinking was like this. *Someone in this group needs to show some class and cleanliness. I'll go wash my hands to set an example.* Upon returning to the table, the pizza arrived. My appetite was up for the challenge. For their dastardly deed to take wings and fly, it had to be directed to an unsuspecting target. Chris Easley cut and passed a very large share of the pizza down to me. He yelled out, over the other chatter, for all to hear, "Coach, can I say the prayer?" His authoritative voice made the team come to attention. "Of course you can, Chris." Chris went on to say, "Thank You, Lord, for our food and the team's finish today. Please give every team a safe trip home. Amen." Raising his head, Garrick said the following in a jubilant voice. "Everybody say it with me." Tom Anthony, Kenny Hobbs and Chad Hall joined in with Garrick and Chris. Altogether they said, "Great job out there, Coach."

Of course, I never eat my pizza without adding cheese. "Good Fellows" also know these things about their targets. My automatic next move after pizza lands in front of my face is to "Pound It." "Pound It" is my six-year-old grandson Aaron's favorite comment for eating a lot of food in fast fashion. I began my speech of gratitude for their effort and results. "Well, guys, I had a great time out there today. Good work. You never quit on me or yourselves." I went on, as usual, "Do you realize if each one of you had been able to save just one stroke each round, you could have won this big tournament?" I was on a roll and had an audience. "Guys, believe me when I say you will win one of these prestigious events. It will come sooner than you or anyone else might think." Into the pep talk, I almost forgot the most important part of having pizza. My mind tried to focus. *Now what is it? I want something to make this pizza taste even better. Oh. Yes. I need the Parmesan.* I spoke up, "By the way, Garrick, would you please pass Ole Coach that parmesan cheese bottle sitting there in front of you?" "Sure, Coach," he replied. I know I don't have to tell you what happened next.

My wife told me that I had to tell you what happened with the cheese bottle. I blame the length of this book on her.

I grabbed that bottle and, like normal, I turned it upside down and thumped the bottom hard. You know how those bottles get clogged up. I thought this was a normal bottle of parmesan. Not so. That lid flew off and landed in the middle of my pizza. Out came the entire bottle of parmesan cheese. It piled up like a sand castle built on Myrtle Beach. I looked down the table. They were laughing so hard that it attracted the Pizza Hut manager's attention. He came over to see what had happened. "A faulty lid huh, Coach?" He continued, "I will send over a replacement pizza at no charge." I think he knew what had happened, but figured his act of kindness would soften my embarrassment. Pizza Hut people are like that, you know. As you can imagine, I was grateful.

The Silent Majority...

I had to keep some of these players' names anonymous. If a prank had a questionable mystique about it that might not be understood or appreciated by my readers, I left name identities out of the tale. Most of my alumni golfers have families and business positions that deem it risky to hope that a wife or employer will laugh with us. These pranks will be enjoyed mostly by the golfers who had a part in them. Names or not, I carried out my threat "it is in the book."

His On-Campus Short Range...

Some pranks happened without me in the picture. However, they did keep me awake at night preparing explanations. I'm still waiting for someone to tell me who hit that wedge shot through his dorm window into the window of the girl's dorm. The golf ball landed in her flower pot. That's the short game I'm talking about. By the way, did you get a date? Did you eventually marry her? If you did, I'm allocating the trouble that episode caused me to a "special" wedding gift.

July 4th "Powder" Prank...

One prank "of sorts" came at the hands of a Liberty golfer who will remain anonymous for obvious reasons. This young man's foolish act earned him a "malicious" charge for bomb making in his dorm room. His July 4th blast did not merit a Dean's "special project" award. When he explained it to me, he said, "Coach, I just wanted to liven up the campus, not hurt anyone." He did not harm others, *thank* God. However, the police did not think it funny. In the 1990s, when life did not include the horrible bombings of today, our campus and city police still did not take to his kind of prank. The Community Judge made it really tough for him. I do hope he is off probation by now.

Much more mature these days, he knows not to play games with explosive devices. His golf game keeps getting better, too. I heard from him awhile back and he told me about using my short game drills for lower scores. This is how I knew he had matured. Using a four iron to chip with was not going to happen back in his bomb making days.

My "Rainbow Rube"...

Beware. This prank is questionable in taste. I recall one of the best constructed tricks ever played on me. The prankster's precursor set me up perfectly. It came during one of my very first trips as head coach. We drove up to the host hotel, a very exclusive place. All the participating teams were staying there. I had heard stories about the host coach. Known for dropping teams from future tournaments if they misbehaved in any way at all, I wanted to make a good impression on our first invite. I wanted to communicate my concern about the situation. So, I told my players how much it meant to me in my sergeant's voice, "Okay, men, listen up. I want you to be on your best behavior. This host coach will not allow any funny stuff." Back came voices in total unison. "We got you, Coach. No Probleeemo."

Each one quietly got their overnight bag, slipped out of the van and began making their way to the hotel. If you believe that "quiet stuff," you need to coach a little league team before coming to this big league "reality check." Instead, out they jumped, clanging clubs and giving out "hoopla" howls. I got a little upset and settled them down temporarily. It was all very stressful for a nervous coach.

While still in the van gathering my things, I looked up to see one of my players standing near the hotel's front door. There he stood just beyond a line of trees. They shaded the door by day and made an attractive show place for a string of bright light bulbs by night. It wasn't Christmas type lighting. These lights gave off a rather romantic effect.

Try to picture a classy, preppy-type dresser with no fraternity to attend. If he had one, he would have been selected president due to his maturity for his age. Every new coach can trust a senior to be responsible. Right! Okay. You are two for two. Believe me when I say in this case two wrongs don't make a right. I could not believe my eyes. There in plain view, standing straight and tall, he hatched his "Get the Coach Frank" prank. Now, slightly bent at the shoulders, a stream of liquid began arching high and to the left of his body. He had his back to me, but I saw enough to be aghast, by the ghastly sight of it. I could not tell exactly what it meant, but I had a good idea. Out loud in the van with no one to hear, I said, "Senior or not, you do not want the "Big Time" Troubbbbbble coming your way. Lord, just let me get there in time to stop a tragedy."

Jumping out of that van, nearly breaking my neck, I ran over toward the spectacle. Yelling at him, trying to lessen the damage being done, I reached full stride. I hoped for the best. Maybe no one had seen him yet. I yelled, "What do you think you are doing?" By this time, I could almost touch him. I didn't know what I would do first, but murder did cross my mind. About that time, he turned slowly toward me and casually retorted his body backward over his right thigh.

At this point, I could see what he had in his right hand. "Coach, I'm just emptying my plastic water bottle." He had a squeeze bottle in his hand with a crooked little smile on his face. After calming down some, I told him that his little joke would go in the book. Oh, yes. I knew way back then that I would have to write a book. What God allowed me to go through had to be in print! Writing it on paper, for my epitaph, has had a therapeutic effect on me to be sure and I hope it will bring unbearable guilt upon those perpetrators. Believe me; I will not hold my breath for that to happen.

Witnessing To Opposing Girl's Team...

I remember taking the team to a Big South Championship and having myself a really interesting night out. Before this disclosure, let me say in their behalf that most of my seventy-plus players over the years were straight shooters on and off the course. I just did not want a good boy to go bad. So, I made it a point to keep a short leash on them. However, they were attracted to the female gender and I wanted my players to find the right young lady.

On the other hand, I never wanted them to be distracted on a golf trip, especially at the Big South Championship. It only came once a year, in April. At the time of this story, the Big South men and women played the same golf course, the same days, just at different times of the day. The school in question had a fine men's and women's golf program. I had been playing in this particular school's yearly hosted tournament, but never again after this incident. My guys already knew this school's female golfers. Foolishly, I was not aware of the attractions that had developed. Call it a coaching blind spot or naiveté on my part, it was still an error. Liberty finally had a chance to finish in the top three teams of a Big South Championship. Only fifteen shots out of first and three shots out of second place, after thirty-six-holes, I cut my devotional and pep talk short, telling the guys to get a lot of sleep, I sent them off to bed.

Most every night when we traveled, I knocked on doors to get a voice count at about eleven o'clock. Noticing their condo door was ajar, I walked in and found the place empty. So, I sat down in the dark and waited. Half past midnight, a tall, thin, lanky guy slowly pushed the door open and peeked inside. "Are you looking for me, sonny boy?" "Oh, Coach. You scared me. We were just about to come back." I let him have my patented *riot act*, "Just about an hour and a half after curfew, you say?" "What time is it?" he asked. I got hot under the collar and sent the first intruder out to fetch his accomplice.

By the way, neither one ever confessed that they knew the time. All five girls from the rival school were at the gala affair. No harm done, having my two guys outnumbered and all. Nevertheless, the men's team of that school whose women's team distracted my players beat our guys by four strokes in the tournament. Who do you think got the biggest laugh on the way home? We led them by eleven shots going into the final round, ELEVEN SHOTS. After our fun night out "witnessing" to the school's females, their male golfers beat my guys by fifteen shots the next day. Do you think my attitude got better on the way home? We had no music and no talking for at least three hours of the six-hour drive. The whole team took the same punishment. The rest of the trip home, I got my frustrations out. "No more witnessing to the other school's female golf teams after hours," I grumbled. I explained my point in several rather creative ways. We finished fourth, again.

Drive-By "Shoutings"…

There were these two best friends who had a bad habit. They took turns yelling at passing cars. You have heard of barking dogs chasing cars. These two, best of buddies, just liked to yell out of the van. Not every car we passed was a target. Sorry. I have not explained this properly. These were not just any cars. They had hankerings for cars with pretty girls in them. I believe their exact words were, "He-y-y-y-y Ba-a-a-a-by." I eventually stopped it. After the boys yelled and she looked over at the van, they shrugged their shoulders and pointed at me. Not only that, one of them began opening the side doors of the van for better acoustics and antics. I yelled back, "Gentlemen, what would I say to your mothers if you fell out that door?"

In both of these previous stories, "Witnessing to Girls' Teams" and "Drive-By Shoutings," these two different pairs of best friends turned out to be great salesmen. All four finally witnessed to, and yelled at, the right four girls. They married "real winners," let me tell you. Ladies, I hope I helped these boys grow up to be better men, husbands, and fathers. All four have become very successful. They are still "fun loving" guys, but with wives and a bit more maturity.

The Whistling Van...

There were others who played tricks on me. Like the time I pulled up to a restaurant. I was turning off the motor, when I heard one of the guys in the back whistle really loud. I looked behind me to see who did it. They were all down in their seats bent over. *What are these rascals up to this time?* Then, I looked out my driver's side window. There, next to our van, sat a couple of good looking girls in a little red sports convertible. Laughing rather uncontrollably, they waved. Holding up my hands, I pointed to the back of our van. At the time, it seemed the right thing to do.

One of the guys said later, "Coach, they thought you wanted them to get in the back of the van. We feel it our duty to report this to the Dean's office." I hope those young ladies saw the rascals in back of me before they ducked down in their squirrelly seats. That little prank brought laughs for several days. It also made me gun-shy when driving near women. The five guys in the van were: Jared Albert, Andy Braddock, Justin Jennings, Mark Setsma, and Dan Willis.

Jared Albert won the VMI tournament as an individual in the fall of 1995. He led Liberty to another team victory, too. It became one of my eleven first-place team finishes and he became one of my seven individual winners. Jared was a smart student who had a lot of talent. His golf shots went neither left nor right. They went right down the middle. His drives flew far and long. His wedge game impressed me most, taking one bounce and a slight back up. I still remember picking Jared up at the Lynchburg airport in his freshman year. I had more recruiting conversations with him than any other prospect to this date in my career. Jared became the only Oregon player to ever play golf at Liberty. A coach's dream come true; he played his best in the rain. Over the years, I've had guys who played really good in rain, like: Yong Joo, Dan Willis, Jon Wolfe, Todd Humrichouser, Rob McClellan, Paul Carey, Andrew Turner, Jeff Thomas, Jordan Mitchell, and James Yoo, to name a few. But, Jared Albert had a different way of coping in the rain. It would start to rain and Jared would not take an umbrella. Instead, he would take off his golf shoes. Jared could beat most players I've ever coached, rain day in and rain day out. He, like a duck, dared it to rain on him. He told me that rain gave him an advantage over the field. I liked that attitude.

Andy Braddock was a prankster debonair. I had many opportunities to see him in his "fun-action-mode." We had our confrontations and comedy, too. At the Wolf Pak Invitational in Nevada, Andy sank a 210-yard tee shot on a tough par 3 over water. With just enough room for me to stand between the pond and the front of the green, I watched Andy's ball land just beyond my feet and roll over a mound and into the cup, which was about four feet onto the green. I jumped up and down with excitement. As I walked off the green, one of the opposing coaches, who had been there for a while, said, "I wonder what you would have done if he had not hit his first three shots into the pond." I responded with a smile, "You will have to admit he just had a spectacular SEVEN!" Andy and I have a good laugh over it still.

However, while on the tee box with him, my attitude was a bit different. After he hit the third one in the water, I stomped off saying, "Andy, I'm going down there and stand on the front of that green. I had better see your ball go past me, or you don't eat tonight." Andy gave me some late nights, too, listening to his well-spun stories. Later that year, Andy won the Washington and Lee tournament and led our team to another much appreciated victory.

Justin Jennings had a 65 (-6) at the UT Chattanooga tournament in October of 1995. Justin came out of a hospital bed to shoot that great score. He had grit. I once told him, "Justin, I feel good about the team when you are in the van." He probably did not believe me. The truth is that I liked to have players with very little movement or manipulation in their swing's take-away and return. Players with a repeatable pre-shot routine made me feel more at ease. Of course, I wanted players to have a good short game. Justin had all of these good skills. Getting the ball in the hole, that's what I'm talking about. He never gave up either. Justin overcame tough things and that made him a tough guy. In his freshman year when he had to redshirt because of a mess up on his home school paperwork, it was hard for him. This meant that he had to wait a year to play. Just after that happened, I had to correct Justin on a small Liberty Way code of conduct issue. He was a tough guy with a good heart. I remember Justin wanting my wife and me at his graduation. To his delight, we attended. He still stays in touch. You can disagree agreeably, and we did it often. Our friendship and love for the Lord overcame our minor disagreements.

Mark Setsma, another "Whistling Van" man, played several tricks on me. On one Big South Championship trip, Mark came down the last fairway in the opening round limping quite visibly. I knew playing thirty-six holes and carrying your own bag was tough. *Maybe, he has fallen during the round.* Then, I noticed that his left ankle looked like a birthday balloon. Asking him what had happened, he quickly assured me it was fine, "Just a small twist and nothing bad, Coach." Come to find out, Mark had a major sprain in an intramural basketball game for his dorm team—*the night before we left*. Thinking he could overcome it, Mark decided to come to the event anyway. He did manage to finish the tournament and played quite well for his condition. Nevertheless, I soon instituted a "no" basketball policy. Mark played great golf for Liberty and became one of six Scholastic All Americans during my twelve years as coach. I did need to watch my back around him. Mark would sneak up, reach around my chest and pick me up off the ground. I frowned on it. A coach is never to lose control. *Ha!*

After implementing my Performance Based Scholarship System, I told the guys to do whatever they wanted, saying, "If you like basketball, by all means play the sport." After all, I recruited guys who played basketball. It usually meant that they had natural talent and a competitive spirit. Now, with my new system, I could tell them to have fun. But I also imparted a new fact. I explained, "Guys, you determine what you make by how you score. However, I don't mean in hoop points. Golf is the sport that pays your bills. You earn that money by the number of rounds played and your scores."

Dan Willis became an explosive factor for us in his senior year. A son of a preacher man, Dan always came across as very subdued in public functions but not in the van, on campus, or on the golf course. I could count on Dan for an unusual set of circumstances to arise. He led the team with an air of confidence in his senior year and backed it up with one fine tournament after another. His 75.2 stroke average for the 1997-1998 year's twenty-eight rounds included sizzling dynamite rounds at the SeaTrail Resort. We won that 1997 Liberty Fall Classic because of Dan's record-setting thirty-six-hole score of 136, eight under par, which tied Yong Joo for Liberty's all time low thirty-six-hole total. He also liked to have fun on trips. His laughter filled the van. Golf trips were better with Dan on board.

CHAPTER NINE

What Others Think Does Matter

Many parents came up to compliment me on the behavior of my players. I had a parent come to me with a question, "What do you feed those boys at Liberty?" "What do you mean, sir?" I asked. *I'm feeding them just as good as the other coaches feed their guys*, I thought. "No offense intended, Coach," the man replied, "I would just like to have my son act as nice on the golf course as this young man from Liberty did all day." Throwing my head back so as not to look too surprised, I nodded like a formal Japanese greeting. In my gracious retreat, I walked toward the next tee box with a proud daddy's bottom lip quivering just a bit.

In the last tournament of my coaching career, a parent from another team came up to tell me that he wished his own son could have an even temperament like my Liberty player. The man went on to say, "Your player had missed ten putts from within fifteen feet." He remarked further, "I could not understand it. His attitude never changed." I thought, *Andrew Turner wanted those putts in the worst way. He could have gotten really mad.* May I say, "Great parenting, Mr. and Mrs. Turner." By the way, those team dinners out on the back porch were just great on our Penn State trips. Thanks for the overnight stays, ping-pong, and eight-ball pool games, too.

Compliments about my players were common occurrences over my twelve years. Most times people just came up to say how much they enjoyed following their son's group and my Liberty player. Words like polite, friendly, good natured, kind, caring, and just plain fun to be around were said at one time or another. Since I told you about their bad moments, I thought I should share some compliments, too.

Augusta College Invitational, April 5-7, 1996...

In a chance meeting five years later, a father told me the following story. His son had graduated from another school. He recognized me and started up a conversation, "Coach, do you recall the day I came up to you at the Augusta College tournament?" "No," I replied. "Well, I had been watching you and your golfers competing for all you were worth." I remembered that part. I had worked for several years to get into that event. Teams were given free tickets to go to the first day of practice for The Masters. The Augusta College event always had fifteen or so teams. You could look in that week's rankings for the top teams in the country and many were in this event. We were playing "stinky" bad. The wind had gone out of my sails. I knew we were never going to get another invitation with this performance. But, for some reason, I had a peace about it all. Maybe I was really walking close to the Lord in my daily devotions at the time. Most likely, I was just worn out and in a prayer mode to survive the disappointment. Anyway, my heart went out to my guys. They were giving it all they had and coming up short. The guys knew how much it meant to me and were hanging an arm around my shoulder to console me. We cared about each other's feelings and felt the other person's pain.

All Of A Sudden, I Knew Why...

It was awful and sad for us all. I could not understand it. We had played so well earlier in the year and we were playing so badly in this most important tournament. "Why, God?" I had asked. Then the answer came to me as the gentleman went on to tell me his side of the story. Now the rest of the story, as Paul Harvey says so eloquently. He started, "Coach Landrey, I came up to you that day and shared how I wished my son had gone to Liberty." I naturally asked him why. "Coach, I could tell that things were not going well for your team. But, the way you guys treated each other and pulled together during the tournament blessed me."

The Man Ended His Story…

"Coach, my son was so unhappy at the time." He went on, "I knew your program was different. I could see it." Finally, he mentioned the bottom line, "I knew with your team being from Liberty University, Jesus Christ played some kind of part in it all." Now I had the answer to my "why" question. He went on to tell me that after college, his son contracted a rare disease. In the process of all his suffering, the man's son had turned his heart and life over to Jesus Christ. The father explained, "When my son told me of his decision, I, too, made the same choice for my life." This story had a miracle ending of two kinds. First, the boy recovered from the illness. Second, and even more important, they both received an eternal healing. Was this God's Divine Intervention back in 1996 in the lives of these two people? Could five guys and a coach, trying to work out a college athletic "desire for excellence," show what Jesus is all about while working through personal devastating disappointment?

Consequences, Or Compassion…

Playing golf for Liberty always represented a privilege. If you violated a rule, that privilege might be taken away even in your senior year or with the last tournament of a career. One time, in my twelve years of coaching, I breached this policy. A player had made a bad mistake in judgment. Trying to decide what to do, I called Dr. Falwell for advice. He asked me if the young man had come to me to confess, or did I find out and confront him with his violation. I explained, "Dr. Falwell, we leave tomorrow and I could not have found out before playing the tournament had he not told me." He said, "Coach, we want to lift people up here, not push them down. I would take him." Being that he had not included other teammates in his bad choice and had come to me with a confession, I took him. However, I did not condone his conduct and he knew how I felt. We went together on that trip with Dr. Falwell's blessings but not with God's blessings, in my opinion.

As a coach, you always wonder if the compassion a person is shown does as much good for them, long term, as consequences? Only time will tell the rest of the story. Early evidence is that it did. He wrote an E-mail and said, "I just wanted to thank you for everything…no way would I have graduated except from Liberty. I am sorry for all the times I let you down. At the same time, I am grateful for you being there for me. I have learned so much about life while being at Liberty. You cared for the guys, sooo much, and we all knew that. No other coach in the world could have looked out for us more than you did."

Seven Things About Leadership We All Need To Know…

1) Others are watching us.

2) Others need help. We can add value to their lives.

3) Agape "sacrificial love" changes things.

4) Compassion wins eventually.

5) Consequences are a serious option and may help.

6) Our reaction "to bad things" happening to us matters.

7) Our efforts are worth it. Don't give up on people.

CHAPTER TEN

What Every Recruit Should Find Out

This chapter will include what every high school golfer and his/her parents should be aware of when it comes to recruiting. Don't take me for the last word on the subject. Information seekers should find other sources, too.

Have Your Own "Swing Coach" Before College…

Teams are in a hurry to get ready for the fall season and qualifying is a top priority. Try no big swing changes here. The player needs to have his or her swing and game ready for the test of their lives. Besides, a coach may have up to fifteen players and he cannot make personal projects of each one. The job of coaching requires several hats to be worn. Even those fortunate enough to have a big budget must pick and choose what he/she will focus on most. To become a teaching facility takes money for staff and tools. Teaching is a full time job, with big salaries to go with the positions. Take the top fifty ranked teams, most of these coaches send their players out to teaching professionals. A college golfer is normally sent to someone the coach thinks can help in his or her particular area of need: mental coaching or swing changes. Of course, the player must always be the one who pays for these outsourced lessons, not the school. I always encouraged each of my players to find a "swing coach" that they could have confidence in at home. We video tape swings for players and they can send it anyplace in the world by internet or mail. Most of the better junior golfers already have a "swing coach." He or she could be a parent. Get someone you like early and keep them through college. I found that most good players needed prompting at alignment and tempo issues which I could help them monitor. But, most scoring problems came from a lack of short game practice and a need for better course management.

College Coaches Recruit, Mentor, Motivate...

Top coaches spend lots of time recruiting at the best junior tournaments. They become a part of the family, so to speak, early in the junior golfer's tour years. Recruiting is treated like a business. They are out on an interview session. Don't misunderstand me, most of these coaches stay within the rules on recruiting. However, their job depends on success as a recruiter and not as a teacher. Most successful coaches have extra financial resources to go recruiting. Smaller budgeted golf programs figure more time in on phones with players and prospect profile research. Finding a niche in my case meant having a lot of 72-74 junior golfers on the roster. It created competition, which helped me build a better program. I subscribe to the "biblical principle" that "iron sharpens iron." Many good players became great Liberty players during their years of intra-squad competition.

Experience in coaching and especially recruiting of players is not something you learn in college. There are no "How To Become A Successful Golf Coach" courses or classes that I know about. You can buy videos and books on how to coach. I have them all, it seems. But, this business is learned the old fashion way, you earn it one tournament at a time and one year at a time. I think it could become a college academic course for credit. It could be taught by a professor, assisted by retired coaches from every sport. At the same time, coaching is a trade that you pick up, while you observe other good coaches in the process of their trade.

May I suggest that prospective players being recruited should make sure they observe those very same coaches? See them work their team in stressful, pressure-packed tournaments. Take notes on how they keep their players calm and focused when the pressure is on. The really good coaches are exceptionally gifted in areas of communication. They are driven to succeed and willing to take up the challenge without discouraging their players. They are driven to find a way. They make the most of what they are given. They ask a lot of questions.

In my humble opinion, coaches who achieve collegiate results accomplish it by the use of some formula they developed on their own in an eclectic fashion. These successful coaches bring together all they have read about or observed and from many sources. They read about successful inspirational leaders and relate that information to their players. They use it to keep themselves going.

As a recruit, you should seek out that person who will motivate you to be all you can be, in golf and in life. Of course, a Christian coach also prays for his or her players. I think the best coaches start in this business at a rather young age, even right out of college. Or, a late comer might study under a head coach for a long time, and when they finally become the head coach these people stay with coaching for twenty years. In my case I jumped in head first without any formal or informal training. My maturation process finally brought some success with it. Like most things in life worth doing, I failed many times before the privilege of success came. The point I'm trying to make here is that high school players need to know what to expect at a college and from a coach before they attend there for four years. Don't take a prospective coach's opinion as final truth for what an opposing school is like either. Do your own due diligence.

You need to visit every school that you are the least bit interested in attending. Make a list. There are two kinds of visits. "Official" visits start in your senior year of high school.

In this visit a college helps you out financially. You have four "Official" visits. You will need to have documents on file at the school before these visits. "Unofficial" visits are unlimited and can be made any time, any year, and without any documentation, but also without any financial help. Both can be very helpful in making your final decision.

If you don't want certain things to have to deal with in college, like drinking, drugs, and cursing, make a list of it. You want to make sure that you ask questions. Don't assume anything. I've had parents of recruits come up to me at tournaments where their son and my team were competing against each other. They said things like, "We had no idea what we were in for" or "If I had only known what he was like" and "I wish my son had come to your school." Now, it is possible that other coaches would say these same sentences were said to them about Liberty or me, too. But, what I am saying is this. Get all of the information possible about the school and the coach. Talk to his/her players. Listen intently to what their answers are to your questions. Find out for yourself what goes on in the dorms at night. Is there a curfew time to be safely in the dorm? Are girls allowed into the male dorms for overnight stays and vice versa? Does the coach curse at his players when they do something wrong? Are any professors at the school anti-God? As parents you may not want these temptations and trials to bombard your son or daughter on a daily basis.

On the other hand, you may be coming from a different point of view. You may be willing to have some of this negative environment, as opposed to a moral set of campus rules and regulations that Liberty's Deans enforce. A rowdy, restless student athlete might be miserable here. A Christian will thrive in the Liberty environment and has fewer bad peer group influences. Foreign players' parents were always glad to know that there were strict rules on drinking and drugs here. They liked Liberty's curfew hours. What is needed is a good match for a son or daughter with a school's campus life along with the coaching style.

Team Practice "And" Qualifying Mean A Lot...

Does the coach have practice sessions? We worked on putting and chipping drills. Ask for a list.

1) Our three-foot wheel drill had four balls placed equal distance apart around the cup. Make them all in a row several times or if one of four is missed start over.

2) Thirty-foot putts up and down slopes were used to learn feel for lagging to within the two-foot area.

3) Four balls were laid three feet apart in a straight line. You make the nearest first and so on, in a row.

4) Four balls were used in chipping drills from four locations around the green. You had to score no higher than eight from each station.

5) Range time involved contests at target greens. Three players hit to a target in sequence. The one whose ball landed farthest away from the flag or target got a letter until two players had spelled Liberty, leaving one winner.

6) Range work included going through the next event's score card, using the clubs required for each shot.

Does the coach hold enough qualification events to help determine who gets into the van for trips? I told my recruits that I would give ample opportunity for them to get into the van by way of qualifiers. At times I had to pick the team, but not before everyone had a chance to prove what they could do. Is there a sufficient golf range facility for the players to work on their games? Are there several good courses that the team uses for practice and qualifying? A lot more questions could be asked. Ask away. Four college years are at stake.

Make a chart with questions. Leave room for answers, listing each school and coach and then compare answers. I always told recruits all that I knew to tell them about what our school expected and how my personal faith in Christ would impact them. I did not hide the fact that Liberty has Christian professors. I explained that most students and athletes believed in Jesus Christ as their personal Savior. I also told recruits that if they wanted to get into trouble doing immoral things they could find a small crowd of students who would do it with them, either from Liberty or some school nearby. I told them they would be caught and dealt with in a fair and judicious manner. I made it known that I had devotionals where I used a Bible to share verses that meant a lot to me. I promised I would try to help them find answers to life's many questions. But, I also emphasized that I wanted to win at golf and would be committed to doing it.

My Recruiting Criteria…

From time to time I would get a question from a recruit or player of mine about how I decided who could play for Liberty and or receive a scholarship. I told them it is simple. "I want really good golfers. They do need to be open to the things of God." I said, "I believe a Bible verse in James 4:8, which says, *'Draw nigh to God, and He will draw nigh to you.'*" I explained, "My golfers can be black, white, yellow, brownish tan or from a different country. You can be sure that he will have the same opportunity to earn a place in my van for golf trips. The scholarship money will be based on their junior golf results to start with and eventually for good performance in competitions as long as they maintain their grades and good conduct." I told my players that I would find extra money for a separate room on team trips for a girl golfer who could beat my fifth best player out. I wanted them to know that my desire to win tournaments outweighed any want on my part to display a preconceived team, in color or citizenship status, even in gender. Don't get me wrong. I always sought out players who would represent our school's ideals. Ideally, my teams were to represent Liberty and Liberty's leader, Jesus Christ. We were to honor the school's traditions and honor the Lord. We were to do it to the best of our ability at all times.

After hanging up from a call to a great golfing recruit, I would make it a point to say this simple prayer:

"Lord, if he is already a Christian or ever will become a Christian, I want him here. Please send this young man to my team. But only if it is the best for him and Liberty."

I Had A Personal Recruiting Message...

I knew nothing about recruiting other than that our daughter had moved to Lynchburg, Virginia, in 1981 to go to Liberty and how much, as parents, we appreciated the school. Two of our daughters met husbands at Liberty, which I told most recruits. My wife and I had bought into the idea of a Christian education for our four daughters, and we moved to Lynchburg as a family the same year that our oldest daughter became a freshman. I told prospective parents that we were happy that our daughters went to Liberty. After telling prospects and parents that sort of information, I told them that I would not rest until we had a winning program and could compete against D-1 talent.

Adamant about telling each prospect to seek God's will for his life, I lost a few who did not want any part of that idea. Believe me; recruiting became a great time to tell prospects that Liberty cared about them, both as an athlete and person. It offered me a perfect opportunity to tell about my personal relationship with Jesus Christ. I will admit I lost many good prospects by using this up-front and honest approach. However, I saved us both a lot of trouble in the process. Certainly a few slipped by my screening and functioned poorly on a Christian campus. They eventually transferred out but not before both of us gained something. Besides, my prayer that God would not send a recruit in the first place unless he was already a Christian or would one day ask the Lord to save him did not end with their transfer.

My High School 4-8 Handicap Player Advice...

One of my big dilemmas has always been the same. How will I get the guys to be all that they can be with the talent God gave them? If they don't make the grade in golf, how can I help them move on with a life lived out for God.

Decide what you want from college golf before you take on a lot of hassle for possibly very little financial gain, if any. At this point, let me say that I always tried to hold a two-day, thirty-six-hole "Try Out" event in the first few days of school. This would allow a fringe player who had shown some real interest in college golf a chance to make the Liberty team. Every year I left one or two spots open, depending on the returning roster. Sometimes I put players from the previous year's team back into "Try Outs." At the same time, I wanted prospects to face reality.

Many high school golfers, playing at a four to eight handicap (76 to 80) at his home course, thought that at college they would be made into a 74 by some coaching genius. I told them that they were probably going to be sadly mistaken. Not that we have not had a few, but the odds were not good for it to happen.

First: A 76 to 80 average in high school golf is usually based on course yardage distances of about 6,000 yards or less. Add four strokes to an average if this is the case. College golf is played at 6,800 to 7,200 yards.

Second: A junior golfer who did not play in a lot of high quality tournaments fell way behind in skill to those that did. It made sense for me to seek out the AJGA players, being that the top programs in Division-1 seemed to be recruiting them. The experience they have gained under pressure at this level of junior golf becomes critical in taking the next step up to college golf, especially up to Division-1. The length of course and level of competition in AJGA events fit most D-1 coaching standards. Many other good junior tours have been started in recent years. Start where you can find good competition and work up to the tour that challenges you.

As soon as a player arrived at Liberty in the fall, his life went into overdrive. The new classes and academic demands engulfed them like never before in high school. On top of that, golf's qualifying school started immediately. We always had our six or seven rounds of Q-Days begin on or about the third day of school. Then, we went from tournament to qualifying, tournament to qualifying, over and over. The spring took much the same routine, with many hours of "brain sessions" and "physical conditioning" going on in January and February.

With coaching staffs and funds in short supply, do not expect much skill development in college. The top twenty programs are recruiting All Americans and only keep about eight players on a roster. Most schools had fewer players on a roster, not more. So, do not show up at school hoping to find some magical teaching facility. You need a "proactive" approach early in your high school years, if not sooner. Read golf books and watch videos. Find a golf instructor or professional at your local club or parent who can help you. Again I say, "Get a 'swing coach' early in the game and keep him/her through college." Practice and compete, practice and compete, practice and compete. By the way did I say, "Practice and compete?"

Make a list of six schools, three ideal college golf programs, and three that you would take if the top ones are not interested. Set up trips to look over these schools. Make out a list of questions you want answered. Make out a golf resume with your last three years of (summer) tournaments, dates, yardages, scores, and finishes. Include GPA and SAT. You may want to pay for an agent's resume internet listing. There are several that will follow the junior tours. Be careful picking the agent. Some have more experience than others.

A Success Formula, For High Handicappers...

College golf scholarships go to the serious and successful junior golfer who has put a lot of time and money into the sport long before college. He/she has been tested in good competition. Competition is a must.

To those junior golfers with high handicaps and little tournament experience who still want to test their game, I suggest that you consider this list of six things to do.

1) Find a school that offers a way onto their team "Try Out." Find a school that will allow you to work at a range or course during the school year if you don't make the team.

2) Improve your golf game, by continuing to practice while at college. Do not let the game slide for a semester.

3) Enter into a lot of quality tournaments during summers.

4) Find a good teacher at home and work with him or her on your game's weaknesses. Keep the golf coach updated.

5) A college player has five years to play four years of golf. Your eligibility clock starts when you take 12 hours of classes.

6) Pray for God's direction in it all. I've listed it last but this should be the first thing done and then continued throughout.

Research Golf Internet Sites…

*www.AJGA@aol.com**www.cjga.com**www.njgs.com* *www.fcwtgolf.com*www.juniorlinks.com*www.sjgt.com www.uskidsgolf.com***www.juniorgolfscoreboard.com** *www.ijgt.com**www.nikejuniorgolf.com,   www.pjgt.com, www.juniortour.com***nationaljuniorgolfclub.com***   www .Links.org***www.ott@usjuniortours.com***and.***www. FutureCollegiansWorldTour@BlueGolf.com. Call the NCAA Clearing House for information on college golf "Eligibility Issues" www.NCAA.org. Review www.golfstat.com and www.collegegolf.com. *God's Best4U*

Another great place to get started is in an FCA Golf Camp during the summers. Contact: www.fca.org for an application.

Don't wait until you read the rest of this book. Do it now and don't delay. I highly recommend all of the above information. Two websites that keep junior rankings of male and female and tournament scores are www.golfweek.org and www.juniorgolf scoreboard.com. Many junior golfers contact an agent to help them prepare a golf resume and then represent them. A player profile is normally sent to all colleges or at least to a list you choose.

Disclaimer: I do not stand responsible for any of the names and or information given in my book because you are the final judge. I do believe that having more information on how to improve your life and game is a good thing.

Seven Things Every High School Golfer Needs to Know...

1) Have your own "swing coach" before college.

2) Perfect practice makes "more perfect" golf.

3) Competition means to seek out good tournaments. Captain's Choice or Father and Son outings do not count. AJGA type junior events plus State Opens count.

4) List colleges: three "wish" and three "acceptable."

5) List questions about morals, education, and golf.

6) Visit each school for campus life and activities.

7) For the three schools showing the most interest, I suggest that you observe these coaches in events. Find out how they communicate with their players in pressure situations and how they react after bad shots. Observe how the players on these teams act and react to situations and bad shots. They will be representing you and you will be traveling and associating with them on a regular basis if they are underclassmen.

Frank with the Co-Founders of Liberty University
(L to R) Dr. Jerry Falwell, Coach Landrey, Dr. Elmer Towns

College golf has good times—lots of laughs, too
(L to R) Jeff Thomas, Tom Anthony, and Coach Landrey

Birthdays and food were both important
(L to R) James Yoo, Todd Humrichouser, Coach Landrey

Liberty Mascot with team on homecoming parade day

A 1992 College Golf Fellowship Bible Study/Golf Retreat
Resulted in Augusta National trip (See Chapter Eleven)

Inside Augusta National's Clubhouse
Coach Frank Landrey and Jerry Achenbach

Liberty's 2000 "Spring Push" Treasure Coast Classic "victory" (L to R) Coach Landrey, Todd Humrichouser, Yong Joo, James Yoo, Rob McClellan and Allen Hill (Chapter Sixteen)

Larry Mize and Rik Massengale Day (L to R) Top: Kenny Hobbs, Tom Anthony, Andy Braddock, Larry Mize, Rik Massengale, Chad Hall, Todd Setsma, & Dan Willis. Bottom: Gary Leeds, Chris Easley, Jeff Thomas, Jared Albert, & Coach Landrey.
(See Chapter Thirteen)

Frank visits with three PGA Professionals (L to R) Coach Landrey, Larry Mize, Rik Massengale, childhood friend Jon Leonard

GT Alumni Golfers Talk It Over
"They had five things in common"

Old Dominion's Jamaica Trip
Coach Landrey and Coach Murray Rudisill
"Twelve years of coaching friendships"

It was always better when Carol attended tournaments

2003 senior Nick Heyland cleans "In God We Trust"
(Read Chapter Twenty-Four for Slogan's Origination)

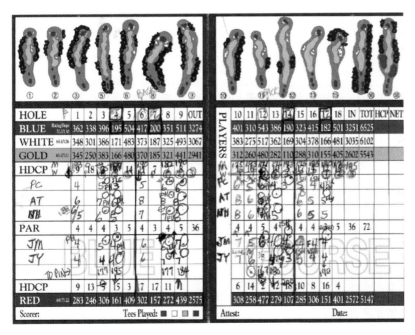

Coach Landrey's Par 3 System
(Actual Score Card Used in Penn State Tournament)

Celebration Dinner after second at William & Mary event
(L to R) Dean Phillips, Son Zack, Andrew Turner, Joe Norman,
Paul Carey, Nick Heyland, and Jonathan Dickinson

These "fundraiser" event winners took home lots of gifts
Coach Landrey's Lynchburg golfing friends: James Shaner,
Bob Goodman, and Brad Shaner joined Frank's sister
Marguerite Meyer-A Vincennes, Indiana, hometown visitor.

NCAA 2003 East Regional Picture
(Left to Right) Top: Chancellor Falwell, Jordan Mitchell,
Andrew Turner, Nick Heyland, Johnny Dickinson, Paul Carey,
and Coach Landrey. Bottom: Joe Norman, James Yoo. *These
seven golfers played the largest number of competition rounds
and held the lowest golf averages.*

Happy Occasion in 2000 Spring Push
(L to R) Top: Todd Humrichouser, Father Mark, Allan Hill,
Coach Landrey, Yong Joo, Bottom: Rob McClellan,
James Yoo

Players asleep in the back .... Coach doing the driving

Coach Landrey's LU logo bag and his putting stroke

"After his retirement, Coach Landrey played more golf."

But, I am ahead of myself. Actually I don't retire in this book. That is a tale for another time. Let me get back to the "tales" in this book, *True Tales of College Golf.*

CHAPTER ELEVEN

One Stroke Wins Augusta National

We were involved with a College Golf Fellowship summer retreat at Reynolds Plantation near Atlanta, Georgia, in June of 1993 when something very special happened. It pays to get spiritually motivated and to attend a College Golf Fellowship retreat. I was glad that we did not skip the Bible study. After the session had begun and we were taking a short break, the moderator told us to mingle awhile.

A gentleman leaned backwards over the chair in front of me and introduced himself. After complimenting me for coaching young men in the greatest game ever, he asked, "How long have you been the golf coach at Liberty?" "I just started coaching this year," I answered. He asked, "Have you won any tournaments?" "No, not yet," I told him. "Well, let me give you a challenge, Coach Landrey." "What kind of challenge, Mr. Achenbach?" "Coach Landrey, when your team and an individual from your team both win a tournament, you call me. I will get you and your player on my home course." A thought flashed through my mind. *How could playing your home course interest me? We play the best courses in the country already.* But to be kind and attentive, I said, "Sir, what is the name of your home course?" What came out of his mouth next would propel us to our first team and individual first place finishes. "Coach Landrey, I will get you both a round of golf at **Augusta National** where they play The Masters Championship."

Kenny Hobbs was sitting to my right and nudged me with one of his long, pointy elbows. "Coach, did I hear him right?" Kenny whispered in my ear. Before I could answer his first question, Kenny went on. "Coach, did he say Augusta National Golf Course?" I nodded my head yes. Kenny dropped a shaking head. It fell right into the open pages of his Bible. He looked to be searching for a verse to claim, to assure him of his first win in college golf. I could tell that his heart had purposed to win a college event, and soon. Kenny lived near the world famous golf course in Georgia. He told me later that he had grown up wondering if he would ever get to play at Augusta. A boyhood dream was growing wings and taking flight in the mind of a talented rising sophomore.

A First Time Victory Is Always Huge...

Now, here is a true story about the importance of just one stroke. October 19-20, 1993, Liberty played in the Davis Elkins Intercollegiate and played a tough UNC Greensboro team in a play off having finished in a tie in an eighteen team D-1 event. What a day we had, with pictures to remember it. JMU placed third, which made us think we could have played against the best in other regions, too. We had not yet moved to the same region as JMU, which happened in 1998. My early teams accomplished a lot.

Our first team win was certainly a mountain top experience. It will never be forgotten by me or those who participated in it. The thrill of our first win far outreached my expectations. We were on the newly opened Gary Player course at Hawthorne Valley Country Club in Snowshoe, West Virginia. The record was 73 strokes for the eighteen holes on the par 72 rock infested and cliff ridden layout.

I was on hand the day that Gary Player had his official opening of the Hawthorne Valley Country Club. I shook my golfing hero's hand and got a signed hat for my trouble. It still adorns the top of a cabinet nearest my home's office door for all to see upon entering. His signed picture hangs just above it. Gary's book, *Golf Begins at 50,* was the first book I bought upon turning fifty. His *"Gary Player on Golf"* video has been very helpful, too.

A Record Remembered: Two Firsts, One Second...

Mr. Achenbach saw a way to motivate Kenny and me. Men who think about others are "special gentlemen." More importantly, his Christian testimony impressed us and he forever impacted our lives. His challenge a few months back made a big difference. We fulfilled both of his Augusta National trip requirements in the same event. Having a team win and an individual win only happened four times in twelve years. Kenny beat his best friend Chad by one stroke to win the individual trophy. He won much more. Kenny Hobbs and Chad Hall placed first and second, respectively, in the very first team victory for Liberty with me coaching, and in Division-1 competition. It would be my first of two coaching triple headers: an individual first and second, plus a team win. Kenny Hobbs won the tournament with a 76-75 and Chad Hall finished second with 79-73. Chad's second round 73 tied the course record. Just a year before, Chad was thinking of quitting golf. Now he was helping Liberty win its first D-1 tournament, getting his college career off and running in a big way. How can I describe my thanks to God?

We won the tournament in my one and only team play off. UNC Greensboro had tied us for first place. Everyone in the van that day remembers the fun we had on the way home. The van was "a-rock-n." The music played loud and all the guys were happily talking about the experience. They talked about our team having a prayer on the putting green before we teed off for the first extra hole. The excitement of teeing off, with it all on the line, took a round of conversation. But, winning it at the first playoff hole was "tops" in the "to remember" category.

Liberty had beaten a very good Bud Hall team on the very first extra hole. Both teams played all five players. The team's five scores were added to get the winner. To his credit Coach Hall would go on to beat us on several occasions over the next few years as wins went back and forth. We had beaten one of the better teams in our 3North Region in just my second year. Liberty had made a statement that we were not going to be taken lightly in Division-1. Liberty had plucked a nice plum.

Let me tell you. I was one happy coach that day and night. Our five-hour ride home was like a trip out to my home mail box and back. It flew by for all of us. We shouted and sang and later ate a big "happy meal." I don't mean a fast food happy meal. I mean a wonderful "steak meal," because we had to celebrate our momentous achievement. Every player contributed to the win and all of us knew that a tradition of winning college golf tournaments had begun. It was no longer my program; now it was theirs, too.

Little did I know that one of the guys traveling that day and playing a solid support role, Jeff Thomas, would one day replace me! God answers prayers. It just takes time for us to see it happen. God's Divine Intervention works that way. Todd Setsma and Daniel Willis rounded out the team for that first victory ride.

Believe me when I say, this coach had no problems with sleep depravation fatigue after that win. I will say more about Jeff, Todd, and Daniel later. They all three went on to graduate as did Kenny and Chad. However, I will focus on the two who had the most at stake in this first team win, Kenny Hobbs and Chad Hall.

I know that Kenny had the most fun. I can still hear that great laugh of Kenny Hobbs. It had a gravely tone, much deeper and mature than other players his age. Maybe his constant battle with bronchial infections had caused his voice to lower one level. We had not been driving long before Kenny leaned over and whispered, "Coach, we did it." "Yes, we won our first tournament," I hollered back, raising my hands off the wheel. "Coach, I think your victory exuberance should exclude a no-hands driving trick," Kenny shot back. I looked over and noticed Kenny's head was lying back on the head rest of the passenger's seat. He had been savoring this experience from the moment they handed him the winning individual trophy. "Isn't that exciting? And you won your first Collegiate Title, too." Then, I waited for his question.

Kenny, raising his body up off the back of the van seat in a deliberate manner, tilted his head and looked over at me with a bit of a crooked grin. He cleared his throat and in a louder whisper, he groveled, "Coach, can you stop the van and call Mr. Piggly Wiggly?" "Do you mean the gentleman we think had some Piggly Wiggly Food Markets, Mr. Jerry Achenbach?" I inquired. "Yes, sir, I have the number." Kenny hurriedly dug into his tattered wallet and waved a sliver of paper at me.

Half afraid that he had changed his mind or possibly had even forgotten it altogether, I waited as the phone rang time and again. A very kindhearted gentleman, golf enthusiast, and wonderful Christian man answered. He agreed to get with me to set a date for an Augusta National golf outing. Kenny was beside himself. Chad still talks about that one stroke. He knows where he could have saved it, especially in that first day's round. Being a great friend, Chad did the Christian thing and joined Kenny in rejoicing.

Had Lots Of Success, But No Augusta…

Later Chad's golfing talents would help propel Liberty to a second D-1 victory. It would come a year later at Campbell. This great team win will be discussed later. I will share a story about Chad at that time which will put a spotlight on his overcoming spirit and personal achievement against the ever-present human challenge of disappointment. Chad Hall had one of his best tournaments during our final event of his senior year in 1996. His performance in that year's Liberty Classic, which was attended by teams like Clemson, Florida State, Wake Forest, North Carolina, East Tennessee State, N.C. State, and Georgia Tech, made the accomplishment even more meaningful. Chad placed seventh in a sixty-player field, many of whom were the best in college golf at that time. Chad made Scholastic All American his senior year, too. But, he missed the coveted Augusta trip by one stroke.

This Bud Is For Me …

There are many great untold coaching stories, what I call tales. Case in point is Coach Bud Hall's drive to a Big South Championship. UNC Greensboro became one of those "friendly" rivalries. Coach Bud Hall felt the same way, as far as I knew of it. Knowing that this was the case, we both chose never to talk about it. Over the years, we had great conversations that could only be described as "Cart to Cart." He usually positioned his golf cart on a hillside where he could see several holes at one time. His long arms folded, he observed it all and it reminded me of a great general looking over the troops. I liked pulling my cart up next to his and breaking up his deep concentration and internalized strategy sessions. I wondered if catching him napping on the hill was possible, but it never happened. I also wanted to know what he was thinking. His coaching style did get results. I wanted to pick his college golf brain trust. While learning a lot about coaching from him, I shared many biblical thoughts, which gave us both a lot to talk about. Who would not want to learn from a man with a gray beard that hung down to his waist? Later, I learned that he had challenged his players by not shaving until they won a Big South Championship. He reached that goal, too. Thank God. We coaches wanted that beard off of him before our own team members started asking for us to do such a thing! I did have a challenge once to shave my head for a Big South Championship. I shot back, "No thanks. My head is not shaped for a Yul Brenner cut."

Here We Come, Augusta National...

Less than ten months from the day Mr. Achenbach made the offer, the call had been made and a date and time set for our visit to Augusta, Georgia. I met Kenny at the front gate. The attendant phoned up to Augusta National's clubhouse for our okay to enter the grounds. As we drove up the famous Magnolia Drive, we talked about those who had made this drive before us in years past. Kenny Hobbs, being a native Georgian boy, knew what this drive meant more than most. Mr. Achenbach met us at the course on that day in May. While driving up to the front gate house, I could almost sense the presence of the world's best golfing talent. What a gracious offer this turned out to be for us. It truly was a golfer's childhood dream come true. After hitting brand new Titleist balata golf balls on the famed driving range, Kenny and I were escorted over to the spectacular par 3 course. Like many past participants in the Masters Tournaments, we played the superbly groomed test of golf using mostly wedges. This occurred before our round on the famous Augusta layout. We had a caddie which is required. The par 3 course was in pristine condition, having only been a month since the 1994 Masters Golf Tournament, which was won by Jose Maria Olazabal.

It was time to play the most famous golf course in America. My first tee shot landed in the right bunker alongside number one fairway. I found out quickly that it was not the trees lining the fairways that counted as much as the precisely placed bunkers. The Masters Tournaments back then did not have rough like today. Those large, undulating, sloping, and lightning-fast greens were treacherously awaiting us on our "never to be forgotten" day of golf. Augusta National Golf Club is certainly all and more than it is made out to be in the best sports writer's most colorful and descriptive words and phrases. However, I was amazed to find the course more wide open than I had ever imagined. My best views of it up until this magnificent day had been from just inside the ropes during the 1961 Masters. My golf hero Gary Player won that year. To watch him pass by my assigned hole for crowd control in my college days was exciting. I had also seen the course from a television camera's vantage point for over thirty years. It was even more spectacular in person walking along with a personal caddic. This golf stroll embedded great pictures in my mind.

On the other hand, walking was a challenge and I was certainly ready for a clubhouse stop at the end of nine holes. Eating lunch in the midst of golf history with pictures and memorabilia on and against every wall kept us both spellbound. The sandwiches were like the course, filled and overflowing with great taste. Mr. Achenbach shared stories of the early days before there was an Augusta National Golf Club. He shared how Georgia Tech graduate and golfing great Bobby Jones obtained the money and plans. He went on to explain how the Masters tournament began and how the first professional tour security staff started here. Insight permeated our gracious host's conversation.

Soon, all too soon, it was time to leave our beautifully decorated accommodations. My meal had barely had time to settle before we reached the second nine's starting tee box. Eleven, twelve and thirteen played tough, just like I imagined those three holes would play. While on the eleventh green, I heard the roar of big, powerful motors behind me. I thought that possibly Arnold's plane had landed nearby. It just so happened that my second shot had found its way onto the large rolling green. My mind should have stayed on the forty-foot putt facing me. Nevertheless, I looked back to see four massive mowers coming down the fairway in a wave formation, each one alongside the other.

Then I realized why I had been hitting the ball a bit fat all day. This professional "mowing team" cut the grass in one direction, always from the tee and always toward the green. The ball rolls a long way down fairways on tee shots because the grass blades lay very close to the ground. Having played my golf growing up with a far less pure and much taller blade of grass my ball sat up more. Even the Bermuda fairways I had played on makes the ball sit up really nice. One answer to my dilemma was to set the club face right up under the ball, instead of the fraction behind it like I had grown accustomed to do over the years.

As you may recall, I had a sloping forty-foot putt facing me. Anyway, I proceeded to three-putt for a bogey and made my way to the par 3, twelfth. I managed to hit the green and missed a short birdie putt. My par at the twelfth and thirteenth gave me a one over score through this popular stretch of tough holes. These three holes 11-13 had been called *Amen Corner* in 1958 by Herbert Wynn, as I remember. Maybe the reason for it went away. I know I said *Amen* making it through those three holes at just one over.

After our fabulous round of golf, my Liberty player and I spent the rest of the day in the clubhouse. We walked into rooms that were used by the best players ever in the game, even one room kept for past winners only. It had been a day to remember for a lifetime. All too soon it was over. I gave Mr. Achenbach a Liberty logo hat, towel, umbrella, and junior-sized golf bag for his highly touted, nine-year-old grandchild. Having made my pitch to Mr. Achenbach for his grandson to come play for Liberty, he smiled and said that he was already headed to an ACC school, which I won't name here. I again thanked our host and waved goodbye.

We headed back to reality, Kenny to his summer tournaments and me to my recruiting and business travels. Our lives had been woven together for a lifetime in one amazingly emotional day. I still have the picture album prepared and presented to me by Kenny. It is prominently displayed in my home for various visitors who want a trip of a lifetime to the green turf of one beautiful golf course.

Chad Hall and Kenny Hobbs are very successful businessmen. They have two children each. Kenny and Jenni have a boy and a girl; Chad and Kristy have two sons.

Team at The Water's Edge with Mickey Hobbs
(L to R) Jared Albert, Jeff Thomas, Mickey Hobbs, son Kenny,
Mark Setsma, and Justin Jennings

My Hero, In Life's Battles...

Mickey Hobbs was diagnosed with a lung disease a few years before Kenny arrived at Liberty. He had a double lung transplant during Kenny's years here. His father and I talked a lot about God's goodness. The fact that he could have a few more years to watch his boy compete in college golf was a blessing that he always remarked about to me. Mr. Hobbs often said, "For me to be able to walk a golf course and watch my son play a few more times is nothing less than a gift from God." This fine father saw his glass half full.

Seven Ways We Can Help Others...

1) Believe that God wants to use you.

2) Decide you want to help others reach their dreams.

3) Be honest with them. Emphasize their potential.

4) Build up confidence in their strengths.

5) Tell them you believe in them. Say so, often.

6) Encourage them. Point out their leadership qualities.

7) Pray with them and for their needs. Watch it happen.

CHAPTER TWELVE

One Good Win Deserves Another

A very successful 1995 spring schedule was well under way. The Campbell event was key, coming before the Big South Championship. My predecessor had taken teams to Campbell's tournament many times and started the rivalry. It did not take me long to make it personal. This was my third time to enter the gates at Keith Hills Country Club in Buies Creek, North Carolina. My previous best here was fourteenth. Although a hostile environment, all participating teams and coaches came with high expectations and were eager to put Coach Crooks and his fine squad of golfers to the test. Everyone wanted to beat the best team in the Big South. Campbell had become a perennial power in the Big South by winning back to back championships in 1993 and 1994.

I soon learned to like the friendly John Crooks. He had a competitive spirit like me. I could identify with his desire to one day get to the East Regional. We often talked about the obstacles confronting us for that to happen. Later, as the battle over the Conference Automatic Qualification into NCAA Regional Sites issue raged, he always had encouraging words for me. "Thanks, John!"

Campbell University has great golf facilities and back then they had the finest college owned course in the Big South. I remember how my mouth dropped open as I drove up to Keith Hill's clubhouse on my first trip there in 1992.

Early in the first round Tom Anthony called me over to a tree. His ball was under it. With branches hanging fifteen feet above, I said, "Tom, you can hit this shot. Grip a seven iron almost at the shaft. Put the ball back in your stance, with hands forward. Land the ball on that leaf in front of the green at the bottom of the hill." "Coach, we have one problem here. I have never hit a shot just like this one." "Tom, you can do this. A seven iron is the right club." I stepped back, again assuring him it could be done. A beautifully hit low shot landed almost on the brown leaf. The ball rolled up and onto the green. It came to rest about ten feet from the hole, a perfectly executed shot. Hanging my arm on his shoulder, I congratulated him on a job well done. Triumphantly we walked together up the hill to the green.

I have at times humorously envisioned in my mind's eye a statue out front of the Keith Hills clubhouse entrance. It is Coach Crooks sitting on a camel, wearing his favorite white wide-brimmed hat, waving a school flag. The Fighting Camels would win even more golf tournaments if this idea was to become reality. The campus is a bit out of the way. Being off the main roads with a rather exclusively small enrollment, many times we passed the school looking for the campus. Did a camel make the first trip? I'm not sure why they have that mascot. Now here we were poised to win in 1995. I had great players that year, 1994-1995. They made me look good. I recall our drive to the golf course for the final round. I will admit I had my doubts that we could make the move needed. Could we actually come from four shots behind in the last round? With Charleston Southern leading and Campbell in second place going into the final day, we were crouched in third place ready to leap.

When we were in the last nine holes of the event, Tom told me I looked nervous. "How can you tell that?" I asked. "You're standing next to me on this seventeenth green," he replied. Normally I hung out at par 3 holes. Tom noticed that at the end of the day, I had been carting from player to player. Aware of my intensity, he knew how to calm me down. "Don't be up tight,

Coach. We will take this one for you." I made my way back to the golf cart and watched as Tom made his ten-foot birdie putt. *Forgive me Lord for not having enough faith in my guys.* A calm peace came over me. I moseyed over, as much as you can mosey in a golf cart, to the eighteenth green, trying to appear confident of a win. Watching my five players finish the fifty-fourth hole was a thrill. Anthony's one under par 71 backed up by his previous two under par 70, helped him recover from a slow start. Having a first round of 77 did not stop him from marking a solid 218. Tom led our team in scoring and ended the tournament in a tie for third place, individually.

Chad Hits His Stride...

Another player who led us in this win was Chad Hall, who placed ninth. It was a special time for Chad and me. Thinking back to how it might have been without Chad, my heart sank as I pondered the possibility of not having him on my team that day. I was glad that he had listened to God. Chad was going to quit the team early in his freshman year. He had been blazing the trail in pre-qualifying practice rounds, even some scores in the mid-sixties. Everyone thought he would be an automatic for one of the five spots in the van, going to the first tournament of the fall.

Then things began to fall apart. He lost his confidence. Like so many good golfers who played for me over the years, things started off very poorly in qualifying. This proved true for many fine recruits in the first year of D-1 golf. To get into the van for our first trip of a season created a lot of pressure, a lot like a PGA Tour qualifying school. Chad missed our first tournament his freshman year because of a high number, "a ten," on the par 4 sixteenth hole. On this day, it happened again. Chad had another big number, "an eight," on that same sixteenth hole. He had missed his second fall tournament in a row. The hole had a much narrower landing area from off the tee at that time, with a drainage ditch to the right and an out-of-bounds off left. The owner of London Downs Golf Course, Mr. Ted Counts, head professional Jerry Conner, and their gifted maintenance staff decided to fill in that ditch. Now the hole opens up for a bail-out right, which avoids the out-of-bounds penalties. Not so, then. Chad's favorite tee shot was a low draw that rolled a long way and it usually stayed in the fairway. His drives held their flight direction better than most, especially on the windy days. Chad hit several disappointing drives on these qualifying rounds that ended up barely out-of-bounds. He had great scores going both rounds until his "big" numbers on the dreaded sixteenth.

After his second time to miss the van, Chad said, "Coach, I don't think God wants me to play college golf." When he and I took a ride in my golf cart, I began with a question, "Chad, have you heard from your dad lately?" "Yes, sir," he replied. "Will you do a big favor for me and talk to him and God before making a final decision?" I asked. "Yes, sir, I will," he replied in a humble voice. I began to explain how decisions do impact our lives. "Chad, your decision to trust Jesus Christ as your Savior was a big decision, much bigger than you playing college golf." He agreed. I added that his coming to Liberty was a big decision, too. Again, he agreed. "Golf is a lot like life. Sometimes you win and other times you lose." He nodded his head in agreement. "Chad," I said, "losing is what I have problems with. You are competitive like me and I like that about you. The other side of being competitive is our questions about the bad things that happen to us when we try our best." I talked about how all of us at times want to quit in life. "Can I make an honest observation?" "Sure, Coach." "Chad, you have God-given talent. So, why should you quit on it? This is just too soon for you to give up on your dreams." I'm not sure exactly what the Lord had me say to Chad. But, to my great pleasure, it was the right thing, at the right time. Back at his car I made one more observation, "Chad, more competition is all you need." Soon after that conversation he won his first tournament, a Ken Roberts' event played at

London Downs with a winning score of 143, one under par for thirty-six holes. Now Chad had helped lead our team in a college victory. It was a triumphant climb for Chad Hall, to be sure.

Knowing You Can Achieve A Big Win "Helps"…

At the awards ceremony, while giving Liberty the first place team trophy, Coach Crooks made kind remarks. He said, "Liberty's D-1 golf program came of age this week. I congratulate Coach Landrey for bringing a quality team that competed fairly for their win." He may not remember the words and they may have been a bit different. But, I remember how his kind comments gave me inspiration to "keep on keeping on." It became a "coaching highlight" that will always be cherished. Thanks, Coach Crooks. Liberty's tough-fought win in a really good Campbell University event ensured me of our ability to compete at this level. Beating the second-place team, Big South rival Charleston Southern, for the second time in a year was sweet. I still consider the Campbell win to be one the most prized tournament victories of our eleven first-place finishes. Having come in my third year to coach and being a top Division-1 field of fifteen teams, it certainly made me happy. Beating a Big South powerhouse like Campbell University, who placed third, rang bells for me. Beating them for the second time in a year helped our D-1 image. During my twelve years, Coach John Crooks represented Campbell University with a "touch of class." Wanting to be a better coach myself, I liked his style. Coach Crooks had a very successful high school and college golf career himself, and he knew what it took to make his players better.

The team I had in 1994-1995 accomplished some wonderful things. Our 1994 fall ended with a second place finish at Charleston Southern by beating them on their home course. Todd Setsma's 73-67 four under par won him individual honors. Tom Anthony's two under par last round 70, Jared Albert's one over 73 first round, Kenny Hobbs' even par final round and Mark Setsma's two over 74 first round all contributed to the team's success. Campbell placed third behind us in a solid field of seventeen teams. This fine fall finish turned out to be our springboard.

There were many program highlights in the *spring of 1995.* The first came at East Carolina with a fourth place finish out of nineteen teams. We beat good programs like: Richmond, Marshall, UNC Charlotte, UNC Wilmington, Duke, Old Dominion, and Winthrop, which made it special. Our next stop was the Campbell first place finish just described. At University of Virginia, we placed seventh out of seventeen teams beating fine programs like: Wofford, Augusta, Furman, Coastal Carolina, UNC Greensboro, Maryland, and East Carolina. Our final tournament of the spring at Carolina Country Club in Spartanburg, South Carolina, with Wofford College hosting, was truly exciting. We finished that event ahead of some well-known golf programs like: North Carolina State, East Tennessee State, Georgia State, and East Carolina. In fact, we were just four shots out of fourth place. Todd Setsma tied for first place, individually, with a sizzling seven under par 137 total. Todd's brother, Mark, was second low for our team and tied for twentieth with 147. Not bad for a freshman. Chad Hall tied for thirty-fourth with 150, followed by Tom Anthony with 155. This team was definitely one of my very best if not the best I ever coached. This team had leadership, character, and class acts all through the roster of players. I really had two teams of equal talent.

The 1994-95 Team Roster…

Participating players were: Jared Albert, Tom Anthony, Andy Braddock, John Hahn, Chad Hall, Kenny Hobbs, Justin Jennings, Gary Leeds, Mark Setsma, Todd Setsma, Jeff Thomas, and Dan Willis. *Note:* Jeff Thomas as of July 1, 2004, became the new Liberty Head Men's Golf Coach.

Seven Things We Need To Know About Trouble...

1) Everyone has it. We are born full of trouble.

2) We are going into trouble, already in it, or coming out.

3) Two people are better than one, don't go it alone.

4) God cares about our trouble. He awaits our prayers.

5) We need to let God help us through trouble.

6) Our prayer to God starts His help to us.

7) Never give up on life. This too shall pass.

Trouble Comes From Three Major Sources...

1) The Devil: Fight Satan with Scripture like Jesus did.

2) The Flesh: Flee from temptations like Joseph did.

3) The World: Overcome the world's pull by focusing on other's needs and getting out the Gospel message that Jesus is the way, the truth, and the life (See John 14:6).

Short Chip Shots***Right Handed

(1) Position feet with ball in the middle, others would say ball on back ankle. Try both.

(2) Flare the left foot out one inch or so.

(3) Swing club back and through same distance and with relaxed hands and pace.

(4) Pick a spot just on the green for a target.

(5) Practice from different distances greenside with your seven through sand wedge.

(6) After determining your roll with each club, now pick a hole and the right club.

CHAPTER THIRTEEN

Golf, Wrestling—Both Dropped

I have found that most good things come with some setbacks. It was a bright and sunny morning. I had been called into the office of then Athletic Director Chuck Burch. Thinking that he wanted to tell me of some upgrade for the program or possibly congratulate me on the big intercollegiate tournament with seven top-twenty teams arriving again in the spring of 1996, I bopped right on into his office and sat down in the big, brown, leather sofa.

"Hello, Mr. Burch. How is your summer going?" With school starting in less than sixty days, my curiosity had been killing me. I had pushed for some financial improvements on our budget with no results. Maybe today would be the beginning of a larger golf budget. While still earning $3,000.00 a year, the work load had doubled. I must admit that I created a lot of work by putting on golf tournaments.

Athletic Director Burch stared at his desk. Then he looked up at me and said, "Well, Frank, I don't quite know how to tell you this very bad news. Liberty's Budgeting Department has dropped wrestling and golf. It will be official come July 1." "But, why just after both programs had such great results in 1995? Our golf program won at Campbell and had so many program building accomplishments." "A needed cost cutting measure, I suppose," Mr. Burch replied. I left his office half mad, half bewildered, and totally dismayed.

How Does God's Divine Intervention Really Work?

As the Lord would have it, I was playing golf the next day with Jonathan Falwell, Dr. Falwell's son. I had never played with him before and have never played with him since. Is that strange or not? Would you say it was just pure chance? Anyway, it came to me during the night before that I should write something up as to why golf should not be cut. With plans to give it to Jonathan the next day, I stayed up late to pray and to work on this paper. My mind and pencil worked until about four in the morning. The explanation told how golf was actually a revenue sport for the school. It detailed the costs of the program specifically related to our operating budget and golf scholarships. At the time, I had recruited a roster of fourteen players with only three scholarships. The revenues generated for the school from those players not receiving golf money well outpaced the costs related to our golf program. As soon as Jonathan and I met that morning, I asked him if he knew about golf being dropped. He seemed surprised. I began pleading my case, "In all due respect to other sports here at Liberty, golf is certainly as much a revenue generator as any other sport. We have no facility to keep up and no staff to support."

The Most Memorable Celebrity Moment...

I told Jonathan Falwell how one fundraiser made golf worthwhile. We had a special testimony by a famous player, Larry Mize. He and I had five things in common.

(1) We both played our college golf at Georgia Tech.

(2) We both had the same golf coach, Tommy Plaxico.

(3) We both had had a "born again" experience.

(4) We both had a Christian friend in Rik Massengale.

(5) We both had a favorite college golf charity, CGF.

129

Winning the 1987 Masters made Larry Mize an exciting celebrity for a fundraiser. He certainly helped us raise local interest in Liberty's golf program. Even "Mr. Sports" Dennis Carter of WSET came out and intervicwed our guests. Rik Massengale spoke as well and had won multiple times on the regular tour. My golfing friend Randy Dunton challenged me to go for it. This helped encourage me. We had more newspaper reporters and TV personalities there that day than my golf program would ever have in one place for one event ever again. I asked Jonathan Falwell to please take my letter to the people who could make a decision to reinstate golf. In it I listed reasons why golf should be kept.

(1) Consider the free advertisement with fundraising events like what happened when Larry Mize came to town.

(2) The value of having Liberty's golfers as human walking summer billboards as they carry their Liberty logo golf bags.

(3) Figuring fourteen student golfers' dollars for attending Liberty less the three golf scholarships given out, Liberty is left with a very large net-plus revenue gain, even after golf's operating budget is taken into account.

Liberty's Golf Program… To Be Reinstated…

My hopes and dreams for golf were rekindled with this announcement. I am still grateful that Liberty kept the golf program as a sport. However, it was only going to be reinstated if I could raise the program's operating budget for one year. With that challenge, there came a promise to never drop golf again. Who would come to my aid in this time of need? I made a list of those that might care enough to help.

Friends Rescue Liberty Golf…

A "100 Hole" Golf Marathon and a Captain's Choice were held which helped raise our 1995-1996 operating budget. Let me thank those who participated in that monumental day. Pepsi helped, thanks to Maxie Wilkerson then, and Sean Councell and Anne Wood since. Many got friends to pledge money for them to play 100 holes. Subway owner/operator Keith Childers helped with awesome subs late in the day. Carol and Harry Betham's wife Susan verified par 3 prizes.

I remember our early arrival on a very cold morning at Ivy Hill Golf Club. In they came at daybreak, one at a time. Brian Betham took golf bags to carts for our participants. Harry Betham shoved hot chocolate into their cold, stiff hands. Later in the day, my golfers took around those awesome "save the cow" Chick-fil-A sandwiches, which were provided by our area's local owner/operations manager, Mr. Jerry Stevens. I recall playing a total of 114 holes. Some played more than that number to help raise money. Among those who participated that day included my Sunday school teacher at the time, David Langley; Liberty's infamous Baseball Coach, Johnny Hunton; and Liberty's Provost Professor, Dr. Earl Mills. Other participants were my team's faithful supporter, Jonathan Falwell, and the one and only lady to play that day, Carol Casaleanova. All took up the cause with me and played their hearts out to raise money. Others that helped me raise funds over the years are David Benoit, Don Fanning, Bob Goodman, Ron Godwin, Tim Hill, Mark Miller, Buddy Moore, Josh Oppenheimer, Jim Knabel, Garry Sims, Jim and Brad Shaner, Paul Sunwall, Thomas Wharton, John Williams, Scott Worthman, Elmer Towns and many parents like Ron Richards, "all my heroes." Rick Smith and Tony Camm helped start the Frank Landrey Intercollegiate in October of 2005. Thanks for the memories.

With us teeing off at around 7:00 A.M., playing all day and to the edge of darkness, a long day ensued. Those were the days that a Golf Marathon meant an endurance test for volunteers. This was a reality check for me, even at the young age of fifty-five. I fell into a bath tub that night at about eleven o'clock. Looking up, I said, "What a fine kettle of fish You have gotten me into this time, Lord!" I think I heard Him say, "You had to go and get golf reinstated."

All I know is that a person needs to get help when the body does not react well to this much activity. I've utilized a chiropractor three times in my life and many physical therapist technicians. I personally have been helped by both over the years as well as medical doctors. I like having a health team in place. It is not for everyone, however. So, I am not endorsing anyone or any stretch plan but physical therapist Shane Stickle and chiropractor Dr. Ed Bauchou have helped me recently. I've listed some stretches that I came up with in an eclectic fashion that helped me get over that bad left heel problem described in the twenty-third chapter. I had to drag that leg and foot all day long.

Seven Sciatica Stretches That Have Helped Me...

Disclaimers: None of these stretch suggestions are sure cures. Consult your doctor before attempting these. Frank Landrey and/or PGI, Inc. accepts no responsibility for any injuries while attempting any of these stretches.

Note: Grasp something to maintain balance on standing stretches. Hold stretches 10 seconds to stretch the hip joint.

1) **Standing: Put weight on left foot toe/ball. Step forward with right leg and hold position then gently rock your body backward. Hold both positions for ten seconds.**

2) **Standing: Fold left leg taking hold of left ankle with left hand. Pull upwards slowly and move leg backwards.**

3) **Step up onto a curb with weight on left foot and toe. Lower your body while holding on to a car hood or post.**

4) **Sitting: Extend legs out in a "Y" and slowly reach to your left foot's toes with the left hand.**

5) **Sitting: Lift left foot up and onto the right knee. Gently pull up on left knee to stretch left hip area.**

6) **Lie down: Place left foot on right knee. Pull left knee to the right with right hand, but keep left shoulder down.**

7) **For a right foot problem, reverse these procedures.**

CHAPTER FOURTEEN

My GCAA Convention Question

My first national meeting with other coaches was very exciting. I observed what was going on during that initial GCAA Convention. It was held in Orlando, Florida. During my twelve years to coach, I met many coaches and found most of them to be friendly and cooperative. Gregg Grost, Executive Director in my last few years, kept it family friendly. As the new guy in the family, I especially liked the open and fair way that issues were discussed. Something struck me odd, however. It was the way in which a team could get to the NCAA post-season tournament. You had to be picked by the National Committee through a national ranking system or by a Region Golf Committee. One thing bugged me. Conference Champions were being left out.

Conference Championships meant nothing when it came to deciding who would go to each of three NCAA Regional sites at the end of every year. *How could this be?* I thought. The next year I went back to the same old, same old. Schools with the most going for them like: weather conditions, budget size, and school name recognition basically ran the convention and came to the same conclusion every year. Schools must earn their way to a post-season NCAA National Regional by participating in the right tournaments. This process, along with other criteria, ranked all schools in a system that favored the more established schools and golf programs with better access to raise budget dollars. The problem was simple to me. The system also favored golf programs, which always seemed to be in the right tournaments. Most schools will never be invited to these events. With the number of allowed tournament days dropping to 24 per team, the higher ranked teams became even more selective in scheduling to only play against very high-ranked teams. Added to this, to overcome the fewer days, the better programs began having more two-day events with fifty-four holes. This required at least one day to be thirty-six holes and that led to inviting fewer teams in order to finish. A net-net result was less access for the more underdeveloped golf programs. We lost out at great events like Duke, Furman, and Virginia. All of this affected recruiting which ultimately determines the quality of a team's golf program. I just could not get it out of my mind. Lesser ranked teams needed a chance to climb the mountain.

After my very first golf season, I could see that the Big South Championship did not mean much to coaches or players. It had become just another event to my own Liberty golfers. During the next year's tournament schedule, I began to ask several other coaches their thoughts. It seemed unfair to me. Other sports allowed Conference Champions automatic berths into their sport's NCAA post-season play.

I remember asking several of my own players and many opposing coaches to pray. I asked for people to help me push for a change. There did not seem to be much interest in this idea. After a lot of negative responses, I asked a seasoned coach to take a cart ride with me just before our own Conference Championship on April 14, 1996. We were having it at Colonial Charters Golf and Country Club in North Myrtle Beach, North Carolina. After expressing my concerns to him about the injustice being done, he looked at me like I had lost my mind. "Who do you think you are?" he asked. He went on, "You will cause your team to lose any hope of getting into the big tournaments. Schools are invited to these key events or don't you understand the system yet?" I left that brief meeting very discouraged and heartsick.

Fast Forward BSC Dinner, Year 2000…

Four years later, that same man came up to the podium during a PUPS Big South Conference awards dinner on April 16, 2000. To start this Palmetto Utility Protection Service (PUPS) sponsored event, the distinguished coach said, "We are here tonight preparing as a Conference to send one of our teams to an NCAA National Championship Regional site." He went on, "We could not do this last year. In fact, it has never been done before in all the years that I have coached. But, we will do it this year." That part I knew. The next thing he said shocked me. "There is one man here tonight that I know believed it could be different. I often told him to stop pushing for Conference Champions to have an automatic berth into the NCAA Regional." This man speaking was short in stature but a giant in desire and talent. He always seemed to have a bit of a tough guy image. Turning his head to the left and toward me, Eddie continued to speak, "I am now here tonight eating my words, and saying, THANK YOU." I sank down into my chair, so as to not be seen so easily. Believe it or not, I was a bit embarrassed. I'll admit it now. My good friend and tough competitor, Coach Eddie Weldon, was talking about me. I thought that would be the end of it. His next words overwhelmed me. "Coach Landrey, would you please stand up so that I can apologize to you publicly." Coach Weldon told our group of Big South dignitaries, players, and coaches the following: "I can remember when Frank Landrey stood up at our GCAA National Convention and asked why Conference Champions did not go to the NCAA post-season tournament, like other sports." Tears welled up in my eyes, like they just did as I'm retelling it all.

My own Liberty guys seated around our table were not aware of the struggle waged in the past that they might be given this privilege. Now at a Big South Conference Championship, Coach Eddie Weldon was saying a nice thing. I was overwhelmed by his kindness and appreciation.

Thinking Back, The Way It Happened...

Tears rolled down my face as I sat back down. While dropping my head on the back of my hand to hide the tears, I pondered the blessing of having one of my very big dreams come true. I sat there in that Big South banquet hall thinking about those GCAA Conventions that led up to the automatic Conference Championship NCAA Berth.

The first year that my mouth began to move for this change proved scary indeed. With about 200 coaches seated all around, I wondered if my legs would support the stand I wanted to take. I hoped that the right words would come out if I did get recognized, knowing that someone else would be received better than an upstart intruder who had not passed through "Coach Protocol." My mind raced ahead. *A Class "A" Professional would make a better messenger. They seem to dominate coaching staffs of the better teams in NCAA Division-1 competition. Others are more seasoned than I and certainly more influential. But, for whatever reason, they have lost their vision for this particular change.*

When my hand was recognized, I began to speak. "Gentlemen, I visualize Conference Championships that all coaches can get excited about. I believe that automatic entry into the NCAA post-season tournament for Conference Champions would help jump start new coaches and give the weaker programs a chance to catch up. Competing for the best high school prospects against the more established and higher ranked teams make it difficult to recruit the better players. As a new coach, trying to build my fledgling golf program, I don't like the present system. One key question comes back to me from every good recruit, which is this. 'What are your chances of making the NCAA tournament?' Prospects tell me that their preferred school tells them they will go to NCAA post-season competition like always. Weaker programs would do better by telling recruits that their team just needs to win a Conference Championship."

One coach leaned over and said, "It will never change." Another nudged me and barked, "Why are you using up valuable time with that garbage? Anyway, what do you know about it." Another said, "Your idea is a mute subject. It has come up many times only to go away." One grabbed my arm, "Hang tough, Coach Landrey. Many want change."

At every tournament we went to the next couple of years, I made sure that the same subject would come up. I had decided that no one was going to forget about it. Every year I brought it up at the GCAA Convention. Finally plans were made to present the idea in a more formal fashion. Opposition to the change stood firm in the beginning. Many times I had my doubts that enough would stand with me. Surprisingly, the idea began to gain momentum and a near final proposal was being formulated in the 1998 convention.

Getting up at 5:00 A.M. that morning was not my cup of tea. My heart pounding harder than normal, I had to get myself ready for today's confrontation and debate. We needed a majority vote from the 200 plus coaches and members who were going to gather soon in the big hall on the final day of our GCAA Convention. At the end of yesterday's joint session there was a "buzz" that hung in the air. How would the rank and file vote? The presidents and athletic directors had to approve anything the GCAA coaches agreed on. The formal request would go from them to the NCAA. We still needed the required votes today.

My energies were focused on running copies of my handwritten proposal. It would make adding Conference Champions more palatable to the better teams. Adding a new feature to the original plan by enlarging the field of teams from sixty-two to eighty-one might satisfy more coaches. Then, not only Conference Champions, but more of the top ranked teams in the national polls each year would go to the post-season bonanza. The idea was that there would always be fewer Conference Champions taken each year than the newly proposed expansion of nineteen teams, because several Conference Champions would also be given entry as a region pick. The leftover spots could be given to programs that otherwise would be left out, resulting in compromise.

Entering the room being set up for our convention members, I stood alone looking around. I prayed for wisdom and God's help. The idea came to me that I should place a copy of my handwritten proposal on top of each person's breakfast plate. If coaches wanted to eat, they had to move the proposal out of the way. I hoped they would scan its contents. A few workers started placing water pitchers around, as I moved from table to table.

A great day followed. Many stood up and said the time had come for a change. Others made it happen with their own individual efforts behind the scenes. Some on the committee felt that it would be the right thing to do and the right time. Others prayed, like me, for it to happen. God gave the increase. Conference Champions had a "Yes" vote. Finally, right won the day. Six years from the first time I stood up, it became a reality and in the spring of 2000 it happened. Praise the Lord! He blessed the many prayers, while we passed the verbal ammunition. Now nineteen more teams, including Conference Champions, participate at three NCAA Championship Regional sites. Increasing the field to eighty-one teams from the previous sixty-two was now reality.

What made me so persistent for change? Maybe my past life in the food business, struggling against the giants in my industry who wanted the little "Barbecue Man" to go away. Maybe it was the Georgia Tech Admittance Department telling me to go away back in 1959 after my entrance exam score was one of the three worst for all entering freshmen. I entered Georgia Tech taking only pass/fail subjects and did prove myself worthy by graduating. College teams will prove themselves worthy, if given enough time for a maturation process to occur, which might take ten years.

Perfect Ending Not To Be...

My mind bolted back to the 2000 Championship banquet. *Icing on the cake would be if Liberty won the first Conference Title, allowing us to make the first NCAA trip to represent the Big South. That would be poetic justice, Lord.*

I had reason to be thinking this way, even though we had never finished better than a fourth in the past. We actually were leading the tournament after the initial eighteen holes of competition. This had never happened before. In fact, Liberty had a player who shot a sizzling 63 the very day of the banquet. Our South Korean golfer, whose family moved to Chantilly, Virginia, made headlines. Yong Joo had broken the Big South individual eighteen-hole record and set a record for the golf course, as well. He went on to win the individual first place trophy by six strokes at seven under par for fifty-four holes. Liberty, however, could do no better than fourth as a team. Ironically, my guys beat Eddie Weldon's men by just a few shots. His many fine teams beat Liberty several times in my tenure, to be fair in my accounting.

It takes more than one player's great golf to beat the "Southern Boys" on their home turf in the Carolinas in early April. Liberty's golfers had only been playing about a month due to some unusually harsh weather, while the Carolina teams had played for two or three months in warmer conditions. Carolina schools have excellent coaches, a multitude of golf courses (we have plenty, too), and practice facilities (our situation is much better today). We always faced an uphill battle come Conference Championship time. My guys had beaten all Big South programs during the regular season while I coached, but at least three teams always seemed to find a way to beat us in the Championship. Maybe I wanted it too much and my guys picked up on it. More than that I really think we need a better way to get ready. *Hum, a driving range with heated hitting stalls works.*

CHAPTER FIFTEEN

Building "Champions" Two Ways

Right at the start of coaching, I immediately began to dream about what the program could be before I had to stop. Mine was a two-pronged purpose.

(1) While my primary task was to recruit the best golfers possible, my next duty was to turn all who came my way into the best possible player they could become.

(2) At the same time, I was eager to put my energies into impacting their lives with the positive message of the Gospel. With over twenty years of experience in giving out tracts and witnessing, I decided to make sure the guys had a good example of what it meant to be a soul winner.

I'll admit that when we played poorly or I coached poorly, I was less apt to do the right thing spiritually. Constantly, I had to work on my attitude. It was an everyday thing. Competition had always brought out my desire to crush the opposition. Too many times in my experience with sports, losing was directly related to feeling sorry for the opponent. Growing up trying to beat my older brother in every kind of competition imaginable and to be the smallest kid in grade school sports, gave me a competitive drive. Trying to turn that heightened emotion off after a tough loss was especially hard for me. I tried my best to be a good sport about it, but sometimes it was more than a small task and failure happened. It is no less true today even at sixty-five years old.

A Desperate Family Stranded...

We had played badly. As usual, it came down to a shared responsibility for our team's poor performance. Nevertheless, I took it very hard. We had an opportunity the last day to beat many top teams. With the event being played on a course that we knew well, it disappointed me. The incident that follows happened while we were on our way back from a James Madison Tournament. The date: October 25, 1998. We had just finished our final round on Stony Creek Golf Course, at the popular Wintergreen Golf and Ski Resort.

While this is not a paid advertisement, I would like to thank Wintergreen for allowing my team to play their beautiful golf course many times, in practice and qualifying. Good people like Wintergreen make college golf happen.

Darkness began to creep into the sky. Finding ourselves way down the finishing list, our hardy efforts on the course had worn us out. I had not spoken two words to the guys since leaving the parking lot. As I scowled at passing cars going by on my left, I noticed out of my right eye a mini van off to the side of the road. Three rather sturdy-built men stood around it. While I knew that a vehicle stranded with the hood up meant trouble, I thought, *No way, Lord. I'm not stopping. Just have them get help from someone else. I don't remember much help today when we needed it on the golf course. Besides, I'm tired and ready to get these guys back.*

My players might have thought I was a giant in the faith that night, being they did not hear what was going on in my head. They just saw and heard what happened next. "Guys, we need to turn around," "Coach, did you decide to feed us?" "No," I answered, continuing my explanation. "Did you see that family standing by the road? I'm going back to see if we can help them out of their jam." The van got really quiet. Maybe my southern boys felt uneasy helping three tough-looking African American men. More likely, they realized this stop would make them miss the school cafeteria.

141

Jumping out, I said, "Hi. What seems to be the problem?" One of the taller men with a wrinkled brow talked first, "Let me tell you how glad we are that you stopped. We've needed help for several hours. The baby in the back seat with his mother needs to be taken to a doctor soon." "Can we take you?" one of my guys asked. "No," said the gentleman holding a towel. "There are too many of us and you have a van full of people yourself," replied the third and shortest man. "Okay. What can we do for you?" I asked. He went on, "With this flat tire, we have no way to lift our mini van." "Guys, open the back of the golf van. Get out that jack. It is under all of your golf bags and overnight totes," I said. Finding it and a flash light, I left them both and some money. When I had prayer for them, tears began to flow. I also gave them all Gospel tracts and personal pocket Bibles and told them that God had used their troubles to remind me what really counts. They all thanked us. Those not working on the vehicle waved goodbye until we were out of sight.

All Is Well That Ends Well...

As we drove off, one of my players asked why I would leave them my expensive jack tool. I explained how I had bought a brand new jack the week before for our team van. The one I had would work best for a mini van or small truck. I told them that I had started to take the old one out just before this trip but at the last minute decided to wait awhile. I explained, "I remember thinking that I might give it to someone." Excitement filled the van and one player said, "Coach, this has been the best golf trip I've ever been on." Others chimed in with spontaneous laughter of joy. I had a silent prayer for the family there on the road and one for my guys. Maybe teams that did better in the tournament passed that family by and just took home a small trophy. We took home much more that would last much longer.

The Homeless Man Finds Shelter "In A Savior"….

It happened during the fall of 2000. We had just placed sixth out of a fifteen team field at the tough Wolf Pack Classic. Had it not been for a disputed canceling of the second round, we would have been in the top three or won the tournament. University of Nevada's Head Coach, Tom Duncan, told me of an open spot in the prestigious Fresno State tournament which would take place in two days. I will always think that Coach Duncan felt badly for how we had stayed out in the rainy, cold, and unbelievably windy weather all day. To be the final finishing team, only to have the other coaches vote to cancel the round seemed unfair, I'm sure. With every team's players having already turned in their signed score cards, it was not just unfair but probably a violation of NCAA competition rules. I heard about that freakish second round cancellation for the rest of my players' careers at Liberty. Coach Duncan's generous offer to call the Fresno State coach for me revealed his "first class" character.

The University of Fresno State Coach, Mike Watney, very graciously let us into his popular exclusive Lexus Classic. Knowing that we might finish last with us having only five players on our West Coast trip while the tournament had been planned with each team having six to pick their lowest four scores, I entered with a certain amount of trepidation. But, with our Golf Stat, Inc. ranking of 116th in the country at the time, it seemed worth the poor odds to get a look at fifteen of the country's top 100 teams. Six of these fell in the top fifty. Having just enough time to drive to Fresno, California, from Reno, Nevada, for our tee off, we left an unjust ending behind. I told the guys, "This is God's bonus."

Driving hard, we arrived in time for our practice round. After the day of practice and some needed range work along with a lot of short game time, I drove our rented SUV away from the Fort Washington Golf Course. We were very tired and hungry. Still, the guys were laughing and having fun. On the way to our hotel, we ran into some very heavy traffic. When I pulled up to a stop light behind a long line of cars, there he stood. *Oh no,* I thought. *We are in a big hurry and my guys have not eaten. I'm tired and need some rest from all this driving and golf.* There in front of us stood a beggar on the corner, with a cardboard sign around his neck. It read, "Work for Food." I thought, *Lord, this guy is not really in need of money for food. He is a fake. Besides, what will the guys think? Okay. If the light stays red until I get there, I will. If it turns green and we can drive on by him, I won't.* The longest red light in history happened that day. When he finally walked back to our vehicle, I rolled down my driver's side window and handed him a ten dollar bill. Smiling and obviously very grateful, he kept thanking me.

Just then, I noticed a tract and pocket Bible in my driver's door. So, I blurted out, "You wouldn't like to go to Heaven when you die, would you?" I had kind of hoped he would be happy with the money and that would be the end of it. My heart just was not into this good deed thing today. After all, if he was a fake, that would be what he would do. Right! He perked up even more and said, "Oh, yes, sir, I would. Please, tell me how that can happen." Putting the van in park, I opened the tract and read it to him, how he was a sinner, how God had come in the person of Jesus Christ and died on a cross to take the penalty for his sin and how he could be saved. I asked, "Would you like to have prayer and settle this with God, here and now?" "Yes, sir, I would," he replied, with tears in his eyes.

I began, "Repeat this after me but say it to God." I started, "Dear Lord Jesus, I am a sinner." I waited for him to repeat. "I realize I need and want 'You' to save me." I waited again. "Please, forgive me of my sin and come into my heart and life." I waited as he finished his prayer, "Lord, save me." Wow! All done with only one light change and no one honking or getting angry behind me, not even my guys in the van. God had intervened in that man's life and in the lives of five college men and one mostly unwilling older guy, me.

"This man made our trip here a success already," one of my guys yelled out. They all cheered and praised the Lord as we drove off. The homeless man smiled, held up his Bible and tract that he had dated and signed, and waved goodbye. We left rejoicing. I could not help but think of the mansion he now had waiting for him in Heaven, plus he had a reason to live and work. As for us, we were off to eat a great meal, stay in a top notch hotel, and play golf in a great tournament. Of course, I will always believe that this man's destination was our reason for all that had happened to get us here.

A Stranger In My Way...

It seemed like a normal day in the life of a coach. I got up early that morning and threw a few things in the family car. Off I drove toward an airport to pick up what I thought would be a solid prospect for our program. I headed down highway 29, going south toward the Greensboro, North Carolina, airport. At about 7:00 A.M., out of the corner of my left eye, I noticed a man walking along the side of the road. With this four lane highway and a divider section between the north and south bound lanes, it was impossible to stop. Needless to say, I did not want to stop. However, not far down the road, I approached a turnoff lane. You knew it would be there. Right! So, I began debating with God, *No way, Lord. I have too much to do and besides he'll not be there if I go back. Okay. I will pull off and think about it.*

I sat along the side of that ramp for the longest time, talking to myself. Trying to reason this situation out, I decided these mental guilt pangs had come from the Lord. Don't ask me how. I just did. At the same time, it dawned on me that I had no business going back there without some food or something to give this needy man. Just then, I opened my front seat middle compartment, thinking nothing would be there. It would show God I tried. Guess what! I found two bags of cookies. Can you believe it? I had stashed them there weeks before and forgotten.

"Okay. So I turned out to be wrong on that no food thing. But, is that enough?" I decided to look in the back. There in my trunk lay a large brown bag with four granola bars. I had stashed those for one of my hunger pang attacks. Placing the cookies, granola bars, and a small pocket Bible in the brown bag along with one of my "But A Memory" tracts, I began turning around.

Driving back, my heart just not beating for this fellow on the side of the road, I still hoped he would not be there. Sure enough, no one had picked him up. I might have known. Right! As I drove up slowly behind him, he whirled around, startled. I stopped the car, got out, and walked up near the front hood. Waving him over, I put the bag on the car and stepped back. Very deliberately, the hump-shouldered, rather tall, thin man wearing a ragged, torn jacket grabbed the bag and lurched backwards. Oh yes, I had also put a twenty dollar bill inside the Bible. He rummaged through the sack, tearing open the cookies. While thrusting two in his mouth, he happened upon the Bible. Out it came. Throwing it onto the hood, he yelled, "Don't come near me. I don't want your Bible. Who do you think you are? Are you a preacher? Just stay away." He braced himself and seemed to be waiting for me to attack him with a hug or something worse. I had no intention of either, although had my Christian "evangelist" preacher friends, Dan DeHass or Norm Pratt, been with me, my spiritual courage would have gotten the best of me and a hug just might have happened. Soon the weary-looking man with his dirty hands and face turned and made a hasty retreat back towards the woods. Taking his actions to mean that our conversation had ended, I quickly jumped in my car.

Then a thought came to me. *I had taken a risk getting out and away from my driver's side door.* I backed up a good safe distance from him, got out, and retrieved the Bible still resting on my car's hood.

Back in the car, it dawned on me that I should give one last go at this guy. Strapping the twenty dollar bill on the outside of the Bible with a rubber band, I made my plan. Driving very slowly, I passed near him, rolled down the passenger's window, and tossed the Bible in front of him. As I drove away, I yelled, "Don't let the money go to waste." With that said, as I drove north on 29, I looked in my rearview mirror to see him pick up the Bible and the money.

Upon making my turnaround a few miles up the road, I realized I would be driving past him going south on 29, continuing my trip to Greensboro. Remembering the three water bottles in my cooler, I recalled thinking that I would have one for me, one for my prospect, and one left over. This is all true. While slowing down and veering off to the left side, I rolled down my driver's side window. As I threw it out, I yelled, "Here is water for you. Don't forget, Jesus is living water." He faced me and turned up a huge smile.

As he shuffled off toward the water bottle, the stranger alongside the road waved his Bible in a joyful manner. As for the "official visit" recruit, he turned out to be a dud and a waste of budget dollars. But, I knew that the trip had been a total success over this one soul who needed a "drive-by-witness" of God's love. It was not a witness of my love, but God's and included a lot of Holy Spirit conviction upon a less than willing servant, if you know what I mean. How many times do we miss blessings? I wonder.

My Three Biggest Coaching Compliments...

My biggest blessings, as a coach, came when three great Christians, Todd Setsma, Todd Humrichouser, and Nick Heyland, told me that their lives had been transformed while at Liberty. All three eventually became Liberty graduates after transferring here in their junior year. Each had nothing but good things to say about their previous coaches. I had made no contacts with these players in an effort to get them to transfer. God sent each one to me, after they had releases. They were all strong Christians before they arrived. In addition to maintaining a strong spiritual and educational situation, all wanted one more thing, to play at the D-1 level of competition. That is why they transferred, not dissatisfaction of a past coach or school. They all came to me with their first two years of accomplishments in college golf and wanted my opinion as to what I thought about them playing at this level. It was my privilege to affirm a sincere belief in their talent.

All three were team leaders and team captains. All three led our program into new heights of success, with important team wins on their watch. Wow! What a blessing these guys were to me and the team members that they played golf with, ate with, slept in the same rooms with, and shared heartaches with along the way during those many days and nights. These three men always wanted the best for their teammates.

In May of 1995, Todd Setsma made this comment…"Coach, my life has been forever changed for the better, because God led me to Liberty. I want to thank you for believing in me and my talent. Thanks for caring about me as a person as well as a player."

May of 2000, Todd Humrichouser made this comment… "Coach, watching you give out and leave tracts for two years revolutionized my soul winning. I've decided to make tracts and witnessing a focus of my everyday life."

In May of 2003, Nick Heyland made this comment…"Coach, only Heaven can record what all has happened for the kingdom with the tracts and Bibles you have given out while I attended Liberty. I was encouraged by watching you do it and intend to do the same."

My Coaching Had Been A Ministry…

My real mission while coaching at Liberty was to send players out from here with a soul winning heart and more on fire for God. Maybe some of my other players will be encouraged to go on for God after reading this book.

Each one of us can make a difference. Move on to God's calling on your life. Be a soul winner. Proverbs 11:30 says, *"... he that winneth souls is wise."* Ponder this verse of Scripture. John 15:16 says, *"Ye have not chosen me, but I have chosen you, and ordained you, that ye should go and bring forth fruit, and that your fruit should remain: that whatsoever ye ask of the Father in my name, He may give..."*

Seven Important Ministry Parts...

1) **Everybody is having a hard time.**

2) **God wants to heal a hurting heart.**

3) **Ask for His help and it shall be given you.**

4) **We are God's healing instrument to help others.**

5) **Use what is already there to minister.**

6) **Ministry is no accident. God will provide a way.**

7) **Blessings await us in Heaven, when we serve here.**

How Does Hot Water Affect You?

What are we going to be? Put all three of these items in boiling water and what difference does it make?

Carrot: Goes in hard and comes out soft and weak.

Egg: Goes in hard outside and soft inside. It comes out hard inside and out.

Coffee Bean: It goes in and changes both taste and color. The bean made the difference. It is made just for the job.

Author Unknown

Question: *What is the taste and color of our hot water? What we are made of can affect others for eternity. Let us seek God and His Wisdom to become better soul winners.*

149

CHAPTER SIXTEEN

2000 Spring Push Falls Short

In the year of 1999-2000, we should have gone to the NCAA East Regional out of the Mid Atlantic Region. My guys beat a good Seton Hall team all three times that we met them during the spring 2000 season. We held a forty-six stroke advantage for those spring events. Liberty was definitely the best team of the two, if the most improved team had been picked. My Liberty team peaked at the best time of the year to represent our Mid Atlantic Region for the upcoming May NCAA East Regional. We had one win that spring with a second place finish and two fourths while beating ninety-eight teams and losing to only eighteen.

Serving as the Mid Atlantic Region Golf Committee Chairman, I felt that we were the best choice for a fourth spot in the region's ranking. One problem stood in our way. Amazingly, we had played against Seton Hall in all five of our fall events. The other unusual thing that happened was that they managed to have a lower team total in all five fall encounters. Liberty was the best team going into May Madness but had not acquired the best overall record for the fall and spring combined.

In the first week of May, our region's golf committee turns in the top six ranked teams to a National Golf Committee, who then picks the final four. Liberty was in the top six, but not the top four. Still, we were without a doubt the better team at NCAA time in the spring of 2000. I pleaded our case to all who would listen. But, in the end, I had to capitulate. As Chairman of the

Mid Atlantic Region Golf Committee, I turned in Seton Hall's name to the NCAA National Golf Committee as the fourth team for our region's final ranking.

St. Johns University was the other team in the top six. Again, for the spring we had a fourteen stroke advantage in our four times to meet, which yielded a split of two wins each. On the other hand, St. Johns held the edge over us for the year by eight strokes with the fall and spring combined.

Another plus to Liberty's account that spring was our win against thirtieth ranked Notre Dame in the Treasure Coast Classic which was played at beautiful PGA Golf Club in Port St. Lucie, Florida. Dr. Falwell has often remarked that our athletic programs need to become competitive with the likes of Notre Dame. Knowing that golf achieved this gave me a good feeling indeed. I mention it to him often.

I will always believe that the 1999-2000 team "set the stage" for our 2003 spring push to earn our first NCAA trip. Our 2000 spring push proved our dream could come true. James Yoo took that vision with him and used it in 2003.

The five players who acquired our team's best averages for 1999-2000 were: Todd Humrichouser, Yong Joo, Allen Hill, Rob McClellan, and James Yoo. Ryan Ferguson and Randy Tipmore added rounds in the mid 70s for solid support.

The 1999-2000 "Key Five"...

Todd Humrichouser was "Mr. Congeniality." Standing 6' 1" and sturdily built, he could have played halfback on the Flames football team. But, to my delight, he was my golfer. His first year was difficult with my asking him to redshirt. He had transferred in and we were loaded with good players. No one likes to redshirt. However, Todd's easy going personality made the request simpler. I remember his first Division-1 tournament. He had stomach problems and low sugar nervousness. I told him to take some deep breaths and let the air out slowly. He followed the suggestion and finished strong. Todd placed seventh in the Big South Conference in his first year of D-1 competition. His talent on the golf course mirrored his ability in relationships.

Todd could charm a cobra out of its venom. I still have a video of him hosting "Friday Night Live," a fun filled evening that begins at midnight on Liberty's campus. Everyone took his cues for their jokes and waited for his perfectly executed spontaneous exchanges.

Todd gained confidence in me as a coach and we became good friends in the process. While he gave his ideas Todd never complained and always functioned as a peacemaker. These leadership qualities made him stand out. Our friendship blossomed his senior year. He led the team with a subtle strength. Todd led spiritually by holding many on-campus team devotionals and led on the golf course by always working hard on his game. Others picked up on his example and we made a great push for an NCAA trip through our Mid Atlantic Region. He always had a good word of encouragement for the underclassmen. While quite a jokester, when it came to golf tournaments, Todd had a serious side. The team knew winning was important to him.

We had our best teams during the years players stepped up and led. A coach can do just so much, but a player can really lead. Over my twelve years I had many who led. I am very grateful to them. They know who they are, I'm sure.

Making Todd my Team Captain proved to be a great decision. While averaging 76.1 in the spring, he brought calmness and confidence into the van. I never saw a player have any more birdie putts than Todd. Had his putter been kinder, he would have averaged par or better. His demeanor never changed. We had many long talks about the meaning of life and golf. Our conclusion always ended up that golf was a great game, but life was what really mattered.

Todd's father Mark and I had several "heart to heart" talks. Mark made great sense and led many of our team devotionals. In fact, Mark, Todd, and their good friends Tom Green and Joe Jacobus came back to help me put on several Liberty/JAE Intercollegiate Classics after Todd graduated.

Yong Joo in his junior year had the best spring of any player before or after him. He won two tournaments, placed second twice and third twice, as an individual. Actually, the only time he finished out of the top five was at Penn State when he finished tied for twelfth. He had the best ever spring average, with a sub par 71.8, for twenty rounds. Yong ended up ranked fifth in Division-1 for Virginia and earned fourth place honors in the Mid Atlantic Region that year.

Witnessing Yong's record-breaking 63 at the Greenwood Country Club in Greenwood, South Carolina, was worth fighting for the program to be reinstated back in 1995. With par 72 for the beautifully quaint, rolling hills Greenwood course, taking it one shot at a time kept Yong's round together until the magic happened. He birdied eight out of his last ten holes with a near perfect day of nine pars and nine birdies. While our team led in only the first round, Yong's solid golf scores led the tournament individually from start to finish. Following up his record breaking 63 with two solid rounds, 73-73, won him the Individual Championship by six shots, at seven under par that spring. Yong Joo and his God-given talent in golf, as great as it had been, could not overshadow his family's witness. Attending their "vibrant and alive" Christ honoring church in Northern Virginia helped me know what made Yong a blessing. Born in South Korea, he moved with his family to America when his father left the military to become a pastor.

Allen Hill, my Australian, played while sick many times. Allen, a sophomore in the spring of 2000, stepped up for us. He averaged 75.8, to lead the team with Yong and Todd.

In 2001, I started a February team fundraiser event. "True Believers" seemed a perfect name with the weather going extra cold that spring. Sean Councell, David Crowder, Don Fanning, Wayne Henson, John Havill, Chris Johnson, Mark Miller, Josh Mullins, Steve Peterson, Frankie Smith, Jay Spencer, Paul Sunwall, Danny Thornton, Elmer Towns, and Ty Woodridge donated $150.00 to play with my guys. This fundraiser event had been planned for an early morning affair to lower our costs. My players were given the opportunity to volunteer as a fifth, leading every foursome of paying friends. Allen volunteered first. As it turned out, he got with a tough group. Fun loving guys Greg Clark, Jimmy Seamster, and my two sons-in-law, Steve Clark and Troy Rice, made up Allen Hill's group. They are all very competitive. I can vouch for it, having participated in our family's "Turk Invitational" outings for four years with these same four men. That is a tale for another time. By nature, Allen is a quiet and unassuming type of person. These four guys will have fun. Add to this equation the cold wind that kicked up and Allen being a down under Australian, who likes his country's 72 degree temperatures, got chilled to the bone. I will never forget the look on his face when I met his group on the ninth hole, with nine left to play. His shivering, shaking body and sheepish grin said it all. Knowing that the guys playing with him wanted his normal, long tee shots and solid putting, I feared for him. Allen yelled back to me, "Coach, we will make it just fine." This event revealed the character of a true team player. I thanked God for Allen Hill.

Rob McClellan was a person who would ask me how to hit a shot and pull it off the first time. Rob played seven out of the eight tournaments during the 2000 push. Averaging 76.5 that spring season in his freshman year, Rob made an imprint on our program that would never leave me. I watched him develop into a fine young golfer. His academic abilities were very impressive, too. He eventually made the Big South All Academic team his last two years. Rob also earned prestigious GCAA Scholastic All American honors in his senior year. While a great student, Rob would never flaunt his mental prowess but kept a humble Pennsylvania attitude.

Rob missed going to the second level of the PGA Tour School in 2003 by only four strokes. I'm sure that his parents are following him in tour tournaments, just like they did while he played college golf. I always enjoyed them coming to our tournaments. Rob left a lasting impression as a player who could take up a challenge and find a way to achieve it. He had not played a lot of junior golf tournaments upon arriving here. I did not know a lot about him actually and after his persistence, I held a "Try Out." Rob beat some of my existing team members in that two days and with his strength, height, and stature, along with solid swing techniques, I could see a lot of potential. He took advantage of his opportunities. He was an amazing success story and I am glad to have coached him.

James Yoo is another player that stepped up for us in his freshman year in the spring of 2000. With seven rounds of 76 or under and a low round of 72 that spring, James made a strong first year showing. His 78 average for the fall and spring combined gave Yong Joo, Allen Hill, Todd Humrichouser, and Rob McClellan solid support. James would be the one player of this group who would see the spring of 2000 push finally maturate, eventually completing the job in 2002-2003 with another spring push. In the spring of 2003 he came back to Liberty after a year and a half at home to lead us to our first ever NCAA Regional trip. James has dual citizenship in South Korea and Canada. I will always be grateful that he returned to finish his eligibility.

1999-2000 Team: Ryan Ferguson, Jeremy Henry, Allen Hill, Chad Howell, Todd Humrichouser, Rob McClellan, Tyler Phillips, Randy Tipmore, Yong Joo, and James Yoo.

Tyler's younger brother played a "big" spiritual part in the success of our 2002-2003 NCAA team. Both brothers learned their Godly traits at home. I will always be grateful to Dean Phillips for his substantial financial gift to the program when I was discouraged. Dean sent his sons and never made any request to get them preferential treatment.

Seven Swing Keys That Every Golfer Needs To Know...

First Six: *Golf Can't Be This Simple,* by John Toepel, Jr.

1) At address: feet shoulder width=balance & power.

2) Alignment: Position body open & clubface at target.

3) Weight transfer: Shift it back and then forward.

4) Keep shoulders relaxed throughout the golf swing.

5) Right leg flexed, with right knee pointing at ball.

6) Weight on inside of right foot at top of swing.

7) Long shots: Pick out a cloud or tree top above the target and hit it. Short Shots: Pick out the smallest target on or near the green for aiming your intended ball flight.

Buy John Toepel's book for a better understanding of his *Five Static Principles*. Sign up for a "free" newsletter at www.conceptgolf.com.

Fighting "Pressure" Problems?

"Choking" is the result of poor anxiety management. Never think about the outcome before hitting a shot. Think positive about your target. Don't try to do more than you are capable of pulling off. Use the club that will allow you to keep your shoes on. One more than you need is better and it will signal to the brain that this is supposed to be a smooth take away. Become accustomed to swinging within yourself, don't overpower the ball. Not everyone can be a Tiger Woods and I even hear him speak of shortening his backswing's length on wedges for more control. Talking to ourselves is considered suspect if in the kitchen at home alone but on the golf course it is helpful. Be nice to yourself. After a bad shot say, *Frank, you are better than that last swing.* Before swinging again say, *I can do this, relax and make your good swing, Frank.* Of course, you should use your own name.

CHAPTER SEVETEEN

The Day I Tried To Shut Golf Down

The idea to close down the golf program came to me in 2001 after the completion of my ninth year. With us having a lackluster year and my energy level down dramatically, the time seemed right to drop Liberty golf. Earning virtually the same take home pay as at the start in 1992, I could not even begin to think of finding a good replacement. After reading my "drop golf" proposal, Director of Athletics Kim Graham reacted opposite of my expectations. Thinking he would agree, I sat resolved to golf ending. Having had the program dropped by the Budget Department in 1995 and reinstated that same July by God's grace, I thought the idea to close it down would please Kim. Instead, he looked up at me and smiled. His next comment surprised me again, "Frank, I can't let you quit. We want a golf program and you are the one we want to run it. Tell me what you need."

Immediately, I had a new purpose. Kim went with me to present a revised proposal to the Budget Department. Again, to my surprise, the proposal was accepted a few days later. Finally, I had enough consulting fee for the day that I wanted to look at being replaced.

In my very first year of coaching, I began praying for a player of mine to come back and take the team over one day. Little did I realize at the time that God had already begun a good work in the heart of that person! In 1992, my first recruiting call went to Jeff Thomas. Jeff had already answered God's call to come to Liberty when he attended and played golf under the first golf coach for a fall semester in 1991. When Jeff did not return to school in the spring, God was doing something in his life. I believe God prepares our hearts for His service, which He sees coming down the road. We can miss it if our hearts stay hurt or get bitter. But, be sure, God has a plan for each one of us. We just need to call out to God with a sincere heart. Jeremiah 33:3 says, *"Call unto me, and I will answer thee, and shew thee great and mighty things, which thou knowest not."*

Jeff came back and played golf for Liberty. After his graduation a neat thing happened. He went to work for me in the barbecue business. Selling and working food shows was part of Jeff's job description. He even took the golf team to tournaments a couple of times. In my twelve years Jeff was the only person besides me to ever take the team to tournaments. I now had time to sell our family's company.

Health reasons and more time to spend with my wife and family made this a must sell situation in 1995. Plus, the business made less and less money every year that I coached. It took less than a year for God to find a buyer, after serious prayers and a lot of leg work on my part. Food shows were more than selling barbecue now. Finding a match was more important, which meant searching out a company that could benefit by having our products and customer base. Brakebush Brothers, Inc. bought the business and hired all of our employees, including Jeff.

After a few short years, Jeff left that high-paying job to get into golf. He soon became a course professional and taught golf at various driving ranges and country clubs. His heart's desire to work with youth in golf was being developed one step at a time. Little did Jeff know that God's preparation would end up with him becoming the next Liberty golf coach! Jeff had to be faithful in the little things, while God prepared bigger things in ministry for him to do.

Soon after my successful May of 2001 meeting with Liberty to increase the coach's pay as well as some budget items, I received a phone call from Jeff. We had talked to each other about the team and his different golf positions over the years, but never about him coming to be my assistant coach. It just did not come up. I had decided to let God move on the heart of my replacement, not me. Jeff said, "Coach, I want to come help you as a volunteer next spring." I got excited in having one of my past players express an interest. It seemed no one was going to answer the call. With me knowing Jeff was coming, I decided to recruit heavily like I had done in the early years of my coaching. The challenge to climb the mountain seemed doable. I made a promise to myself that I would leave Jeff in good shape with talent when my day to step aside came. It was like God had now laid Jeff's name on my heart to pass him the torch.

Having let the team's roster drop down to eight players during my ninth year, I now wanted to recruit upwards to fifteen players. I promised Jeff that when the time came to step aside, I would recommend him to replace me.

Jeff followed up his call to me with action. He and his wife, Heidi, also a Liberty graduate, moved to Lynchburg, Virginia, in the spring of 2002. It had been nine-and-a-half years since I started coaching. His first semester to volunteer had involved getting to know the guys. He became good competition for them. Due to my age, I had lost my golfing edge for D-1 course distances. Jeff worked on his own golf game, while challenging the guys to get better. He played in some regional and national professional events, too. Jeff also gave me his opinion when I asked for it.

The Bible tells us that two do God's work better than one. No one has explained it any better than my own pastor. Dr. Jerry Falwell's message on "The Power of Partnership" helps a person see this truth. Verses given in that message were: Matthew 18: 19, Judges 20:11, 1 Samuel 14:6-7, Exodus 17:11-13, Genesis 2: 18, and Ecclesiastes 4:9.

Some benefits of partnerships given by Dr. Falwell were as follows: Partnerships increase our effectiveness, empowers our prayers, multiplies our impact, shares the load, brings more people to Jesus, and helps us do greater exploits for God. I will always believe that Jeff made me a better coach.

With Jeff wavering a bit on his decision to complete his Class "A" Professional status, which had been started, I highly recommended that he continue advancing it. Completion came soon after he became Liberty's Head Golf Coach. Looking back at everything that happened during the twelve years I coached, Jeff Thomas succeeding me was nothing short of God's specific intervening over and over in both of our lives. How else could all of this come about? Keeping in mind that each of us will choose our own reasoning about such things, I can live with you thinking that this was definitely nice but certainly not Divine Intervention. On the other hand, if I am correct and there are times that God wants to intervene in our lives for special blessings, why take a chance? Don't miss the blessings God has waiting for you because you are not willing to open up to His leading. Eternity is a long time and Divine Intervention matters for a person to share it with our Creator.

Seven Observations Concerning Divine Intervention...

1) Few people understand it. Fewer people talk about it.

2) Few sermons are preached about it. More are needed.

3) We would do well to investigate it in more detail.

4) It comes to us from above. Only God is Divine.

5) God is not our good luck charm. It is all about a relationship with Him (Romans Chapter 1).

6) Looking backwards we can best understand it.

7) If we pray for His wisdom, each of us can know more about His Divine Intervention.

CHAPTER EIGHTEEN

My Decision, Do I Step Aside?

At the completion of my tenth year, 2000-2001 golf campaign, I decided that we needed a new system to determine how much scholarship money a player would get each succeeding year. The system in place had not produced the results I had wanted. Players promised they would work hard over the summers, but most came back only slightly better. Some returning players convinced me to give them as much or more scholarship money than the year before although their average golf scores improved only slightly. Many of the scholarship players went home, took a summer job, and did not practice or compete. Those that worked hard on their games and played several good summer events usually earned their scholarship money. I knew they would earn it with a system based on performance, too. Needing to find a way to recycle my four scholarships (dollars) from non-producers to new recruits and worthy returning players, I continued to pray for an answer to my problem.

Having considered a change for years, I woke up one night with an idea to base scholarship money on performance. My motivation could have been a sign over my friend's office door which simply says, "Show Me The Numbers." He once told me, "It is results that changes things. After all, that is the American way." I realized that the parable of the talents was God's warning to Christians of the importance of performance. Deciding to try it, I prayed for God's wisdom.

I contacted prospective recruits and discussed it. They liked the idea of carving out their own scholarship, based on their golf performance. Some really good junior golfers were even willing to attend Liberty without financial aid their first year, knowing they could earn up to a full scholarship in the future. If a prospect had great junior golf credentials, he would get a lot of money the first year, but future money depended upon him keeping sharp. Players could increase their next year's scholarship amount by producing lower golf score averages in competition, along with staying eligible. After getting approval from the A.D., I changed my way of determining the amount I gave players. Eventually, the system allowed me to befriend and pull for everyone to do better, letting their results take care of the end of the year deliberations. But, the conversion really did shake things up.

The changeover was difficult. Having scrapped my old system, handing out scholarships based on *hopes and dreams*, I had one very good returning junior decide that my new system did not provide him enough scholarship money for his previous year's performance. Understanding his concern and trying to make adjustments to my system, I still could not satisfy him. Although I eventually tweaked the system to include year end adjustments for individual accomplishments, bad weather, sickness, and bad rules decisions, it had not come in time to keep my best golfer. He had already decided not to return. This hurt and set the golf program back big time.

My implementation sent team morale on a downward spiral in the 2001-2002 year. With freshmen making up half of my team, I faced a lot of rebuilding problems, too. My new system did free up a lot of scholarship dollars to bring in top recruits. That was a positive and it proved to be the fodder needed to build the future, which I believe resulted in our 2003 NCAA trip. Starting the 2001-2002 year with twelve players, I had numbers but very little experience with six freshmen, two sophomores, three juniors, and one senior. Having some internal discipline problems along the way, and very little success in tournaments,

I started thinking about stepping aside. I seriously considered it during my tenth year. I had become weary of the well doing, so to speak. It seemed as though God did not want to answer my prayers. *Have I come to the end of my dreams? I want what is best for the team.*

One thought often popped into my mind. *God does not care about your little project.* I tried to remind myself of Scripture, having read about the sparrows. Even though they are little, God did a great job taking care of them. Zechariah 4:10 says, *"For who hath despised the day of small things?"* I decided that even if my golf program is one of those little things, God expects me to give Him my very best. This attitude of faith and trust had prevailed during my occasional times of discouragement. I had often heard it said, 'The measure of a man is what it takes to discourage him.' Now in July of 2002, I was seriously considering stepping aside, having felt my time for team success had passed me by.

I mentioned my dilemma to a Christian friend. He told me, "By you already having teams and players win several tournaments, and individuals make Scholastic All American, along with the one player winning the Big South Championship, these were no small accomplishments." Continuing to console me, he proceeded, "Your memories of lives changed are worth the invested time. Keep praying for wisdom." With a grateful heart that someone cared enough to take his valuable time to encourage me, I decided to take his advice.

Good Memories Came Back...

I considered the past. Thoughts came to me in questions. *How about that plane trip and near death episode, just to get started as a coach? How about those pranksters early on? How about those early teams that paved the way for bigger and better things? How about that first win at Snowshoe, West Virginia? How about the program's second win at Campbell?*

How about the Scholastic All Americans and our prayers for that to happen? How about the 1995 fundraiser at Ivy Hills Golf Club to keep the program going another year? How about God's Intervention to keep Liberty from accepting my own offer to shut the program down in 2001? I had all of these "heart issues" to consider. These questions brought back great memories which turned into pictures.

A Marriage Prayer, At Thirty-Thousand Feet…

One such memory was with a golfer and his ofttimes date. My degree in counseling from Liberty came in handy more than a few times. Players asked me about a lot of personal decisions. Sometimes I just went ahead and offered my opinion. Tom Anthony is a case in point. I would tell Tom to marry that beautiful girl. "Which one, Coach?" he would joke back. "Tom, the young lady you brought to Christmas dinners," I replied each time with a smile. I could see a lasting relationship for these two. While no wizard, I am a good judge of "style and substance."

In January of 1999, my wife and I were on the way home from a trip to Israel. It had been four years since Tom's graduation. While making my way to the back of the plane, I heard a faint voice in the dark. It came from the right side of the aisle. I heard the voice again, "Hi, Coach Landrey." I leaned down to find out who was behind the greeting. "It is Rachelle, Coach. Remember me? I'm the one who dated Tom Anthony, one of your golfers a few years back," she said. "So, how are you two doing these days?" I asked. "We don't date anymore, Coach," she replied. "Rachelle, I want to pray for you two to get back together." "Okay. But, I don't think anything is going to change now." God honored that prayer and a couple of years later they were married.

I often preached to the guys in the van about marriage vows. "Guys, my mother gave me the following advice. Son, a woman can take a lot of mistakes from a man. But to have an affair with

164

another woman is one thing that she will never quite forget. She may try to forgive it, but forgetting is what God does best, not women." I often told the guys about my own marriage and how I got back with my high school sweetheart, after three years of being apart. I told them about our second chance and how our two salvation stories came after marriage, another second chance story. Decisions do matter. I warned them, "Be sure that you are not the least bit interested in your girlfriend before you say goodbye for the last time. Do not lose a soul mate! Life is too short and soul mates are few and far between."

Tom and Rachelle bought a restaurant. You should try it when you pass through Westerville, Ohio. Call "The Chili Verde Café" for directions. Tell Tom that Coach Landrey sent you. Have him sign this book. Many times I've thanked Tom for his help during my first coaching year. I needed a helping hand on my shoulder at times, to be sure. Returning the favor with my reconciliation prayer for Tom and Rachelle means a lot to me. Rachelle and Tom have a son and a daughter.

Have You Asked Her To Caddie Yet?

Todd Setsma transferred to Liberty as a junior. He wanted to try his golf skills against D-1 competition. After an adjustment period, his game took off. In Todd's last year he won at Charleston in the fall and went ten under par on his last two tournaments of the spring. He was the only golfer to ever be presented Liberty University's prestigious Rock Royer award. Only one athlete is awarded this honor every year. It is presented to a senior for excellence in academics, character, and talent. He also made Scholastic All American his senior year.

Todd came to me one day and said, "Coach, I think I've found the girl to marry!" "Has she ever been with you on a golf course?" "No. Why?" I spoke frankly, "Are you still planning to play the Tear Drop Tour when you graduate this year?" "Oh, Yes! Is there something I should do?" Tipping my hat back a bit,

165

I said, "Well, I suggest you get her out on a golf course and ask her to caddie for you."

A few weeks later, Todd came back to me very excited. "Coach, she is the one," he proclaimed. Then he told me that she had not only caddied for him, she actually liked it. Melisa not only traveled with Todd on that Mini Tour, she carried his golf bag. I was so pleased when Todd and I were on the Golf Channel together along with his lovely caddie, Mrs. Setsma. The interview happened because Todd was an alumni player from Liberty University and at the time was ranked in the top twenty-five on the Tear Drop Tour.

Todd and Melisa were being interviewed at London Downs, his home course in college, where he was playing in a Tear Drop Tour event. They wanted to interview me as his coach at Liberty. I was proud to say that I had coached him for his last two years in college. I'm sure that his previous coaches are proud of him, too. During his college days, Todd went to the golf course between classes and on Saturday mornings. He constantly worked on his short game and the results were evident in his scores. I always used his dedication to motivate my new players to do more on their short games.

A few years later, Melisa had to stay home and have their first baby. She was carrying for another Setsma, so to speak. Todd opted for a sales position soon afterwards. I guess it is just too hard to replace a good caddie. Karstan Manufacturing Company, the maker of Ping products, now has Todd represent them in the Orlando, Florida, territory. He is still taking care of the little things like he did with his short game practice and the big picture is taking care of itself, like what happened in his college golf scores.

Two Got Married While In School...

Kenny Hobbs was the first player to get married before his graduation time. When he came to me and asked my opinion of his idea to be married in the summer before his senior year, I asked if getting married would make him the happiest man on campus. Smiling like only Kenny can, he thanked me and would later tell me that marriage helped his golf game, too. Living near Orlando, Florida, he represents Nike Golf, Inc. He and Jenni have two children, a son and a daughter.

The only other player to get married, that I knew about, while still on Liberty's golf team was Andy Weissinger. However, I might add that he turned pro on me soon after his wedding, before I could see his college golf blossom. Andy led the field in his first college tournament as a freshman. Two under par will lead lots of tournaments, I told him. He finished in the top ten of that event. Another thing that I could count on from Andy was a detailed in-depth team devotional. I'm glad to have coached Andy.

My Decision, When Do I Step Aside?

On another occasion and under another leafy oak tree, I decided to call my brother Richard. It seemed a good idea to discuss with "big" brother my thinking about stepping aside. His advice was to stay at it until I knew for sure that the time was right to step aside. I guess he could tell that my heart was not in leaving it all behind, yet. He said, "Just remember, you are the final one to decide. It does not matter what you've told someone you might do. You are still the head coach, until such time as you officially step aside. Do what you want." Warmth washed over me. It might have been caused by the sun breaking through that old oak tree. It might have been the "heart to heart" with a family member, which warms us all. I took it as a warm embrace from God. No one knows these things for sure, but it certainly fit.

I needed more information on why I should retire. In fact, this is how I've learned to follow God's leading. Right at that moment I did not have enough information to make such a serious decision. I was to go forward by faith. The time to step aside would come, but not now. God had intervened with His Scripture, my family, and many friends, as well as good memories lodged in my mind and heart, for just such a time as this. The many fun times spent with my teams and all those wonderful mountain top experiences helped to stop me from coming to the end of myself and jumping off too soon.

My strength to carry on had been revived, with past memories and future hope both stoking the competitive fires still burning inside. Thankful for Jeff Thomas and his help, I could go on a little longer. I marked it up as more of God's Divine Intervention in behalf of a very unworthy Christian.

Seven Things To Know For Making Good Decisions...

1) Decisions require us to process information.

2) We must accept the task to gather the facts.

3) It is good to keep a file on your topic or dilemma.

4) Seek counsel from trusted family, friends, and pros.

5) Pray to God for His wisdom about your dilemma.

6) Wait for decision crystallization to occur.

7) Make your decision. Learn from the outcome.

Not every decision is God's perfect will for my life. I'm not able to read God's "will" like a newspaper. Prayerfully, I do my best to follow biblical principles, while bathing choices in prayer. This process will come to a place where a decision is required. Living out Proverbs 3:5-6 helps me. Don't misunderstand. I am not saying that doubts never come into my pin-head mind. When facts don't add up and my "faith factor" does not solve my quandary; I lose sleep, say prayers, ask questions, and stumble like a lost sheep.

CHAPTER NINETEEN

Year Starts With Poor Fall Results

We started our 2002 fall season with a so-so finish at the James Madison Invitational. It was played at their home course, that "frisky" delight of a challenge, Lakeview Country Club. JMU's Coach, Paul Gooden, had invited my team because we had been ranked in the top ten several years. Maybe he had grown to like my competitive drive and pesky determination a little, too. I'm sure he saw himself in my desire to reach lofty goals. I considered it a privilege to play in Coach Gooden's top rated Mid Atlantic Region tournament at the start of our new year.

Coach Gooden deserves an introduction to my readers. More of a John Wayne "leading man" type, Coach Gooden stands about 6' 1" and has dark, wavy hair. It is graying and thinning some now. Mostly easy going, he is a bit of a funny jokester. Some might humorously call him an "agitator." Honestly, he is just a fun loving guy in my opinion.

One example that comes to mind happened at a Penn State tournament. Paul had been talking to Villanova's Coach Moran (part of a two brother Joe and Jake Moran tandem-tag coaching staff). Coach Gooden yelled, "Coach Landrey, does Dr. Falwell allow you to wear a hat in his church service?" Knowing it was a trick question, I paused before answering. "Well, I'm not sure about hats being worn in Dr. Falwell's church service. I can tell you this much. If a person realizes that they need, plus want, a Savior and ask Jesus to save them from their sin, they will be saved. They could then wear a hat in Dr. Falwell's church service and not lose salvation, even if he kicks them out of church for it." Coach Gooden smiled and looked at me like he had forgotten his "leading man" line for a moment. Then he said, "Well, I just wanted to know why you wore your hat while you ate at the Olive Garden last night." While he joked a lot, Coach Gooden was always a gentleman. Unlike many "leading men" types, he was well liked among other members of the same *Coaching Guild* who were struggling with their own bit parts. While savoring this opportunity to fire back a little "swash talk" for the many years he dished it, I will fondly remember him as a friendly but fair competitor.

Nevertheless, he was my arch rival. I might say that the last time I met with him, he had trimmed down and looked to be pushing for a new role involving a thinner, albeit a younger looking "leading man." *Could it be that he is getting "leaner and meaner" for another ten-year billboard run as JMU's Head Master of the Links?* Let me assure my readers and fellow coaching friends that Coach Gooden definitely always knew his team's ranking against the region's top ten. He keeps all stroke differentials and Head To Head standings handy. Like prizes in a hen house, the *Old Rooster* knows the dangers in the barn yard. He always has a fix on the fox and his own requirements to secure one of the four prize hens in the Mid Atlantic Region for that year's NCAA Regional.

I must say that Coach Paul Gooden always encouraged me. When I asked questions, he listened and tried to be honest in his opinion. When I told him of my interest in moving to his Mid Atlantic Region, he agreed it made sense. Always a fair and gracious host, he made certain his events had good rules officials. A large Mid Atlantic Region field played there and my guys liked his tournament's daily lunch packages, too.

While our first round score was okay, Liberty's second round 286 tied our program's third best for eighteen holes. Joe

Norman's brilliant 68 (-3) helped make that happen. Andrew Turner's fifty-four-hole even par golf led the team. Although our team's 867 was the third best for a fifty-four team total ever for our program, we fell willfully short finishing ninth among eighteen teams. It told me two things.

First: Mid Atlantic Region teams were getting better every year. Our players needed to improve more each year, too.

Second: Liberty had not played this short golf course as well as the competition, which told me we needed work on our wedges, "120-yards-and-in" game. The wedge game has always been a weakness for my teams, due to not having a short range facility on campus. While having London Downs Golf Club's short range area available to us and the Poplar Forest Golf Course's short range, we still need our own.

After the James Madison tournament, my guys traveled back to campus somewhat saddened by our initial outing of the 2002-2003 year. As for the work on our games, efforts were doubled on putting, chipping, and wedges.

McLaughlin Invitational, Second Fall Event…

We drove the mountains of Virginia, Pennsylvania, New Jersey, and New York to the highly touted St. John's event. I always looked forward to a Frank Darby run tournament. A rapid speaking "New Yorker," Coach Darby's personality claimed a classic individualist work ethic. He was someone you felt you would like next to you going into a burning building, and he could have won the "old west" with his energy and grit. This particular tournament was to be held at beautiful Bethpage Red. The guys could not wait to see it.

Red's twin course, Bethpage Black, at this State Municipal Park, was host to the 102nd prestigious 2002 U.S. Open just three months before. My guys made sure to get pictures in front of the U.S. Open plaque. Mr. Dave Catalano and the Bethpage State

Park employees pulled off a golfing marvel, while Tiger Woods added the major to his list of titles won.

My junior golf sparring partner at Lawrence County Country Club was the incredibly talented course setup genius for the Open. This is a matter of opinion, I suppose. Many U.S. Open contenders would like to catch Tom in a dark alley. Tom Meeks, "Meeksie," the USGA course setup specialist, had something to do with the outcome as he was in charge of virtually everything that went on inside the ropes. Meeksie and I had more than a few golf duels in our younger days. Both of us had money to burn from our caddying profession. We spent many a day out knocking down flagsticks. I saw him on television during the 2005 U.S. Open being interviewed about his retirement. *Hum…* *Maybe he and I will have a home and away match at Lawrence County Country Club and the Vincennes Elks Club with us both retired. Meeksie will not set up either course.*

This Bethpage Red Collegiate Invitational would pose a big challenge for Coach Darby's talent and hosting abilities. Due to the heavy rain overnight, we were faced with a difficult choice on the tournament's first scheduled day of competition. Either we would be calling off the first day's round, make it a one-day tournament, or try a different format than I had ever coached. It was decided that every team would play together, with their coach as the official counter. Had each team been assigned an independent official scorer instead of that team's coach, I think that format would have been better.

College Golf's Traditional Format…

During my coaching years, a player from three different teams played together. These five threesomes made what we called a wave. Arriving at my team's initial par 3 hole, I would meet the first wave which had each team's number "five" man. Then the number four man and so on. Number one players on a team's posted lineup sheet passed by last. This number one spot for our team was played by the person who felt best in that high profile position, as much as being the best player on our team. Most coaches did have a favorite lineup. In 2002-2003, I put our best player (meaning lowest average) in the fifth spot many times. He just liked to get off early. However, after the first round had been completed, each player's score determined the team's one-thru-five lineup. I hope this explanation helps in understanding how college golf is played. Parents often came up to me and asked how they could find their son's group. A tournament program and this information could help a lot.

Experimental Format Not For Me...

In this experimental format, playing a whole team together, my first/last thoughts about the concept were/are negative. This idea met with a lot of opposition before the round was played. Even "easy going" Coach Gooden had serious doubts. I did appreciate Coach Darby trying to find a way to make it a thirty-six-hole tournament. Liberty did not play any better or worse the second day. There were teams that played much better in the whole team format, as opposed to the traditional way. It was obvious that they liked the new "experimental" format. Those teams that did have much better scores on the first day also had coaches who were above reproach and well known for integrity. From that angle, there was no problem. However, I felt uneasy about me calling rules for my players. When I left the first tee, I could not stop thinking that if Liberty played exceptional golf, some coach or player might say that I had let my guys get away with rules infractions. I wanted to avoid all appearances of evil. My attitude affected us negatively making the guys nervous. Our first day's total was 301. The next day we went back to a normal tournament format, with three teams playing together in waves.

The previous day's tension hung over us like a cloud and we could only score one stroke better than the first day. Liberty posted a nasty fourteenth place finish among the eighteen teams. Normally a 75 average put us in the top half of the field. However, the Bethpage Red cards a 70 par, which makes a big difference. To place high in tournaments these days a team must average no higher than one or two over par per counter. Competition in all eight D-1 Regions has gotten much better in recent years. It bodes well for NCAA college golf. Anyway, Liberty's Mid Atlantic Region ranking plummeted with our first two tournaments being very poor performances.

River Landing Intercollegiate: Fall's Third Event...

We held five qualifying rounds and lots of range work from September 30 thru October 12. Totally convinced that the guys were ready for this one, I told them as much. It may have artificially raised hopes in their minds, to a detriment. We went through our normal team tournament preparations on the 13th of October. On October 14, Liberty teed it up with some of the finest teams in the country. Again, results were disappointing. Even though we had played poorly the first thirty-six holes, we had an opportunity on the last day to beat some good teams and one very key team in our MA Region. We failed to capitalize. The last round's miserable rainy weather got the best of us. Our trip home did not go well for my cold, rain-drenched companions. My normal human decency (assumption could be disputed) did not prevail. Some of the nicest guys I had shared rides with over the years got plenty of cold air over the driver's right shoulder. They knew things were not good.

When we drove onto campus, I told the guys that I might decide to change my qualification system for the next trip. Letting them out, I prayed at the back of the van with them for me to have wisdom to make a good decision about qualifying for ECU's event. My sleep patterns worsened after that twelfth out of fourteen team finish at UNC Wilmington. Trying to decide what to do about the upcoming East Carolina trip's lineup did not help matters.

This particular team's lack of effort in bad weather made me determined to change my normal qualifying process. Assuredly, I would make some kind of example of this group. Players back at Liberty, awaiting their chance, deserved that those on a trip give their best effort every single competition round. One thing I knew, based on my own high school and college athletic experiences, the coach needs to be the keeper of the gate on some issues. For example, I never wanted anyone to make fun of another teammate or to slack off without some kind of penalty for it.

A Marine's team spirit and physical toughness is built into him by the "drill sergeant." That is what the military regiment of strict discipline and conformity is all about. They hate the sergeant until superior achievement comes. When those inoculated become "men of valor," a bond is forged that makes friends for life. I wanted that for this team. Therefore, those who fell short had to pay a price. I wanted to deepen the flame burning within each one. Granted, every attempt to refine metal could damage it. This is the risk every demanding coach takes.

Fall's Fourth: The ECU Pirate Intercollegiate…

Bradford Creek Golf Course, here we come. After the team's lackluster showing at UNC Wilmington, I decided to shake up the squad by picking all five players, which was very unusual. We normally qualified-off for some spots. But, I had other fish to fry. First, I wanted to see if we had any potential left on the sideline that might help us in the spring. Still, sending four untested freshmen and only one experienced player, a junior who had played well at UNC Wilmington, would most likely be disaster. Second, I wanted to send a message to the four who would most likely have made the trip had they finished well at UNC Wilmington so as to prove that anything less than 100 percent efforts would not be tolerated.

We finished seventeenth out of nineteen teams at ECU. Explaining things to Coach Williams, I expressed my deep regrets for our failure to perform better. His understanding and support, along with his assurance of an invite for the following year, strengthened our friendship. One positive thing came out of the ECU Pirate tournament. A highly touted Florida freshman got his big chance. His 75 average for fifty-four holes made him Liberty's second best, which allowed Jordan Mitchell to earn himself a spot on the team for our last tournament of the fall in Savannah, Georgia.

Fall's Last Event: "The Liberty/Crosswinds Classic"…

I had decided to host a tournament at Crosswinds Golf Course because it had easy access for Florida coaches. Also, it had an airport handy for northern teams. The opportunity to host here came about after my inquiry on the previous year's spring break trip. Knowing they had a great lighted driving range and lighted par 3 golf course, I had stopped for my guys to get in some valuable practice on our way to Florida. Finding the Crosswind Golf Club members and staff interested in having a College Intercollegiate event, I began planning for the next fall.

The Highway 95 par 72 layout proved to be a good test of golf. The minor distractions with planes flying overhead added to the excitement. Liberty's 296-295 team scores beat back a good Navy team by three strokes to take first place. Two tough Florida teams, Bethune-Cookman and Florida A & M, tied for third in a field of nine schools with a team total of 600. Rutgers and their up-and-coming Coach Maura Waters took fifth place. I told my players this was a fine win against good competition and that it set the stage for a spring push.

Finally, we had played up to our potential. Freshman Jordan Mitchell, in his second tournament, stepped up with a 74-71 to tie for second place individually with my "Stocky Irishman,"

Paul Carey. Sophomore Jonathan "Home School" Dickinson added 75-73, for ninth. Paul's nickname came about by way of a female sports writer's exuberance while Jonathan's was self imposed, having had home schooling. Liberty won the final tournament of the fall. Nick Heyland's 76-74 and Andrew Turner's 75-76 secured the win.

Leaders Lead Even When They Hurt…

I must finish this chapter by sharing two more true stories. Neither has anything to do with golf performance but both have a lot to do with Divine Intervention in my humble opinion. It is in the looking back that we see how God did it.

The first is about a sophomore, Gary Hui, who had made trips and had had some good golf scores. Nevertheless, Gary decided to return home to Duncan, British Columbia, Canada. He is going to college there and helps his parents run their fine golf course, Duncan Meadows Golf Club. But, before leaving Liberty in his second and last year here, Gary did something that helped our program make the NCAA tournament. It was not him firing a hot round that made the difference. Instead, while the team was competing in Savannah, Georgia, in our last 2002 fall event, I got a call from Gary. "Coach, I just want you to know that we are praying for the team." Here was someone who had not gotten to play all fall, but he wanted us to do well. I told the team that night in our devotional what had happened. We won that event and it became our first of three tournament wins during that 2002-2003 campaign. Upon arriving back in Lynchburg, there was Gary Hui waiting for us. Standing in the headlights at midnight in a light rain, Gary was a one man welcoming committee. Inviting him into the van and out of what was now a downpour, I asked Gary to have the night's final prayer, which he did with distinction and substance. Gary Hui made a huge difference in our team's overall success. I say, "Thanks Gary, all the best to you."

The second story involves two wedges, many prayers, and a glad reunion. An amazing and yet weird thing had been going on that fall whenever I played golf. It seemed a small thing, us swapping wedges that year before he left school. Now, every time I used his wedge I felt a need to pray for James Yoo even though I had tried to forget the guy who left the program unhappy with me. Nevertheless, one night I sat up in bed. Out loud, I said, "I'll ask James Yoo to come back and offer him a full spring scholarship!" That was the amount of money he would have received the year he left and because of the change in my scholarship system, which was the reason he had left school, I had the amount of money needed at the middle of the year to now give him. The next day I spoke to Paul Carey, knowing that in his freshman year and James Yoo's sophomore year they had been together a lot. But, I was not sure how well they got along, having noticed some conflict on a spring trip in 2001. I did not want to bring unrest back into the camp. I was happy to have Paul tell me that if James came back it would assure us an NCAA trip and that they would get along fine. Paul thought offering James a full spring scholarship was a great idea. The next day I spoke to his two sisters, Grace and Esther. They liked the idea. After a couple of turn downs, James agreed to pray about coming back. By Divine Intervention, James made the right choice and joined Liberty's team of destiny.

Our Mid Atlantic Region ranking had been in the top ten for several years but after a poor showing in the 2001-2002 campaign followed by the fall 2002 season, Liberty had fallen to seventeenth in the Mid Atlantic Region ranking. The Mid Atlantic Region Committee Chairman and George Washington University Head Coach, Scott Allen, would later say, "Liberty went from seventeenth to fourth place in one spring season. It was an amazing turnaround, which proves it can be done." Coach Allen led our Mid Atlantic Region in integrity, and I wish him and his team success in the future.

CHAPTER TWENTY

2003 Miracle Spring Turnaround

Excitement filled the room. Our first meeting of the spring 2003 season was underway. Coach Thomas, at my request, had set forth in writing some mutually agreed upon goals. One was to make an NCAA trip. It was my job to emphasize those goals. "Men, mental toughness will be required for us to be victorious at our spring's Conference Championship. We will work on mental toughness for the next few weeks along with physical training. Make no mistake, this team still has a good chance of going to our first ever NCAA Regional. It can be accomplished in one of two ways: by winning our April 17-19 Big South Tournament or by being selected from our region. It is truly doable with our wealth of experience and the addition of James Yoo." The guys let out loud "hoots" and "hollers" for James. He had already been accepted back into the fold. Having played in his sophomore year with Paul Carey helped, too. James knew that Paul had highly recommended that I call him. Even though I had spoken to him by phone and prayed many times for his return, I was still pleasantly surprised when he actually arrived.

It was time to bring them up-to-date on the difficulty ahead. I began, "Guys, our fall 2002 golf results represented a very slow start toward our goal. Even though we had some record-breaking rounds, our best finish for the first four fall events was ninth. However, hope was renewed in the last fall tournament when our captain's prayer came true." I went on to remind them of the story of how Nick Heyland wanted us to <u>win</u> a tournament and added it to the list of team goals during our first fall meeting. I continued, "It finally happened at the Liberty/Crosswinds Fall Classic. This can be our springboard to a 'spring push' like what happened in the spring of 2000." James remembered that great finish and let out a "whoop" quite unlike James, a quiet South Korean.

Coach Thomas gave more spring goals and closed in prayer. Soon after this meeting, Coach Thomas, at my urging, accepted a head golf professional position at Poplar Forest Golf Club. The downside, he could not travel with the team.

Spring 2003 Team Looks Good…

In many ways, things held lots of promise for the Liberty golf program. Junior, Paul Carey, had averaged a smart 73.2 for his thirteen fall rounds. Freshman, Andrew Turner, had the second lowest fall average for ten rounds or more, at 74.9. Andrew, my first "lefty" golfer, had played exceptionally well for his first college golf season. Having played as the team's number one man several times, he had gained a lot of confidence. Four players were at 76, with five or more rounds: Freshman Zack Phillips, sophomores Joe Norman and Johnny Dickinson along with senior Nick Heyland. Another very bright spot surfaced with freshman Jordan Mitchell playing in the last five rounds of the fall and averaging a sizzling 74. He even managed a second place tie with Paul Carey in the final event of the fall. We had a new ringer to go with them. James Yoo had returned. Somehow I knew this spring would hold something special for the guys.

My January and February mental preparations pushed the guys to think positive. Along with some spring physical training, running and stretching, I held many sessions on the mental side of the game. This year I decided to emphasize "mental strategies" to get the team ready for our spring push. It was apparent that we had to forget the past and at the same time not become fixated too much on the future. Somehow, we needed to learn to stay in the present. GolfPsych and Peak Performance Golf Insights newsletters helped me stay on theme. Their materials reminded me to stress one shot at a time and stay in the present, as did other materials.

I included a lot of team devotionals in practice sessions and tried to find Scriptures which would challenge them. Joshua 1:7 spoke about being strong and of good courage and in 2Timothy 1:7 we are told not to be bound by our fears. It all helped the guys think good thoughts. It helped me hold the players responsible before God. I explained that staying in the present was "biblical" thinking and pointed out that Philippians 3:13-14 says, *"...This one thing I do, forgetting those things which are behind* (past-our fall season), *and reaching forth* (present-mental and physical preparations) *unto those things in the future* (future-our spring season), *I press toward the mark for the prize (NCAA Regional)..."* Plagiarizing these verses I stressed the biblical idea to go on.

While concentrating on building confidence, I stressed realities, lecturing from two of Dr. Rotella's books, *Golf Is Not A Game Of Perfect* and *Golf Is A Game Of Confidence.* Reading different sections to the team in our pre-spring training sessions, and later in college golf trip pre-game meetings, prepared them mentally to be patient and practical. It is my pleasure to help sell a few more of these books.

We worked on learning to think like champions, by reading together the testimonies of great professional golfers in the book *Golfers On Golf.* After running ten times around the top and five times up and down the stairs, I had my players sit in the stands at Liberty's basketball facility, the Vines Coliseum. I had them read from *Golfer's On Golf.* The many quotes from golfing greats like Gary Player, Arnold Palmer, Ben Hogan, Tom Kite, Jack Nicklaus, Ernie Els, Bobby Jones, Bob Toski and Tiger Woods opened my players' minds to having winning attitudes.

Reading Gay Brewer's comments, "Be brave, be bold, and

take your best shot," I told the guys that we needed to apply his thinking this spring and be willing to give it our best shot with no half-hearted efforts allowed. I told them his quote was special, because it reminded me of the day I played eighteen holes with Mr. Brewer, the 1967 Masters Champion. "Guys, my second shot went over a row of five or six trees at the Quail Creek Country Club in Robinson, Illinois. It dropped onto the green and rolled into the cup on the very first hole yielding us an eagle "two" for the card. Our PGA Pro-Am best ball team had birdies on the next two holes then a par and birdie. We were five under after five. Mr. Brewer held his hands up and asked where we were playing next week. Mark Michael and Richard Cannon were contributing members in that foursome. By the way, the next week I was still selling barbecue and Mr. Brewer was playing in another PGA tournament. We both knew what paid the bills. Addressing the guys, I said, "There is a moral to this story. Anything can happen. We will have some of our best shots and scores. Believe good things can happen."

A Geico-Direct Win Gets It Started Right…

Before this first spring tournament we had been working on our wedges and short game. Two new drills were implemented in the Geico-Direct practice round. The guys were willing participants, which was a good sign.

The first drill was what I called *LU 100s: A Lay-Up Drill.* This is short for Liberty University 100-yard "lay-up shots." To impress this idea, I had the guys drop a golf ball at the 100-yard marker on all par 5s during practice rounds. It helped them see the best places for a lay-up shot and gave them confidence to actually do it. All five players competed for the nearest to the pin prize. A dessert at that night's meal went to the winner for the four par 5 holes played in the practice round. Of course, we all shared in the winner's spoils. One dessert and six spoons made quick use of it.

Course management deemed it necessary to lay-up on certain par 5 holes. I picked the 100-yard markers as the best place. I would not like to know the number of tournaments that we finished two or three places down the list of teams because of players going for the green on their second shot. When the trouble up around the green was not worth the reward/risk factor and did not merit an attempt, I was irate if a player went for it. On these par 5 trouble holes, I tried to make the guys consider the odds. This particular team abided by my warnings better than any of my past teams.

Why risk a big number when a mishit that did not catch the trouble would leave the third shot in rough, short sided or thirty yards out. It is my opinion that the touring pros do not want to leave themselves 30-50 yards out, that old *dreaded-in-between*. One touring pro was asked what club he would use from 40 yards, to which he replied, "I'm not sure about that, but I do know what I would do if it happened a second time." The inquisitive questioning reporter could not resist. "What is it that you would do the second time?" "I'd fire my caddie," the pro told the interviewer. Touring professionals work on a favorite wedge distance; usually it is 70-100 yards. They will often leave themselves at this distance on treacherously long par 5s, short par 4s, or chip outs from the trees after errant drives or fairway golf shots to greens.

The second new drill, I called *LUDs: A Short Game Drill.* LUDs stands for Liberty "up and downs." In this drill, there is a captain for the day. He picks a spot around the green to drop a ball after every par 4 has been played by the team members. The five players must drop a ball from eye level, with no rolling it around by the club head for just the right perch. They were in competition to see who could chip the ball onto the green and putt it into the cup in the least amount of strokes. This was done for par 4s in the day's practice round. There was a dessert awaiting the winner.

The idea for these two drills was to help the guys get used to certain shots that would come in handy during the event. Playing from 100 yards out (Drill 1) helped the guys think about laying-up on those tight par 5 holes. Chip shots, just off the edge of greens (Drill 2), allowed them to become familiar with the grass around the greens, which was especially important at new courses in a different part of the country. Plus, they worked on making short putts in the same drill under pressure. I believed in adding an intra squad competition factor, which gave the drills added fun and more of a tournament feel. Building more experience under pressure made sense to me.

Hunter Army Golf Club turned out to be just the right place to start these drills. The rain poured down. My guys showed up with a heart for the work. James Yoo made his debut as a returning Liberty golfer. James got off to a great start. His performance was good enough for a Division-1 tournament individual first place trophy. Second place individual was none other than my "Acemon" freshman, Andrew Turner. "Acemon" was his nickname and he proved it this week. The two of them led us to our second straight team victory. We had picked up in the spring where we left off in the fall. The course played 7,030 yards and the rain poured down for two days. Par had been changed from 72 to 73 the first day. Par changed to 74 the second day because of rain damage to the course. The Liberty guys stood tall in their first test of the spring 2003 season, coming out on top of several quality teams.

Second Event: Third Place, Beating All Region Teams…

After winning two in a row, last of the fall and first of the spring, the guys wanted the Treasure Coast Classic, too. Hosted by St. John's University, the event in Port St. Lucie, Florida, at beautiful PGA Club, was going to be a good one.

We arrived early afternoon on March 12 with enough time to have a casual practice round. This had to be a good tournament for us. The guys knew how much we needed to beat all Mid Atlantic Region teams. The night before the first round of the tournament, I held a devotional and covered some team motivational topics. Each player read from *Golfers On Golf*. My first player to read spoke boldly, "It was Tom Kite who said on page 64 that he never short changed himself on dreams." I jumped in, "Guys, tomorrow we begin to chip away at our dream." Another player read Bernard Langer's advice, "Treat each putt as a separate little task without worrying about what has gone on before or what will come after." I closed the motivational time by asking them to think like Ernie Els. "Guys, Ernie said, 'Hit fairways, hit greens, and sink putts.'"

The guys responded well with a first round score of 294. But, we struggled a bit the second round with high winds. Our thirty-six-hole team score of 598 ended up in third place, in a field of nineteen teams. Two Florida teams beat us, but they had a lot more opportunity to practice in the Florida weather before the early spring event. We held our own with Mid Atlantic Region teams, beating them all.

The Birth of SITTAWAGA...

We gained more than momentum at the Treasure Coast Classic. It was here that we acquired our spring hustle chant. It happened like this. I was in the PGA Country Club clubhouse snack shack when freshman Andrew Turner came in to register his score. Before going over to the computer and the person tallying each player's results, Andrew rushed up to me and exclaimed, "Coach, did you see? We stuck it to St. John's U." St. John's University was the host school for this event as you may recall. In fact, Coach Frank Darby was at the laptop computer waiting for Andrew to bring him his score card. Overhearing the rather loud proclamation, Coach Darby decided to make his feelings known in no uncertain terms. Being a half-wrestler and half-boxer body type, you felt Frank could back up harsh words. Feeling that his players' turf had been trampled, he took up for them. Having had several discussions over the years, positive and negative, the result being mutual respect, I liked Coach Darby's flare.

Coach Darby's work setting up college tournaments always earned my admiration. Frank made it a point to express to me his admiration for tournaments I hosted, too. When playing in my events, Coach Darby always did our scoreboard lettering the night before for me. His board expertise gave our tournament a look of professionalism. Coach Darby worked hard to produce a very competitive golf program at St. Johns, and I respected him for it. He also knew that I worked hard for our program. This kind of mutual respect often made two coaches friendly competitors, but it still left lots of room for good rivalries. We both wanted our team to end up one shot better than the other. *Maybe we wanted it more than our own players did at times.* I felt that I knew a Coach Darby that he himself did not know existed. I could see the competitive spirit in his soul.

Anyway, I assured Coach Darby that my player meant no ill toward him or his team; but that Andrew had heard me talk about the "key" teams to beat in our Mid Atlantic Region. I went on to explain that I had stressed the importance of beating a tough St. John's five in my team meetings, because of how far ahead they were in strokes. I'm not sure Coach Darby ever totally accepted my explanation.

Out of that comment by Andrew came a problem and an opportunity. The problem was that I needed to make sure any future excited outbursts or comments were kept among our team. On the other hand, this was an opportunity for me to capture the high-spirited determination displayed by my freshman. I had always wanted more of it. I could not seem to get enough "spirit" displayed to carry us to a coveted NCAA trip. As we continued our spring break trip, I decided to seize the moment. Many ideas came to my mind as to how to use my freshman's competitive spirit to our advantage. Finally, I settled on it. I needed one word, with each letter as part of a team slogan captured in a single sentence.

As I prayed about just how to do all of this, a thought came to me which included some key letters. I capitalized them for emphasis. "SITTAWAGA" seemed to me to be just the right word. While my players would know what each letter of it meant, other teams and coaches would not be inflamed about the saying. It could become our team's rallying call, which we could all feel good about.

SITTAWAGA

S-Sock
I-It
T-To
T-Them
A-Always
W-With
A-A
G-Godly
A-Attitude

The phrase *Sock It To Them, Always With A Godly Attitude* and the word SITTAWAGA was talked about all spring. I said the phrase and the word often. Soon the guys were saying the phrase and word to one another.

Back At Liberty, After Spring Break…

I decided to give the players a review of things covered in our January and February meetings and before spring break by retelling a true story. My memo went to all nineteen players. It shared key mental hooks and was written for them to ponder before qualifying for the William & Mary Intercollegiate. What follows is the main body of that memo.

"Qualifying & Tournament 'Pre-Event' Range Work"...

(1) Work on your tempo before qualifying and event rounds. Every golfer's range work should include getting relaxed and in a rhythm. Place a club down parallel to each target line keeping the front of your body parallel to the club and target.

(2) Use your complete routine every time you hit a shot, which prepares your mind and body to take the practice "range game" to the score card golf course.

(3) Hit three balls each with all three wedges (I have four). Using shorter shafts first will safely loosen you up. It also helps your rhythm and tempo. Then hit every other longer shafted club in your bag twice. Finish by hitting three drivers. This totals twenty-five range balls for my warm up.

(4) Then head to the practice green for putting practice. Work on three footers all around the cup. Then stroke putts up and down a slope to golf tees or cups, thirty feet in length. Get a feel for the length of stroke needed for each.

(5) Drop three balls at the edge of the green and chip with a seven iron. Land each ball just on and get a feel for its roll and distance, always trying to hit the first ball with your next chip. Do the same with a pitching wedge and sand wedge.

Remember, Dr. Deborah Graham, of SportPsych, Inc. said, "Champions maintain dominance by making every shot and putt of equal importance. They strive to put 100 percent concentration into each shot..."

"Inside The Box" Thinking, A True Story

Be sure to work on mentally staying "inside the box." Allow me to explain it with this true story about a golf match not long ago. A friend of mine teamed up with me against a bunch of young college "Lions." Jon Leonard and I took on three other teams of two players each, in an eighteen-hole "best ball" grudge match. Jon's age of sixty-four and mine at the time being sixty-two made us three times their age. So, we played tees up from the farthest back "flat belly" tees.

The game was on. I had a couple of problems to overcome. One, I had not warmed up properly due to being rushed to the first hole by the opposition. Secondly, I had not played golf with my friend for many years. Being that I did not want to let him down, I allowed this to put undue pressure on me. These two poor decisions precipitated my "third problem," which was thinking "outside the box."

Stepping up to a short 360-yard hole, I pulled out a driver when the narrow fairway called for a safer selection like a long iron to protect against the golf ball going tree hunting. My macho mentality and "outside the box" thinking landed my ball deep in the woods, starting me off with a double bogey. I did the same thing on the second hole with similar results and arrived at the ninth hole six over par, which didn't help our team. With no tempo or rhythm, I had limped along for eight holes. Jon had carried our team up to that point. Assuring him help was on the way I began "inside the box" thinking with a one shot at a time mental resolve. Relaxing my shoulders by rotating them up and down, along with being somewhat warmed up after eight holes, my rhythm and tempo was getting better. Good self talk which is part of "inside the box" thinking helped, too. On the par 4, ninth hole, I began with encouraging self-talk using my high school and college nickname "Geno." *Geno, we can beat these rascals if you just don't give up. You can make a difference in this outcome. You've done it before and you can do it again. Maybe today is that day.* Some people call this being cocky. Not true. Thinking "inside the box" means being focused. I finished my personal pep talk as usual by repeating another little jingle that I had instituted. I said,

Targets-Targets-Targets
One-Shot-At-A-Time
Leave-It-Behind

Getting myself to think "inside the box" on the next fairway shot made a good swing possible. On the green, it also helped me stroke my ball on the line envisioned. Imagining the speed needed for that line, I used a practice stroke intended to send my ball the distance needed to reach the cup or a foot by it. Just before the actual putt, I told myself to make a smooth, slow take away. Doing so would help keep the putt on line. I watched with great glee as it went in the cup. I had finally helped Jon with a birdie "three" and our team was on the move. We combined to contribute five more birdies down the home stretch. At the eighteenth we had pulled to within one stroke of two groups and flat even with the third pair.

On the last hole of the day, my tee shot rolled down the fairway about forty yards past one of the competitors, Paul Carey. I'll admit it was my best drive of the day and his worst. On the other hand, it just so happened that his and my teeing ground were within ten yards of each other giving me a small advantage. For purposes of a "fair and balanced" retelling, Paul did contradict my accuracy of this story. You know how those college guys are, being sleep deprived; their minds can get pretty foggy on "tit for tat" details.

Back to my story, I took out a five wood for my second shot on the par 5 eighteenth and made the following statement "out loud" so that Jon heard. "Geno, relax the hands and tighten the bellybutton muscles. You can do this." To my delight (a bit surprised, too) it landed on the green. Coming to rest just twenty-five feet from the flag, I had a great opportunity. Could I make a "two under par" eagle on the final hole to seal the win? I put that thought out of my mind and refocused. Using the same "inside the box" putting thoughts as I did at number nine, the ball rolled exactly on the line I had picked out and it wound down a sloping green and over a ridge. The left to right breaking putt plopped "bellorlorlorla" down and into the cup "plop." I kid you not, it was a dream come true. My partner Jon was the first to congratulate me. Others on the green had their heads down in their hands and were not available for the high fives and hugs that were passed out. We had finished the final nine holes at seven under, with a winning score of 29 to go with our first round of 37, making our eighteen-hole total a 66 on the 72 par, 6,700 yard test of golf. What can I say? It was a fantastically fun-filled day. Looking at our six competitors, with a smile, I humorously said, "Guys, it is always more fun to win. Vince Lombardi was right!" Of course, I have since been taking lessons on how to be a "better sport" from my regular Wednesday competition: Bob Goodman, Russell Tyree and Jimmy Shaner. I'm told that there is a deep seeded problem. Winning has always gotten me into trouble, especially when I laugh a lot. Can't a guy have some fun? Of course, I'm not that funny when I lose, or have you noticed?

As my six players climbed into the van for our trip home, I gave "Big Jon" a "big hug." I have fond memories of Jon and of meeting his son Jon Leonard Jr. who was a college golf superstar himself, in his day. As we drove away from their family owned and operated Francis Lake Golf Course in Lake Park, Georgia, my mind drifted back to our last tournament. We had just come from our Florida spring break trip and a third place finish at the Treasure Coast Classic. Stopping off at my childhood friend's place was special.

The story and memo had a point. "Inside the box" thinking actually works. I must give some of the credit to Peak Performance Golf Insights (1-888-742-7225) and GolfPsych (1-888-280-4653). Their fine newsletters and information were used often in my thinking process. On page 92 in the book, The Eight Traits of Champion Golfers, cofounders of GolfPsych share the following 1994 quote by Mark McCumber, "All year I concentrated on 'Forget the last shot.' The only thing you can control is your attitude."

Third Event: A William & Mary Second Place Finish...

Next on our schedule was a very big Mid Atlantic Region tournament. The KINGSMILL Intercollegiate was held in Williamsburg, Virginia, on March 24 and 25, 2003, at the oft-times used PGA Tour stop, to be hosted by College of William & Mary. Almost everyone in the top twenty from our Mid-Atlantic Region would be playing in this key tournament. The fifty-four-hole event required us to play thirty-six holes on Monday and eighteen holes on Tuesday. Before leaving Lynchburg, I had my guys play the Kingsmill River Course while standing on the London Downs driving range. Each Kingsmill hole's required shot was to be hit with the appropriate club until they reached what would be the green. I wanted them to do it while going through their full, complete routine. The guys did not like the idea at first but soon it became fun and I think it turned out to be helpful.

The day we arrived for our practice round William & Mary's Coach, Scott King, was busily pointing and gesturing. I had nothing but admiration for this man, who had come into the coaching ranks after me. He had not once looked back. Filling some very big shoes, Scott did a great job for William & Mary. He replaced Joe Agee, who had blazed his successful coaching career over a thirty-five-year span. A very capable Jay Albaugh took over for Scott in my last year. But, for this huge Mid Atlantic tournament, Scott King's past tournament hosting integrity, to run it right, meant a lot.

It was a bright, cloudless day during our practice round and the guys were happy to have this opportunity. Everyone had expressed confidence in one another during our LUDs and LU 100s. The two winners shared their desserts after our fine meal at a local steakhouse. My evening devotional was followed by a pre-tournament message. It all fell in line with my SITTAWAGA team strategy. After passing the golf books with quotes of golfing greats around for each player to read a positive mental message, I prayed and sent them to bed. It was midnight and my day had started at dawn. Personal reflection told me that I was very fortunate having had the privilege to coach such fine young men. I slept really good that night even in a strange bed.

The Williamsburg Inn did their job with a timely wake-up call for all three rooms. Of course, my two alarm clocks made sure I was already up an hour before the call. Breakfast came next. Then off to the course we went. The music played softly. I drove slowly. The guys went about their personal warm-up and I did my thing by picking up a golf cart and loading it with umbrellas, food snacks, Gatorade, and water. Everyone had settled in for a long twelve-hour "Links" day. Although Coach King had thought of everything, the weather did not cooperate and a cloudy day caused dusk to come early. Darkness cut the lights off after our team's thirty-fourth hole, resulting in us losing shots to par in the thirty-third and thirty-fourth holes. No team finished all thirty-six holes before the day's play was halted by the officials who decided the unplayed holes and the final eighteen holes would be finished the following day.

That night at our team devotional and strategy session, the guys committed themselves to waking up with an attitude of confidence. We read Scripture and quotes from our list of team devotional books. Knowing that we could not afford to lose more strokes to par, I assured the guys that our two morning holes would set the tone for the rest of the day. I recapped the situation one more time, "Guys, the final day's eighteen holes will be played right after we conclude the previous day's leftover thirty-fifth and thirty-sixth holes. Start off right. Pick targets and play one shot at a time." I closed the meeting by asking Zack Phillips to pray. Little did he know how much his sincere words blessed his teammates and his weary old coach!

The next day my guys came out with the hot hand. Birdies on both holes by Paul, while the other three counters for the round made two pars each, allowed us to accomplish our first goal of the new day. Instead of losing strokes to par, we gained two. It gave me a good feeling about these guys. They could accept a challenge and still be able to return their minds to a focus of playing in the present, a shot at a time.

A Special Moment Set The Stage…

All tournament players came in for a short break after the completion of the previous day's round. The event's officials took time out to remake new team parings based on how we had all finished. Positions of all eighteen tee box locations and pins on the greens were changed. During this down time and because of cold weather, I took my guys inside the clubhouse to have a brief team meeting before the final eighteen started. Inside in warmth, I passed out hand warmers and my congratulations on a fine finish for the two holes. My advice was to think of this as the start of a new tournament. Refocusing ourselves on "in the box" thinking and staying in the present, I sent them back out to chip and putt. Just before teeing off for the final and third round, Zack Phillips called me over near a tree. Zack had qualified in Lynchburg to play in the tournament as an individual. His interruption was not a selfish complaint because of his disappointment in not getting to play. Rather, Zack asked to have prayer with me for the team. After hearing him pray, I called the guys together and had him pray with them. Zack proceeded to pray for God's blessings to be on each one of our players. He expressed his gratitude to the Lord for allowing him to be along. Zack asked God to give the guys peace of mind during the round. He prayed for them and me to be patient on the golf course. The five players representing Liberty knew his prayer was special because of what had happened to him.

A college golfer gives his all to make it into a tournament. A player can go on a trip as one of five players on a team or, like Zack did in this event, as an individual. This means that his score cannot count for the team, but he can win the individual tournament title. It is a great experience just to play in a college

194

tournament. Playing as an individual is the next best thing to playing on the team. Zack had played great in the fall, scoring 74 and 76 in his first college tournament. He followed that up with two rounds of 72 all in his freshman year. But, our tall, slender Zack had struggled a bit in the spring. William & Mary would be an opportunity to show his game's progress inside competition. However, when we arrived I learned that an extra team had been entered which filled the field. Zack was not allowed to participate. A disappointment like this can be devastating, but not for our man Zack. He turned his lemons into lemonade. Zack Phillips bounced back from the initial hurt and decided to become a *one man booster club*. He became the "spiritual leader" for the other five players who were representing Liberty. He inspired me, too. His prayer for the team had been just what we needed at just the right time. Starting the last eighteen holes in fourth place, the guys were up to the test and Zack's prayers did get answered. Finishing the last round strong, we beat a very good ACC Maryland team for the first time that year. Excitement was "alive and well" on the way home. Finishing second out of nineteen teams set the stage for a spring "comeback story" that would be heard all around the region as well as throughout most of Division-1 golf.

Fourth Spring Tournament: The Liberty/JAE Classic …

We had very little time to enjoy the accomplishment, because I would soon host our own Collegiate Tournament. The Liberty/ JAE Classic was set to be played the next Monday and Tuesday. Sunday afternoon it snowed five inches and many thought our event would be cancelled. My hour drive to Smith Mountain Lake was filled with a flurry of large white snowflakes. I prayed for a clearing in the weather. My prayers were answered. Coaches had often told me that they liked my tournaments because I had a direct line to the "sun-god." As a side thought, I fondly recall George Mason's aspiring Head Coach, Linda Gaudi, asking me to pray with her team in the Best Western Ocean Reef's parking lot at Kill Devil Hills, North Carolina, in my last year to coach. It happened just before Old Dominion's second and final round to be played at Seascape's Golf Course in Kitty Hawk, North Carolina. After the prayer and politeness, it was off to the course to compete for a win. Every team had their eye on the prize. Once in the cockpit of that vehicle, my mind began to work on how to outwit the opposition. We finished tied for second with friendly rival, Wofford College.

In this case, I had gone directly to the "Son-God." Fortunately, The Water's Edge holds water (snow, too) very well and a little sunshine worked a golfing miracle by Monday morning. We were able to have the event and even more important, we won. Defeating two top district teams, JMU and GMU, along with seven other teams helped our ranking. Now we were in real contention to claim the fourth spot in our region and consequently an NCAA trip.

*Short Sand Shots***Right Handed*

(1) Stand away from the ball with your body in a sitting fashion, while positioning the ball in the middle of your feet.

(2) Position feet at an angle slightly open to your target.

(3) Dig feet in for two reasons: to check the sand depth and to place your body lower, compensating for gripping down.

(4) Lay open your sand wedge club face with blade edge pointing at target. Do not roll it over during the swing.

(5) You can experience this feeling by using the right hand only (for right-handers) in your practice sessions before competition.

(6) Slap the sand at the appropriate spacing behind the ball to have the sand flush it out on the green to desired distance.

(7) Swing along your feet-line which will help cut the sand out from behind the ball. Use a smooth tempo throughout.

CHAPTER TWENTY ONE

How I Came To Write This Book

For many years, I searched for that one key thought needed to start writing any book. Maybe others need to find something else. It all came together for me while attending a Liberty University Flames Club meeting. This particular community booster luncheon, also called the "Talk Session," was held on April 15, 2003, at Billy Joe's restaurant in Lynchburg, Virginia. Coaches in season spoke weekly. Liberty's Coach Brant Tolsma, whom I had come to respect as a coach and Christian, spoke first and told the group he wanted Divine Intervention to win their tenth straight Big South Track Championship. I was inspired by his talk and his willingness to make a public announcement of his need for God to "intervene." Of course, I must give my son-in-law Bryan Bauer credit. He helped me figure out laptop software.

Coach Tolsma explained to me later that his prayer request was for God to give him wisdom to coach the team and for runners to have exceptional courage. He said, "I did not mean for God to wave some magical wand over the competition to make my team mysteriously prevail." You can read more about Coach Tolsma's accomplishments and thinking in his book, *The Surrendered Christian Athlete,* on the track web site, www.Liberty.edu. There are many differing opinions on what Divine Intervention means. Just ask someone. Bob Bonhiem, a Flames Club Member and retired wrestling coach, sent a letter stating God would never in any circumstances stoop so low as to "intervene" in an athletic contest. In his letter, he wisely asked, "What about the other players and coach?" Good question. I've often said while on the golf course that God does not care about golf in any way shape or form. Billy Graham, as I understand it, once said, "Prayer never seems to work for me on the golf course. I think it has something to do with my being a terrible putter." While this statement was meant to be humorous, I agree to a degree. Golf is not the kind of life and death event requiring God's altering of an outcome supernaturally just because of a selfish coaching prayer. Maybe that is why I came alive when Coach Tolsma used Divine Intervention terminology in his request at the Flames Club. Since Coach Tolsma has clarified his comments to suggest that "wand waving" is not God's way in sports, I guess he would fall closer to the view of Coach Bonhiem.

After my experience at the Big South Championship which you will read about in the twenty-third chapter, I should fall in behind them. However, I decided to give God the opportunity to do it. He is God. Right! Divine Intervention is His thing, when and where He chooses, even in sports. For a trip to the NCAA tournament, I decided to even request Divine Intervention. *God could bless me and my golf team. It is up to the other coaches and players to do their own praying. If they out-pray me and my guys, they deserve that extra blessing or benefit that might make the outcome different. Let it be known. I decided to test God's mercy.*

My Divine Intervention Announcement…

As the Lord would have it, I spoke next and told the group "of the faithful" about the strange rain-out at Princeton. I explained, "It was like we were not supposed to play this past week." I did not tell them that my guys grew closer on the trip or that they enjoyed the weekend together. The guys slept in, ate late, and watched the "Masters." Each day we played a little 8 ball at the local pool room. They came back to campus totally refreshed.

On the drive home from Princeton I pondered the happenings of this confusing trip. At the writing of this book, I now know that the rain-out was a blessing. Looking back, I realize that the Princeton course is a bit tricky as we found out on the following year's 2004 trip. In fact, I doubt we would have made the NCAA trip in 2003 had we played there that weekend.

Addressing the Flames Club members, I said, "The rain-out does keep our hopes alive for the Mid Atlantic Region's fourth spot and an NCAA trip. We still have hope of a good finish in the last big region tournament at Penn State," I continued, "A more pressing issue is our upcoming Big South Championship. Being that we will leave in four days for it, I want you folks to pray for God's Divine Intervention at this tournament." I've wondered, did God only hear the last part of my prayer? Did He really have a part in it all? After all, my prayer for an NCAA trip was answered just not in the way I thought it would happen. Remember, I'm not sure how much God cares about golf. But, I know He cares about individuals. I've lived it and seen God do "Divine things" in my family, in business, and as Liberty's golf coach. After that day at the Flames Club, I could not get Divine Intervention out of my mind. The more I thought about it, the more I realized that God had Divinely Intervened in my life on many occasions. Thus, the book's overriding message finally came to me-*Divine Intervention*. I hope you have seen it as you've read this book. I've not heard much preaching on Divine Intervention. Assuredly, I'm not the greatest person to write about it. Certainly, I do not hold any special insight nor have I heard an audible "Word" from God. I just had it come up in my search for life's meaning in sports, of all places.

Big South Championship Results...

We met Wednesday morning at 6:00 A.M. to leave from the Liberty campus. The night before, I had told the five going to *"Meet Me At The Chain."* Morning broke, but just barely, when we left Lynchburg. The first three hours of the drive to Sunset Beach, North Carolina, passed by fast while the guys slept. The only sleep my college golfers got came on golf trips. As we drove south down highway 29, I had many thoughts. *Yong Joo had taken home the individual champion's trophy in 2000. Would this be the year we brought home the team trophy? We certainly have the talent and a good mix of experience with two juniors, one sophomore, and two freshmen. All have played great this spring. Yes, winning is a real possibility.* As a fog settled in, we rode on and I thought. *The Big South Championship looms ahead of us. I am as excited as I have ever been about our chances to finally win a Big South Championship,*

After four hours on the road, we stopped for a fast-food breakfast. Six hours from the time we left campus, I drove onto the beautiful grounds of the SeaTrail Golf and Resort. I recalled turning my SeaTrail/Liberty Intercollegiate over to a friend, Elon University's Golf Coach, Bill Morningstar, who continued the event's tradition for college golf. Coach Morningstar was much more than a long distance runner and track coach. He could run a first class golf tournament and was in charge of securing the site for this year's Conference Championship. I had lobbied for the Big South Championship to be held at SeaTrail. Having been a tournament host here several times, I felt at home. Finally, a conference title would be determined on a course I knew.

Arriving on schedule, with an hour to spare, I had enough time to feed them lunch and get in a good warm-up session. We teed off for our practice round at our appointed time. This was always important to the coach, more so than to the guys. I did not want to miss a practice round tee time, especially for a Big South Championship. Coaches have this awful feeling that, just maybe, their team would not have a practice round if they missed the assigned tee time. At least I considered it.

The reason for a practice round is to let players get to know the course. We did that, too. For me, however, it was also to determine clubs to hit on par 3s. There were predetermined tournament distances for par 3s, which a coach made sure to know prior to each new tournament's practice round. To have my players use a tee box that is thirty yards off from the ones used during the official days caused unneeded confusion. It could cost a team several strokes.

I always marked down the wind direction during every practice round and reminded my guys that every time we met at a par 3 for the next three days, I would record the distance, wind, and club of choice for each player that day. They were instructed to come to each par 3 tee box, figure their own yardage to the pin, and tell me what yardage they had figured. It was my job to confirm it was right. If I came up with a different number, I would ask them to refigure theirs. We discussed the wind, amount of it, and from which direction it came. We noted if it would help or hinder the ball flight. Example: Players with a predominant right-to-left ball flight (draw) meant that the ball would fly farther with a right-to-left wind. Then, with all of this information, they made their own club selection. My job at that point was to add confidence by assuring them they could perform well with the club they had in their hands.

Regrouping Is Part Of Coaching...

The SeaTrail Jones Course had been a 72 par on the clubhouse scorecard for SeaTrail Resort play. For the Big South Championship, it had been changed to a par 70. Moving tees up turned par 5 holes into long par 4s. Hole number eight became a 465-yard par 4 and the second change was at number eighteen. It became a long 470-yard par 4. These two holes would prove to be our downfall. Had they been left as par 5s, I do believe we would have won the tournament. Of course, I have some Carolina coaches who would dare to differ with my analysis and prediction.

As usual, I recapped the outcome to my players in the van. "Men, we only lost the Big South Championship by fourteen strokes as a team. Had players who counted for Liberty saved one shot in nine of those rounds and two strokes in three rounds, we would have won our first Big South Championship by one stroke." The sadness that enveloped me on the way home was indescribable. It is shameful to let a sport do this to a person, with all of the tragedy in our world. But, life does not seem to work that way for me. Somehow, a sporting activity becomes my focus and captures my emotions totally. I told both freshmen that I had so hoped they could go to the NCAA National Championship four years in a row. *Now, the possibility of making our first trip seemed all but gone.*

Knowing that we needed to pull together for our last tournament, my pity party had to end quickly. The next statement that rolled out of my mouth came even before we were to make a fast food stop at McDonalds, which was a mile-and-a-half from SeaTrail's front gate. "Guys, that was then and this is now. Let's eat something. We will need our strength to SITTAWAGA at Penn State." Cheers went up from my disappointed but not destroyed college golfers.

While driving back to campus, I pondered all that had happened to us. *Divine Intervention had not worked in our favor, for sure.* Deciding not to blame God, my thoughts turned to the guys. Realizing that we all had worked hard in preparation for the Big South Championship, I began to count my blessings. *Three firsts, a second, and a third-place finish and now a fourth place at Big South was still a great run for our team. Besides, I could have made better decisions on par 3s, which certainly would have helped.* I decided to go back to the drawing board. First, I determined to treat these players like the winners they had been all spring. *One way to assure them that I had put the Big South results behind us would be to feed them a great meal at a special place.* My mind was made up, I knew what to do.

About an hour out from Lynchburg I asked them a leading question. "Is anyone back there getting hungry?" "Sure, Coach, where can we go?" one brave heart asked. Telling them about a special steak house just up the road, they all let out a loud "whoop" of approval. We had the biggest steaks in the place and definitely became united in our cause again.

Upon arriving back on campus and at the pick up location's chain, we formed a circle behind the van. With arms on shoulders, prayers of gratitude went up to God. James Yoo prayed, "Thank You, Lord, for giving us the opportunity to compete at the Big South Championship, for a safe trip home, and for a great steak."

Following my hug for each, I sent them to their dorms. It was back to reality, studies, and tests for them. As for me, I had fish to fry. Of course, I saw myself as the "fish" being fried. Having told the Flames Club of my desire for God's Divine Intervention, I knew my experience at the Big South Championship had to be told. Folks were always kind to me when I spoke at the Flames Club, but "mercy," it was hard for me to give my report when we did not perform as I had hoped especially after my predictions of a good result. This would certainly be one of those times.

A Personal "Fish Fry" Flames Club...

When I walked into that large open room with tables set for lunch, the first thing that caught my attention was the podium standing alone out front of the group. All too soon, my turn came to tell our story. I explained the fact that three fine Carolina teams, Charleston Southern, Coastal Carolina, and Elon University, had managed to beat us, leaving Liberty with another fourth place finish. Rounding out the eight teams were Winthrop, Birmingham Southern, High Point and Radford. They already knew the results because everyone at our meetings always got a weekly sports report when they entered the room, thanks to "sports information" staffers.

I tried to explain to the Flames Club members my disappointment. "Actually, it was an unbelievable outcome for our team in the way we finished. How could I understand it? If someone had told me that my two freshmen would place second and ninth, individually, and we would still not win, I would have called them foolish. Andrew Turner's second-place finish earned him an honor no player of mine had ever achieved before. He was named the Big South Conference Freshman of the Year. Jordan Mitchell placed ninth in a tough, sixty-player field. While being happy for them, it was no Big South earned trip to the NCAA Regional for us as a team." This was my way of breaking the ice before I told about the strange way God had responded.

Let me close this chapter by forewarning you that the next chapter describes what I think was my own encounter with God. Did God have a hand in how the PUPS Big South Championship played out? Did He send me a message? Was I thinking I could use God as a good luck charm and He decided to teach me a lesson? I have pondered all of this and much more, just from these three incidents that I will share in the upcoming chapter. You will hear me ask God to "intervene" in behalf of my players. This next chapter will be my lame attempt at an exercise in "God thinking," as I examine how He dealt with a "born again" rascal like me.

What I am saying is that God will treat one kind of personality and salvation background differently from another. If you recall, Joseph was basically a good person having some bad luck. But Jacob was known to be a stingy, deceptive conniver until God changed him and renamed him Israel, which means "Prince with God" or a blessing, adding "value" in the Spirit while still struggling with the old nature from time to time. It is a great picture of the ongoing struggles we all face on a daily basis. Oh, by the way, in case you were wondering, I am the Jacob personality. Most of you know the Jacob me and not the "Prince with God" side. Did someone say, "I heard that!?"

CHAPTER TWENTY TWO

God Is Not My Lucky Charm

My head was down with my eyes fixed on the top, flat portion of the plain brown podium. I stood motionless, dressed in all black clothes to show my attitude and state of mind about what had happened. I began my Divine Intervention speech, "I'm not sure that enough of you prayed." Raising my head slowly and smiling, I said, "I know you prayed, but those prayers were not answered the way we wanted." I started my story. "The beginning of any tournament is hectic and a bit frantic. Of course, as coach, I tried not to let my players feel the tension. One problem was that my college guys seemed to be unaware of the importance of making it to their first tee on time. No matter how much I stressed it the night before in our team meetings, they still managed to hang out at the driving range or practice green way too long. The penalty applied for failure to follow this "on time" rule was two strokes for any player not at the tee for an appointed starting time. If a player missed their tee time by five minutes, they would be disqualified for that day's round. I did not want to play four to count four because I had lost my fifth to a late start. As always and to my delight, we found a way to meet our deadlines and all of the Liberty players got off the first tee in a timely fashion."

Pausing for breath, I went on, "Because of the push to get everyone up that morning, fed breakfast, to the practice area, and the first tee, my mind was not on Divine Intervention. Later in the day, when a couple of my players had crucial short putts, I decided to apply my thinking of what Divine Intervention meant to me. Just before an important five-foot putt, I asked the Lord to please give the player a calm spirit, to help him stroke the putt with confidence, and for it to go right into the cup." I smiled and told them that he made it. Continuing my story, I said, "However, after as many putts were missed as were made, I forgot about giving any more Divine Intervention requests on golf greens."

My Divine Intervention "Boomerang"...

A few people laughed. I continued, "Later in that Thursday's first round, I could not resist asking for Divine Intervention again. This true story happened on the eighth hole. On this par 5 hole turned into a par 4, one of my freshmen stepped up to the tee box. Things had been going pretty good for him. By having the honor to hit first indicated to me that he had beaten the other two team's players on recent holes. That was a good thing. This hole required a tee shot of 280 yards, just to leave a second shot of 185 yards. The green sat twenty or so yards beyond a small creek. A player needed to have a really good second shot to reach the elevated green surrounded by sand. The odds of having a bogey or worse were high. So, I asked God for Divine Intervention, to help my player hit his drive into the middle of the fairway about 300 yards." I was into this story now with everyone waiting for an outcome.

I went on, "Now comes the unbelievable part. Jordan Mitchell could not see me as he prepared to hit his tee shot. I was hiding, as I often did. In fact, my whole body was nestled amongst several very large trees. I stood behind one situated along the far left side of the fairway about 270-yards out from his viewpoint. Watching it all over my right shoulder, I peered in and out from behind my tree. Confident that Jordan would hit his normal straight down the middle tee shot, my Divine Intervention prayer seemed almost needless. After all, Jordan was the one player on our team who, more than any other, split the fairway on a regular basis and drove it 270 to 300 yards. On the other hand, I figured with the difficulty of the hole, God's blessings on Jordan's tee shot could not hurt." Stopping for a breath, "Folks, you won't believe what happened next. His abnormally high hooking tee shot came straight at me! Remember, I'm standing in the left woods. Landing just a few yards from where I was and onto the backside of a mound, it bounded forward and nearer to me. Bouncing left, it gained speed as if shot out of a cannon. I could not believe what I saw next. It hit a tree just in front and a bit to my right. I kid you not. If the ball had made contact on that same tree just one inch to the right, it would have bounced out into the fairway, in perfect position. Instead, it hit one inch or so to the left of the tree's center and careened left again. This time it whizzed in front of my face. The ball rolled less than one yard beyond a series of white stakes located about ten yards in the woods." I paused.

Looking up, I said, "Shocked by what had happened, I watched as his ball rolled and stopped a few inches out-of-bounds. After walking over to it, I confirmed the situation. While personally witnessing this unbelievable bit of bad luck, my mind computed that "something weird" had just happened. Astounded by all I had seen, I leaned up against my tree for just a few seconds. Regaining my composure, I realized that more coaching duties were calling me.

Looking back toward Jordan who was awaiting word on his fate, I motioned with my arms. Hands high in a wave fashion, I threw my arms in the direction of the out-of-bounds stakes. I then had to signal for him to hit another. This time his tee shot went far right into more trees. There were many other places that I could have been, other than this hole at this very spot and time when this happened."

You Want Divine Intervention Again, Do You?

I shook my head and went on. "After leaving Jordan with his troubles, I journeyed to more par 3s and then to the final hole. Having positioned myself just behind the eighteenth green, I watched in horror as my players one by one made bogeys. When our number one man finally arrived, the thought came to me to ask for Divine Intervention again, this time for him. He was approaching his third shot. This was the second of the two short par 5s turned into very long par 4 holes. Four of my Liberty players had already finished their round and were sitting or standing just behind the green. This was our team's normal show of support for teammates."

I paused and began again, "Pulling my guys aside, I asked each to pray for Divine Intervention that our anchor man would finish with a par. We had all heard that his score could be really good, which our team needed. What happened caused my heart to sink even further than seemed possible. His third shot fell short of the green, dropping into the greenside bunker and in the one place he did not want the ball to end up. The pin was cut near the edge of the green, leaving a steep slope down to the flag. Knowing not to leave his next shot in the bunker, he overcompensated and hit his ball thin, low, and hard. His fourth shot landed on the green's downhill slope, beyond the flag, and skipped across to the other side of the green. Faced with 70 feet back to the cup, he three putted, resulting in a triple bogey. My heart sank deep into my chest. Needless to say, I did not ask for Divine Intervention during the final two days of the 2003 Big South Championship." I concluded, "One thing for sure, God is not in the business of being my '*Lucky Charm.*' I am '*Divinely Sure*' of that fact." Many laughed and my point was well received by all who had also from time to time searched for answers from God.

To appreciate this factual account, you need to understand where I'm coming from in my Christian faith. My pre-Christian life had shades of the Bible trickster, Jacob. I have many of his weaker personality traits. Even though I had gotten saved and was now living with a new, more compassionate heart, God needed to put me in my place. My Divine Intervention prayers got His "Divine Attention." I figure God did not want me to get the wrong idea about how "His Intervention" works in behalf of Frank E. Landrey. What I mean is this. If Coach Tolsma asked God to keep a pole-vaulter's bar from falling after being tipped as his all-star went over, God could answer his prayer and not be concerned that Coach Tolsma would head to Vegas for a little financial windfall. I believe Coach Tolsma has a "Joseph-type personality," while Frank E. Landrey has a "Jacob-type personality."

I recall a recent incident in a Lynchburg, Virginia, congregation. Just after speaking for a good cause, which was to be followed by an offering to buy Bibles, I sat down in a pew up near the front. As it turned out, the church took up their offering first. When the plate went by me, I fumbled around for my wallet. By the time I had my money clip out the plate had passed. Continuing to look, I found a one dollar bill and a twenty dollar bill. Thinking I should give something, I followed the ushers out to the counting room. *If I can catch up, I'll place a folded one dollar bill in the plate on my way to the restroom. No one will know. Besides, I need the twenty for spending money.* As the Lord would have it, I could not catch up and got there just before the counting room door closed. Reaching inside, I dropped the dollar in the plate that now was being held by a young lady in the counting room. As I walked on to the restroom, conviction overwhelmed me. On my way back to the sanctuary, I knocked on the counting room door and handed the same lady a twenty dollar bill saying, "I gave you the wrong bill." My point is, Jacob gave the dollar and Israel gave the twenty.

As I walked away, she said, "Mr. Landrey, it is great to put a face with your name." Stunned that she knew me, I turned around. "My husband is so-and-so, the head professional at such-and-such golf course." I smiled and said, "Tell Jerry I said hello." With that, I made a hasty retreat back to my pew. We just never know when the Spirit of God might be trying to bail out the "old you" and an embarrassment that could certainly tarnish a testimony. Of course, I had to go and tell it all to you folks. But, I know you will keep my little "struggle" secret between us "golfing friends."

But, to get back to my Big South tournament Divine Intervention golf story, I closed the speech to the Liberty Athletic Booster Club with a look forward. Sharing my concern that we had never played well at Penn State, I told them the truth, "Having missed a great opportunity to go to our first NCAA Regional as the Big South Champion, our dreams all come down to this final event of the year." I tried to explain why we never played our best golf at the Big South Conference or Penn State, by saying, "Maybe we always play bad at these two events because the guys are preoccupied with end-of-year grades and tests. Maybe my wanting it so badly has put too much pressure on them. All I know is my players' minds and focus seem to be elsewhere." I thought to myself, *There I have said it.*

I got on to good things. I explained, "This is the best team I have ever taken to Penn State. We need to win or have a very high finish for any hope of making our NCAA dream come true. Your prayers will be appreciated."

Of course, I did not ask for them to pray for Divine Intervention. Instead, prayers in general would need to be whatever God laid on their hearts. As for me, my prayers would no longer be to ask God for supernatural control of putting outcomes, ball flights, or final scores for my players. I still believed in prayer, but no longer did my thinking include magical interactions at my beck and call. I'm sure Jacob understands, if no one else. On the other hand, I do believe that God performs miracles everyday that include angels unaware and mystical interactions with human beings on a daily basis, just not out on my golf holes, number eight or eighteen, at the Big South Championship.

CHAPTER TWENTY THREE

SITTAWAGA "Sizzle"

After the Flames Club talk, I made my way back to campus and held a team meeting with the five players going to Penn State. Our meeting consisted mostly of mental preparation. After going through the course score card, hitting each club needed for that hole and especially working on iron shots to their four par 3 holes, I asked the guys to join me in the van. Passing out bottles of water, I said, "Guys, relax in the air conditioning and watch a video." I inserted a spring of 1995 team tape, which I had pre-set at that year's Campbell trip. It blessed me to see the guys enjoy a previous team's victory. Excitement filled the van. My goal reached, I began to speak. Explaining we had one more breakthrough coming to us, I pointed out that there were still a few teams who had us down strokes and in head to head stats, win-loss records. "Guys, the good news is as follows. Every team we need to beat will be at this last tournament." Standing in front of them, slightly bent at the shoulders and moving from side to side, I hammered home one thought, "Count on it, Penn State tournaments have at least one rainy day to contend with every year. Be ready for it." I asked them to pray before they fell asleep in their dorm rooms and to thank God for the opportunity to play golf for Liberty. Figuring they needed to be reminded that this was their time to shine, I said, "Men, leave all your troubles behind on this trip. We must focus on our task at hand, make no mistake about it."

Sure enough, when we arrived at the Penn State event, the weather report was calling for rain. It was to be no different than past years. I did not share with the booster club, but I wondered how our team would react to rain. Player attitudes on a five-man team matter even more during bad weather. Mental acceptance of the rain makes all the difference in winning or whining.

After a full day which included eighteen holes, practice green, and driving range work, we headed to the Outback Steakhouse. Soon, we were back at the hotel and in our nightly team meeting. April 25th was upon us. Opening my trusty devotional book, *Experiencing GOD Day-By-Day*, I began, "Guys, the title for tonight's devotion is CONTENTMENT." I continued by quoting Philippians 4:11. "*Not that I speak in respect of want: for I have learned, in whatsoever state I am, therewith to be content.*" With most eyes finally on me, I went on, "Tomorrow you will find times when your circumstances will seem overwhelming. Decide to be content. Contentment means a personal resolve, which includes patience and persistence along with a determination to accomplish the task at hand."

Each Of Us Has A Second Chance Gift…

I told them that contentment frees us to appreciate all the good things available from God. "Tomorrow you begin a tournament that is a gift from God," Continuing, I shared how we were a team of second chances. "Guys, I need to tell you something about our program's past. Golf was reinstated after being dropped from Liberty's list of sports. In my own personal case, I considered quitting two years ago. James Yoo took his second chance offer to finish his college golf. Paul Carey had a second chance when he talked about dropping out of school his sophomore year. We got past it together. Andrew Turner got a second chance when he decided to come back after his first semester. We talked through it together. Jordan Mitchell had a second chance when his career was jump started in my coach's pick at ECU in the fall. After missing our previous tournament, our senior and captain, Nick Heyland, had to take a tough sophomore, Johnny Dickinson, to the last hole in qualifying to make this trip. All of us are second chance participants." I explained, "Last year when coming to Penn State, we left four of our best five players at home, for reasons that don't matter tonight. Because of that, we finished dead last. Because of that poor showing last year, Coach Nye was not going to extend us an invitation this year. But, later he decided to give us this weekend opportunity. I will always believe prayer changed his mind. It is like a second chance." After a slight pause, I said, "Christians are second chance participants in life, freed to live for God." Standing to make my point, I made a request, "Men, while it is just a golf tournament, let us make the best out of our second chance."

Let The Greats Of The Game Speak Out...

Opening up a book that we had read from several times that spring, I started with the following by Payne Stewart, "I'm just myself and I hope that's good enough. I've given up trying to be somebody else. I've found out what works for me. And what works for me is just being Payne Stewart." After acknowledging my great admiration for Mr. Stewart, I said these words, "Guys, you five in this room have what it takes to accomplish all we need done tomorrow."

With that statement, I passed James Yoo the same book, *Golfers On Golf.* "Read your quote from one of golf's great players, Ernie Els." I had the pages marked. James took up the book and began, "I'm constantly looking at my grip, posture, and aim. Golf is my living and I can't afford to take anything for granted." I broke in, "Check these things in the morning, during your warm-up. Set a club down in front of your feet and parallel to your practice target line. Align your body. Check your grip pressure; lighter is better. Stick your behind out and get good posture." James passed the book to Nick or Niko, as the guys referred to him. He responded immediately, "A bad attitude is worse than a bad swing." Explaining it, I said, "What Payne is saying here is that tomorrow we are going to fail at times. Go to the next shot and give it your best effort." Nick passed Paul Carey the book. He spoke in his Irish brogue, "Peter Jacobson said this about six footers. You can't do it unless you've imagined it first." I jumped in, "Does everyone agree?" All did the bobbing-head, dashboard doll trick. Andrew read Tom Watson's thoughts on desire, saying, "Desire is the bottom line. You've got to have 100 percent desire. Anything less is complacency." Andrew Turner passed the book to Jordan Mitchell while I reminded the guys of what my friend Jon Leonard told them when we visited him and his son at their golf course in Georgia during spring break. "Jon challenged all of you to give 100 percent of what you have everyday. We have two more days to finish this dream season." I asked Jordan for the last quote of the night. He spoke softly and yet with a deep conviction, "Coach and teammates, Tom Kite said this after winning the 1992 U.S. Open." Jordan went on to read Mr. Kite's quote, "I didn't play my best golf, but I kept focused better than I ever had. I stayed in the present tense all week." Taking the book, I closed in prayer.

They picked up golf shirts, gloves, and two sleeves of balls for the next day's thirty-six holes. As they left, I said, "Liberty is the place God wanted you to play college golf. Be content to do the best you can tomorrow on every stroke you play. You will walk away with your heads up high no matter what happens." I told them to turn off the television and get a good night's sleep, knowing that tomorrow's thirty-six holes would be grueling.

April 26, 2003, "A Very Long Day"…

In most college tournaments the golf coach has a golf cart. Penn State does it differently. Like at both post-season tournaments, the NCAA Regional and Finals, a coach must walk

214

the course. Players always walk and carry their golf bags, but usually the coach has a choice. This was especially bad for me. My left foot was giving me fits with incredible pain. All spring, I had used the golf cart to our team's advantage. In years past, I had demanded my guys be responsible to bring an umbrella and towel that had been issued at a pre-season meeting. If it rained and they had forgotten their umbrella and towel it was too bad for them. They got wet and their club grips got soaked. In the last few years of my coaching career, I decided to give out umbrellas and towels in pre-season and provide an extra one to be used on trips in case they forgot theirs. Along with the umbrellas and towels, I carried in my cart the following: extra water bottles, Gatorade, fresh fruit, and all kinds of snacks. They especially liked "Balance Bars," which I always gave out to my players during qualifying as well as practice sessions, and in tournaments my last two years. I must have looked like the "bag lady" in a golf cart, but it was effective, especially in bad weather. My job was to get them what they needed when they needed it. I accepted the challenge, like a boxing coach. To play thirty-six holes in one day is not easy, especially if it is hot, cold, or rainy. Carrying all of this for them made their very long day a bit easier.

My conviction to make life simpler for them came from a Bible verse, Mark 10:44, *"And whosoever of you will be the chiefest, shall be servant of all."* Then in the fall of 2002, I read leadership books written by Dr. John Maxwell that advocate leading by example. I decided to add value to their lives in any way possible, which helped my players know that I was in this struggle with them. This Penn State tournament was going to be different because I had no cart. Nevertheless, I would need to walk and sometimes run from par 3 to par 3, a total of eight times that first day. Of course, walking and running for me involved dragging that silly leg and bad foot.

Penn State: The First Round-The First Day...

As we played the first day, the rain fell. When my senior, Nick Heyland, came to the first par 3, I could tell he was having a difficult day but he told me he would get it together. I decided to ask Paul Carey how the rain was affecting him, he being the next to arrive. He said, "Coach, I play 80 percent of my golf in the rain at home in Ireland. I say, let it pour." We had gained some confidence for ourselves as a good harsh-weather team, having faced it several times in the spring season. That plus the lesson learned at UNC Wilmington in the fall had worked to prepare us for the biggest day of my coaching career and their lives as college golfers. My freshman, Andrew Turner, of Lititz, Pennsylvania, at the first par 3 tee said, "Coach, I hope it pours." I smiled. He had challenged the conditions with enthusiasm. Both Jordan Mitchell and James Yoo had positive outlooks as well. All in all, I was satisfied with my first "rain-attitude" checkup.

Four Liberty players had it going their way through fifteen holes. I picked up bits of information indicating they were all under par. But, I saw bogeys and double bogeys on the very last hole, a par 5. Nick Heyland finished his round first and carded an abnormally high score. This meant that I had to count on the next four coming in for us to stay in the hunt. Our dreams would become a nightmare if we had to count an 82 in our team's total.

As Nick double checked his card for any possible mistakes, I observed a sadness that seemed to be overwhelming his countenance. Going right back out on the course for a second eighteen, I knew we were all but sunk if Nick could not get his mind in gear. Liberty needed him to step up if we hoped to finish the tournament in the top three. With my heart in my throat, I walked up to Nick just before he was to tee off. You never know just how a player will react when confronted with a reality. Getting my face nearer to his, I quietly said, "Look at me." He slowly turned his eyes toward mine. In a resolute tone, I said, "Nick Heyland, you are not going to finish out your senior year with 80-80-80. Do you understand me?" With him not having an 80 but rather an 82, it just seemed to be the best way for me to let him know that I was not going to let him take a week off during the biggest tournament of his life and of my coaching career. He turned to walk away with head lowered. Putting my hand on his shoulder, I gently pulled him closer and whispered louder, "Do you understand me?" He jerked his head up and with eyes wide open said, "Yes, Coach, I understand. I'll do my best for you." Nick had a good tee shot and went on his way. I did not ask God for Divine Intervention for him. I did pray for Nick to have wisdom on shot selections and for him to play to his abilities, if at all possible. Right on that tee, I begged, "God, help me to be what the guys need today."

Junior, Paul Carey as well as freshmen Andrew Turner and Jordan Mitchell came in with solid scores for a rain round, 71, 75, and 72 respectively. When Paul Carey asked how his roommate Nick played, I told him that he had an 82. Quickly, I predicted that he would not go over 73 in the final round of the day. He agreed. Having teammates believe in each other does matter. When the other two players asked me how Nick played, I told them that he could not help us this first round and sent them back out with assurance that Nick would help the team in the second round of the day.

James Yoo, playing number one in our lineup position, was the last player to finish the first round. I waited with anticipation and excitement that he might pick us up with a low score, which would set us up good. A team can mark a good total if at least one player finishes deep in red numbers and the other three counters stay in the mid to low 70s. We had our three in the mid to low 70s. When James met me earlier at number seven which was our sixteenth hole, a par 3, he had gleefully said, "Coach, I've just made three straight birdies! I'll post a good score for you; I'm one under." With a good feeling about the possibilities of a low team score, I observed James. A coach watches his players from a distance to see what their demeanor is like. It gives them a good idea what the last few holes have been like for their player. To my dismay, James looked a bit disappointed in himself. I could see at least one of the reasons. He had short sided himself. Penn State's Blue Course has a pear shaped green at the ninth hole, our eighteenth. With the morning's cup placed in the top right neck of that pear, I could see why his head was down. James had left himself a tough third shot. His ball, just to the right of the green, had come to rest in high rough. He was just a 56-degree flip wedge away. A birdie was possible, but the slightest miscalculation could result in a high number, too. He had no choice but to try a flop shot, with a safer shot leaving him possibly off the green. My worst fears came true. As his pitch shot fell short of the green and into the sand, it left a difficult fourth shot. With the ball resting on a down slope and the pin just beyond the bunker's edge, he came out long and over the green. James finished his first round with double bogey, par, double bogey on his last three holes. His disappointing three over 75 was heartbreaking.

When James came off the green, he jerked his bag up and over his right shoulder. A few yards away, he threw it on the ground and stared up above the trees in utter frustration. I eased up along his right side. Grasping his left shoulder with my left hand, I quietly whispered in his ear over his right shoulder. "James-e, I know you are upset over your poor finish." He shrugged his shoulders in agreement. I continued my pep talk. "Listen to me, James-e. Hold your temper for us. We cannot accomplish our dreams without you fighting through this disappointment. You need to be in these next eighteen holes with us. We are a team and you are the heart of it." James smiled and gave me that determined South Korean look. "I'm in it, Coach. You can count on me."

After all five of my guys teed off for the second round, I made a quick retreat to the scoreboard. It was just as I suspected. Our team total of 293 had fared quite well against the field of fifteen teams, even with our bad finish. I was pleasantly surprised to see us in third place and just one stroke behind the host team, Penn State. A very good Western Kentucky team led. Coach Brian Tirpak always did a great job with his players. I knew he was on top of his game, them posting the low round of 287, one under par.

It occurred to me that if my players realized how high up on the leader board Liberty had finished, they might be encouraged by it. So, before going to the first of four par 3 tees for the day's second eighteen holes, I found a scratch pad and made a list of all fifteen schools and their team scores. With a plan in my mind and the "scoop" tally-card in my pocket, I made tracks to our team van needing to first pick up a cooler with drinks and a bag of snacks. I ditched some rain drenched wet towels that I had exchanged for dry ones. Perspiration dripped from my brow. The walk from our van to number fourteen irritated my leg big time. Having started our round on the back nine again in the afternoon, this was my first opportunity to have contact with the guys on the second eighteen. I knew that it was a "must do" situation, to get them through this tough 189-yard hole from the back tee. Standing on the elevated tee box, with water in front and sand all around the small sloping green, it looked like a postage stamp. Fortunately, the rain had kept the wind quiet and softened the green which made it hold golf shots much better. My guys liked firing golf shots like darts at greens with mid-irons.

Soon the first of my five players approached the par 3 tee. I quickly showed Nick the tally-sheet I'd made up with the first round's team results. As he walked off the tee, going to his brilliantly played shot, which had landed just ten feet from the cup, Nick looked back, and said, "Coach, I'm giving it my best effort, I won't quit." Paul was shocked at how high up we had finished. As Paul walked away, he smiled, "All the best, Coach." One by one, the guys blessed me as I saw their eyes light up with the good news. Smiling, I told each, "We are in the right place, at the right time, but we do have more work to do today."

Doing the SITTAWAGA S-i-z-z-l-e...

As each one came by me at par 3s I said things like, "You are the man." "You are as focused on your game as I've seen you all year." "I cannot tell you how glad I am that you came to Liberty to play for me." They were not just words of encouragement. I meant what I said and their eyes reported back that they believed it. They knew that my words were true. Of course, I believe a person plays their best when they want to do it for the other team members, a goal, and coach. Some coaches get the job done by instilling the "fear factor." Other coaches resort to the "push and shove" tactics. This last one definitely does not work in the sport of golf in my opinion. I had tried to get my point across while keeping a good spirit.

Closing out the second eighteen holes, they all finished strong. Four of the players ended up with sub-par rounds. Nick Heyland had a three under par 69. He tied James Yoo who finished well on the last three holes this time and carded another three under 69. Andrew Turner's two under 70 and Paul Carey's second one under 71 rounded out our best team score ever recorded. Hallelujah, they did it. Our nine under par 279 was good enough to move us into position to win the tournament and certainly in sight of a top two or three finish, which would give us our best chance to make the post-season NCAA Regional in years. Jordan Mitchell held his own with an even par 72 to go with his team saving first round even par 72. We had finally put on the SITTAWAGA S-i-z-z-l-e!

Preparation Meets Opportunity...

That night in our devotional and strategy meeting, I told the guys about all who were praying for us. We read quotes from Bob Rotella's book *Golf Is A Game Of Confidence.* I read three headliners from three different pages in his book, including 18, 41, and 81 all in sequence: "To play golf as well as he can, a player has to focus his mind tightly on the shot he is playing now, in the present." "Nearly all golfers would be better off if they forgot about the score as they played." "Acceptance is critical after a bad shot and an angry player can't really execute a pre-shot mental routine."

I pulled out Harvey Penick's book, *And If You Play Golf, You're My Friend.* I read great lines like "Give Luck a Chance." You will find that story on page 77. It is about Coach Penick telling Davis Love how to have better scoring. Mr. Penick told him how Bobby Jones made the point that while a putt left short of the hole obviously did not go in the cup; neither did a putt that went past the hole. And there are more three putts coming back from beyond the cup than there are from just short of it. After watching Davis putt 30 footers for a while, Mr. Penick said, "Son, I want you to try to get that ball to die somewhere around the hole. Work on your speed, your touch. Just roll the ball up there near the hole, and they'll start falling in. The idea is not to try to make every putt from this distance. You want to roll the ball to die at the hole." I read how a couple of weeks later, Davis was on the seventeenth at Harbor Town with a 30-foot putt. He sank it and won the tournament. His excited father phoned Coach Penick that night. Speaking to Coach Penick, Davis Sr., said, "He told me, 'Dad, I did exactly what Mr. Penick was talking about. I rolled it up there and gave luck a chance to happen and it did.' "

Out of another great book titled *Golfer's On Golf,* the guys read different sayings one by one. Gary Player, "The toughest thing for most people to learn in golf is to accept bad holes and then forget about them." Payne Stewart, "A bad attitude is worse than a bad swing." Nick Faldo, "You can get caught up in being too nice and just playing along. You have days when you need to turn it on." Paul Azinger, "I do some form of breathing exercises during a pressure situation. It definitely helps. Every time before I hit a key shot, I take a deep breath and cleanse my mind." Bobby Jones, "Long ago I learned that no putt is short enough to take for granted." After winning the 1992 U.S. Open, Tom Kite said, "I didn't play my best golf, but I kept focused better than I ever had. I stayed in the present tense all week." I concluded with a quote by Bob Toski, "I came to the conclusion that successful players had the Three Cs: Confidence, Composure, and Concentration." Capturing the moment, I ended the meeting with, "Guys, this is an opportunity to apply the Three Cs."

The night ended as usual by bowing our heads. I prayed, thanking God for each player on our roster. I knew we were playing for those back in the dorms on campus, too.

April 27, 2003, The Game Is On…

The next morning we got up refreshed and met downstairs for breakfast. With our team being in the final group, our morning tee time came late, at ten o'clock. We made our way cautiously into the parking lot, after most teams had already teed off. Penn State parked vans just beyond the eighteenth green. Placing the vehicle's gear in park, I shut off the motor and turned sideways to my players, "Guys, it is time to pray." I had long since stopped asking players to pray just before a round. This never worked for me. The player who prayed seemed to always perform badly. Maybe he felt a need to do more than his best. To keep them from feeling this added pressure, I had long ago changed to personally doing all pre-game prayers. Today's round would be no different. I began by making a request. "God, help us to be a good testimony, stay relaxed, and able to accept a bad shot. Help us to never give up on ourselves or on our team's goals."

I had arrived an hour before our first tee time. This was normal for my teams. Those who were to go off first got out and began to chip and putt. Other team members sat in the van and collected their thoughts and or prayed until it was nearer to their tee time.

Our previous day's thirty-six-hole total of 572 (-4) had jumped us into second place going into the final round. We were now tied with Maryland University. Our combined two-round team total was low enough that it distanced us from most teams including a fine Towson team. Coach Brian Yaniger's players scored well the second round but had fallen too far back in the first during the rain. *Of course, I now know that they came back to win the next year, in 2004. It did my heart good to congratulate Coach Yaniger, too.*

The last round's pairings of the 2003 Rutherford set the stage for an exciting finish with the final wave of threesomes being Penn State, Maryland, and Liberty. About fifteen minutes before our first tee time, I called the guys together. We stood in a small circle, off to the side of a practice chipping area located just behind the Penn State clubhouse. We joined in a wheel of arms and I prayed. There would be no high fives or laughter here. Pulling them in close, I whispered, "SITTAWAGA, SITTAWAGA."

Standing on the first tee, one thought kept me praying. *How would my guys hold up under this kind of pressure?* Having a chance to make the NCAA Regional caused even more pressure on Liberty's players. They knew what must be done, but could they do it? As they all teed off, I began to think. *Now, it is up to me to gather myself for the challenge ahead.* The region's last poll ranking had Penn State first and Maryland second. Here we were in the final group of the day playing golf with the two leading teams of the Mid Atlantic Region, in the biggest tournament of my career. This was reason enough to have a good set of the jitters. Feeling confident that a first or second place finish would secure us an NCAA trip, I hoped that third or fourth place would do it, too. Of course, it all depended on who would beat us. This was truly a time for preparation to meet opportunity. A fall and spring schedule had come down to this one last day's round. I knew my guys were tired, like me. But new energy seemed to flow freely to us all. Of course, all teams and coaches experienced the same feelings that come with tired legs. I prayed that my guys would find the energy needed to finish our dream tournament in winning fashion.

Knowing my job would be to have a smile at all times, I determined to have a "happy face" on for my guys. I'm the one in charge of our "emotions," you might say. Often, it became my job to remind them to forget about the last hole and refocus for this one shot at hand. It was my job at times to set an "on course" eighteen-hole scoring goal. Players cannot handle a day's pre-picked scoring number, like a 74 goal. Most assuredly, I did not set scoring goals for today's players. That would be a coaching mistake. I wanted them in the present, at all times. Thinking ahead or looking back, either one is a "no-no" course management mistake. We wanted none of these errors today.

Paul-e Could Take A Challenge...

Occasionally you find a player who has an abruptly short and unusual swing routine or one who can take an "on course" challenge. Paul Carey fit perfectly for both of these oddities. Paul should have been nicknamed "Money" or "Iceman." Time and time again, he birdied the last two holes when we needed it. However, I did on several occasions need to set "on course" goals with Paul during rounds. In his last two years, I learned that it was possible to do it and wish I had realized it sooner. Whenever I noticed his head down after four or five holes, it cued me to jump start him. I would drive my golf cart alongside him and start a conversation or I would find him sitting on the very end of his golf bag waiting at a par 3, or in the fairway during a "play delay." These conversations went something like, "Hey, Paul-e, how's it going?" His patented answer came back, "It's not going to be pretty, Coach." That was my cue to set a scoring goal for him. I would start, "Okay. How do you stand to par now?" He shot back with a wrinkled brow, "I'm four over after just five holes, Coach." My answer was simple, "Well,

that's not good, but you are the one guy who can bring it back."
I asked, "Would you like a bottle of water?" "No," he replied, as
though he did not deserve one. "Here's the deal, your new goal
is a 75," I'd say. His head would snap up. "But, Coach, I said
I'm four over par and par is 72 on this tough course." I calmly
retorted, "I didn't say it was going to be easy. I said you are the
kind of guy who can bring it back." His normal response was a
slight smile and comment like, "I'll do what I can, Coach." As
he walked away, I remarked, "See you at the next par 3, Paul-
e." Paul Carey would almost always bring it back. A few times
he actually gave me a card with 73 or 74 on it, along with his
infectious Irish grin. I watched Paul play the first three holes.
He was relaxed, swinging loose and in control with his compact
swing. Today, goal setting would not be needed. Paul-e had
rhythm.

Finishing What You Start Is Sweet…

While waiting for my players to come through the first par
3 hole my heart was beating so fast that I feared people standing
around could hear the rapid pounding. Out of the corner of my
eye, I noticed Penn State's Coach Nye coming up the fairway.
Casually walking over to a nearby tree for what he might think
was a hunt for shade, I wondered what he would say. A lot of
times in a tight tournament score, an opposing coach is tempted
to try some gamesmanship. "Liberty's players look sharp and
confident today, Coach." Still not sure about his sincerity and
not wanting to be overconfident or boastful, I remarked back,
"I do appreciate the kind words, but it is very early." Later, I
realized that he was being a friend and trying to reassure me that
my guys were holding up fine under the pressure. I felt good
after Coach Nye's encouragement. I wanted to say "thanks," but
it seemed inappropriate at the time.

Later that day, when it looked like we had a chance to win
the tournament, I went to the awards scoreboard area to pray.

"God, if it would be possible to fulfill Scripture today, I like Matthew 9:30, which says, "...and the last shall be first." Being that we were last in Penn State's tournament in 2002, maybe we could somehow finish first in 2003."

Their Fabulous Finish...

It came down to Penn State counting four birdies against our four pars on the last hole. Had it been the other way around we would have forced a play-off. That would have been very exciting. As it turned out, we finished the tournament behind Penn State. In a way, I knew it was the right thing.

The Liberty Flames finished the last day's round with a team total of 288, even par. Team Captain Nick Heyland had come through again for us with a one under par 71. Paul Carey led the team in scoring with 214 (70.5 average for three rounds) and placed ninth individually. Our team's fifty-four-hole total of 860 was good enough for a second place finish. Our four under par total became the third best fifty-four-hole team score in Penn State's tournament history. Liberty's golfers proved in grand fashion that they could play against the best and not fold under pressure.

It was the second time in a row for us to beat Maryland, a fine Atlantic Coast Conference team. Coach Tom Hanna, a determined coach rivaling my competitiveness, immediately found me after our final hole to add his congratulatory handshake. JMU was a strong third in the region and we had now beaten them for the second time. Coach Paul Gooden was quick to congratulate me on Liberty's success.

Soon we headed for Lynchburg, with trophy in hand, but this tournament meant much more than a piece of memorabilia. Excitement bounced around the van on the six-hour drive home. I called our #1 fan. She made goodies for us all year and deserved to be notified before anyone else. My wife was as happy as I was about the team's finish. Alumni were next to call, and the drive home was great.

Divine Intervention Possibilities…

I think that Divine Intervention actually happened here. God blesses persistence, patience, prayers, and faith, but not always in the way we ask. I've listed six reasons for success:

ONE…God sent me nineteen very good players and a great group of dedicated Christian guys in 2002-2003.

TWO…James Yoo decided to come back and finish his golf career at Liberty, and he won his first event as an individual. That set the tone for our team's amazing spring 2003 rally.

THREE…Two people are better than one. Jeff Thomas and I, together, made a better coaching staff than me alone. Having the school increase my consulting fee when they did and getting Jeff's phone call at the time it happened was big.

FOUR…Mental toughness learned in newsletters from GolfPsych, Inc. and Peak Performance Sports allowed us to stay focused on the golf course. Dr. John Maxwell's leadership principles, Dr. Rotella's confidence insight, and quotes of great players were a huge help.

FIVE…My new Performance Based Scholarship System allowed me to give large scholarships to two exceptional freshmen players, Jordan Mitchell and Andrew Turner.

SIXTH…At just the right time, Dr. Falwell would preach one of his "Don't Quit" sermons. Having heard him speak over a thousand times in the last twenty-four years, I've benefited from his four major sermon categories. They are:

Get Saved, by putting your faith and trust in Jesus.

Get Going for Jesus, by telling others what has happened.

Get Right, by confession, for fellowship with the Father.

Don't Quit on God. After all, where can we go?

Having gone through the Get Saved stage before arriving in Lynchburg, Virginia, I knew this message was a good one. Because of testifiers like Bertha Fravel, Donna and Bob Hagemeier, Pastor Ron Kerr, as well as Georgiann Sims Leonard, on December 27, 1970, while sitting alone on a front pew of the First Baptist Church in Vincennes, Indiana, it happened. God had given me His promised Supernatural "increase." This wonderful "life change" that occurred for me can become a reality for anyone. Some people thought that my life looked great on the surface. With a measure of success in business, sports, and family, I managed to put up a "happy face" in public most of the time. But under that facade, I was going down for the third time. My wife Carol and I were at our end, with me gambling and drinking.

As an unsaved person, I was "born again" when I asked Jesus Christ to come into my heart and life by saying a prayer very similar to this, "Realizing that I need and want a Savior, Lord Jesus, please come into my heart and life. Save me from my sin. God helping me, I will live for You." My tiny bit of faith attached to God's amazing grace did it. I had forgiveness of sin by the blood of Jesus Christ (Ephesians 1:13). His Holy Spirit had sealed me until the day of redemption and I immediately had potential to live a victorious life for Christ (Ephesians 1:13-15).

As a young child in the pond a block away from our modest home in Woodlawn, I went down for the third time. My sister held my older brother's heels as he reached out and grabbed my hand to lift me up. My older siblings pulled me out of a "Gravel Pit," just in time. Jesus pulled me out of a "Fiery Pit," just in time. This is His specialty. Was getting saved, moving my family 640 miles away, and becoming golf coach happenstance or Divine Intervention?

One final note: Dr. Falwell has often said, "All of our failures are prayer failures. Nothing of eternal significance happens apart from prayer. Prayer can do anything." Jeremiah 29:12-13 says, *"Then shall ye call upon me, and I will hearken unto you. And ye shall seek me, and find me, when ye shall search for me with all your heart."*

Coach Landrey Challenges Paul Carey to Refocus His Efforts while He Discusses Paul's Par 3 Club Selection.
(Read Chapter Twenty-Three for Conversation Details)

CHAPTER TWENTY FOUR

Our 2003 NCAA Trip

By May 13th, school was officially out. Thousands of Liberty students were packing cars and vans to go home. My five guys going to the East Regional had been told the night before to "Meet Me At The Chain" at 9:00 A.M. sharp. Those going to the post-season tournament were told by dorm officials that they could keep things in their rooms until we got back. But at eight the next morning they got an edict for everything to be out of their rooms that day.

James Yoo pulled up behind his dorm for quick packing. It just so happened that a campus policeman drove up at that time and proceeded to give my junior a warning ticket for illegal parking. This led to two other players getting upset. They thought the campus officer had given James a ticket that would cost him money and unwisely got involved verbally in an overly-heated debate. In fairness, the campus policeman was just trying to do his job, albeit too excessively and authoritatively. Having this done on a very hectic day for us did not help. That conversational exchange developed into a "for money" ticket being issued to a second player. As the Lord would have it, Dr. Falwell drove up. Visibly upset, I told him our dilemma. "Brother Frank, it will be okay. You just take the young men on this trip with no thought about what has happened here. Trust me. Things will straighten out here before you return."

Atlanta, Here We Come…

I took the team to Auburn, Alabama, through Atlanta, Georgia, deciding to have our overnight stop come in Atlanta, near Georgia Tech's campus. I wanted to show my guys the dorms in which I had lived while an athlete there. Shortly after our arrival, I found the guys a place to hit balls. Before heading on to the south side of Atlanta, I took a walk down memory lane and treated the guys to a ride through Tech's campus before a surprise stop at the *Varsity*.

I never thought I would come back to the *Varsity*, bringing my own team as a college coach. My *GT* college meals at the *Varsity* included one each of three or more of the following: chili dog with cheese, death burger "all the way," fried peach pies, fresh cut french fries, and a frosted orange or chocolate soda. I must confess. My youthful stomach pangs bowed to its lure more than once a day, especially on weekends when a three-time trip sequence might occur. This was my normal eating out schedule from 1959-1963. Of course, I always ate the great meals at our Georgia Tech athlete dining table. Steak was my "meal of choice" there. Some say I can still out eat most college players. *Is that a compliment? Hummm.*

The Varsity Story: "Gordy's Goal"…

I told my guys what I had read and heard. It goes like this. The original *Varsity* came into being in 1928 just three years after Mr. Gordy had dropped out of Georgia Tech. He told his classmate friends that he would make $20,000.00 before they graduated, that was a lot of hot dogs back in the 1930s. The *Varsity* is now considered to be the world's largest drive-in restaurant. It seats eight hundred inside with twenty-four rooms and 30-40 one-arm chairs in each, plus a television, parking for 600 cars, and all on two city blocks.

Two Vagrants: A "Second Chance" Wish...

Having played basketball and golf against Auburn in my *GT* days, I told the guys that I never thought I'd be back as a coach at either location, The *Varsity* or Auburn University. And, I certainly never dreamed of being back as a Christian. I shared with them that during my own college years, I was not interested in becoming a Christian. I was reminded years later by my best *GT* basketball pal and now fellow brother in Christ, Johnny Herbert, that Coach Hyder took our team to church. Now we will dance in Heaven with King David. In some strange way, I feel we will know a little something about dancing in the spirit. I think I will laugh a lot doing it.

This night, with our meals piled high, my guys and I had prayer together, which was a normal thing for us to do. After the feast, I led the way down a set of steps past the french fry section. Making a left turn, going past the food factory located opposite the restrooms, we went out the doors to our van which had been parked on the backside of the restaurant. The fellow sitting just on the other side of that exit door had his hand extended, to catch my eye. He got a Gospel tract. I also handed him a pocket Bible with money in it. Another fellow noticed my generosity and walked up to my driver's door, which I had just closed. As he looked rough and tattered, I did not roll the window down at first glance. With him motioning for me to do so, I reluctantly did. He immediately asked if I had any more of what I gave the other man. I felt obliged to give him a tract and Bible. After looking in my wallet for a five or a ten, of which I found none, I slipped a larger bill in the Bible. Jordan Mitchell must have seen me slip money into the Bible and asked the amount I gave. Telling him that God knows, I remarked that it was a way of showing gratitude for my own salvation. I explained, "If money helps them know that I care, maybe they will be more apt to read the Scripture verses." Not thinking about the money but rather the spiritual message that went with it, I kept a lot of thoughts to myself.

I watched the poorly dressed, haggard-looking man depart. Unshaven for days and hair a mess, sprouting every which way out of his head, he quickly shuffled up the street. Slightly bent at the waist, hunched over with arms tucked into his belly, I assumed he meant to protect the money. Holding the Bible like a fullback carrying a winning touchdown on a wild Georgia Tech football Saturday, he darted away. We were only a block or so from the famed Bobby Dodd Stadium, located on the Georgia Tech campus. My new friend, obviously down on his luck, had with him at that moment more money than he had seen in months.

Gazing back at the vagrant, I told the guys in the van, "But for the grace of God, that could have been me." As we drove off, I yelled, "Don't spend it on booze. God wants to bless you!" He managed to throw one hand up but walked a little faster. Knowing that it most likely would be used in the wrong way, I prayed for the man to be saved. God can change any heart. I knew it to be true. God can take the urge for a drink away. I knew that to be true, too. I recalled a preacher saying, "What he will do for one, He can do for you." I could dream of meeting my "fraternal friend of fate" in Heaven one day. If he had honestly looked up in a genuine repentant prayer, we would one day have a happy reunion.

I continued to drive south down highway 85, heading to our hotel. It was the day before our "dream tournament" in Auburn, Alabama. Later that night while standing in the hotel's parking lot with Jordan Mitchell waiting for his musically talented sister, who lived in the area, I felt sad. Thoughts broke my heart. *My two new friends from the Varsity were now trying to find a place to sleep.* Soon Jordan's eyes lit up as his sister's headlights flashed before us. Soon she was singing several of her hit songs, while Jordan played his guitar. It made our night go quickly and helped my guys to stay loose. After a fast couple of hours, it was over, and she departed. We settled in for a good night's rest, knowing that tomorrow would bring excitement and challenge.

Off We Go To Auburn, Alabama...

We left Atlanta early on May 14th. The 100-mile drive proved to be an exciting time. We had great anticipation of the opportunity at hand. Most of the twenty-seven teams participating were ranked top fifty in the latest polls. There would be "three" Regional Tournaments going on at the same time around the country, with a total of eighty-one teams competing. Coach Mike Griffin and his fine school, the Auburn Tigers, was this year's NCAA East Regional host. Ten teams would come out of each of the three regional sites, making up the thirty team field for the NCAA Finals to be played in Stillwater, Oklahoma, two weeks later.

Now was our time to show the collegiate golfing elite what we could do. Just coming off of three firsts, two seconds, one third, and one fourth in our last seven tournaments, while posting eighty-three wins against only seven defeats, gave me great confidence. We were also looking forward to having the opportunity of avenging our only poor showing of the spring, a Big South Championship fourth place finish. Charleston Southern had beaten us by fourteen strokes. They were rightly awarded the East Regional spot for winning our conference. We wanted to even the score with them. The fact that our last tournament was a second place finish, with a four under par 860 score, made me confident.

We entered the parking lot on May 14th at about eleven o'clock for our practice round. Our school's name was on a ten-by-eight inch sign hanging near and beside teams like: Auburn, Clemson, Duke, East Tennessee State, Florida, Georgia Tech, Georgia Southern, Georgia State, South Carolina, Tennessee, and Wake Forest. *Our conversion van looks like it belongs*, I thought. I had pictured it in my mind, Liberty's van sitting among the best. Ours was the only van that honored God and Country. Upon buying it, I pledged to God I'd acknowledge Him with it by inscribing above the windshield these four words, "In God We Trust."

I hoped that we could put together a SITTAWAGA Sizzle like we had in the second round at Penn State, to show what our guys really could accomplish at this level of competition. I certainly believed we had "guns loaded" and "in the van." Like always, we prayed before the guys put on team shirts. After stretching, they made their way to the putting and chipping green to be followed by a lot of driving range work. I mingled with some coaches and sized up the place, finding out what time the coach's meeting would take place. Coaches always needed to seek out details concerning tournament pairings and rules for an event. Then, I rounded up the team for our practice round.

When James Yoo came back to school in the spring, he continued to use his Liberty golf bag, which was blue with red lettering. I told him the NCAA rules might not allow a color to be different from our new, red bags, which the other four had. Having used his blue bag all spring without a problem along with having become a sentimental favorite, James could not imagine that his blue bag would be rejected. I told him that the NCAA post-season regulations were a lot tougher than season regulations. On the other hand, our golf bag dilemma was not plainly spelled out in the paperwork. Sure enough, a tournament volunteer working the first tee gave James Yoo a wrinkled brow and frown. "No red bag means you play no tournament golf." My heart stopped momentarily. Concerned that my second best season average might get too upset to play, I swallowed hard. James explained that it had Liberty on the bag just like the red ones. The man said angrily, "You're in the 'big time' where things are done right, son." Fortunately, planning for all possibilities, I had my personal red Liberty golf bag with us. Otherwise, we would have played with four players, to count the best four, instead of five to count the best four scores for our total. The volunteer even made us use duct tape to cover up my name. That same man made a speech to our team before we were to take the tee box. In a gruff voice, he said, "You are to take only one tee ball and one fairway shot on each hole. When you get to the green, you can chip and putt but keep up with the group ahead. Violate any of these rules for this practice round and you will be pulled off the course."

My other junior and best season average, Paul Carey, stepped up and promptly hit his tee shot into the right woods. Pulling out another ball, the unfriendly man stepped forward, "Son, I said only one tee ball per player." I wanted Paul to let it go in fear the man might have authority to pull him off the course before our practice round. Just then, Paul put another ball on a tee. The man bellowed, "Young man, did you hear me?" Before I could say anything, Paul turned to him and said, "Sir, when a ball is lost, I always have the right to hit a provisional." The grumpy man turned and walked away.

With the confusion before leaving Lynchburg and these distractions at the start of our practice round, I wondered how my team would respond. After calming everyone down, I established club selections for all four par 3 holes. Knowing this was the biggest thrill in their golfing lives, it seemed right to ask them if they wanted to continue using my par 3 system, writing down clubs used daily and having our consultations on wind and yardage. To the man, they assured me it helped more than it hurt them. Any par 3 system has a tradeoff. Some coaches work par 3s with their team and some leave it up to their players. Either way is certainly acceptable coaching strategy. Not allowing coaching carts, to get from par 3 to par 3, meant that I would miss some with my bum foot and leg anyway.

It was 5:00 P.M. by the time we finished our practice round and a cookout was being served. Barbecue chicken and ribs are two of my big weaknesses, having sold barbecue for thirty-one years and trying my competitor's products. None were any better than this. Of course, I thought ours was just a little better. That is why I named our company, "Landrey's Famous Foods" and believed our pit-cooked "Live-Fire" wood flavored meats would eventually be famous. I had believed in my product and now in this team.

One very good thing came out of our NCAA trip. As good friends gathered around great barbecue, I met and thanked a coach who had helped me get started. Coach Puggy Blackman lifted his head out of his plate of ribs and smiled, "Well, I knew you would make it here one day." I extended my right hand in a gesture of friendship, thanking him. "Relax and enjoy the fruits of your labor, Coach Landrey." One other time I was scared to death and he had been there for me with a lot of wisdom and some great advice. My comments to Puggy, as he stood there with a College Golf Fellowship National Representative, mirrored these words, "I will always be indebted to you for your openness and helpful attitude back when I started coaching."

As usual, Coach Blackman's team was participating in another East Regional. They placed seventh and made it all the way to the NCAA Finals. He had represented his new school, South Carolina, quite well. I would expect no less. Another goal of mine had been achieved. With a promise to myself of an NCAA meeting of our two teams, while on the way home from my Atlanta Q and A trip eleven years before, I had come full circle. The weight of that uncertainty had been forever removed. God had blessed our efforts.

Auburn University Runs A Great Regional...

The fine people hosting the East Regional at the beautiful Auburn University Golf Course were very polite and helpful. I made sure to thank them, telling my players to do the same. College golf takes place because members are willing to give up their golf course. It is extra special when these same people make you feel wanted. Auburn volunteers did it just right. Of course, there is always one bad apple. Once we got past him, at the beginning of our practice round, it all came together. In all fairness, I guess he had a bad day. I knew him from when he coached and remembered a "tough cop" type. That's okay. I also remembered him being a fair-minded man, too. So, I chalked up our run-in to mostly our lack of experience in the big league. His attitude may have been a heart problem. Maybe our attitude had a part to play. Christians are expected to go the extra mile and maybe we could have done something different, too.

While we were out on the course, a huge screen had been erected. With it sitting just to the right of the clubhouse, people could check out the results from the parking lot. Information scrolled across the screen constantly throughout the day. It was used as a scoreboard for tournament standings and for *Info Messages*. A giant tent sat on the golf course side, next to the huge information screen. Providing a lot of shade for the weary, we ate under the big top and it came in handy on the tournament's hot days. Walking to the course from our van, we passed by the big screen, the giant sized tent and past the two huge BBQ cookers. News media, coaches, family members, and interested spectators sat under the tent at long tables, watching the screen for results.

Our first round started off shaky on the 7,207 yard par 72 monster of a course. Bad luck put us back on our heels. Then, we made a move with three players under par. It helped Liberty post in the top ten early on, along with my friend Coach John Affleck's Binghamton Bearcats. Seeing that listing on the course scoreboards made me dream a bit. But, with the favorites teeing off later that morning along with our own course management miscalculations, which yielded some big numbers, we fell back. Having our first day's team score twenty-five strokes over the average round for us at Penn State, I knew we were in for a tough three days. Even though the last two rounds were better than our first day's performance, we never got our game on track.

What we needed was one big round like at Penn State. It did not happen. I still felt good about the tournament, in that we did accomplish some of our goals. We had beaten the Big South Champion, Charleston Southern University. We did not fall apart and finished two teams ahead of our NCAA announced twenty-sixth pick while beating three teams.

Liberty's first ever Division-1 East Regional was history. I had believed that we could do a lot better. This time we fell short of my goal to be one of the top ten teams. One of my players, after he had finished his golf eligibility, told me that he always knew I believed it could be done but he had to admit that he and other players at times did not believe it enough themselves. It was not until that day that I realized I had failed to communicate my confidence in their games to the degree that they could see themselves good enough to accomplish the unthinkable.

"Big Plans" For "The Future"...

While making the long drive home from Alabama, I had a lot to be grateful for. My mind raced as I pondered all that had happened. Already thinking about next year's prospects of a return trip, I was making plans to go to Yale's fall MacDonald Cup preview tournament in New Haven, Connecticut. It would be on the very course where the NCAA East Regional would be played in May 2004. *By playing that course several times in the fall, we would have a much better chance to finish in the top ten and make it to Virginia's #1 Course "The Homestead Resort" for the finals.*

Having already given my request to Yale's friendly, savvy Head Coach Dave Paterson, I had high hopes we would get an invitation. *Next year we just might climb into that elite field of thirty teams.* Dreaming again, I could see us in our first Division-1, NCAA Championship Finals. Only time, good planning, and lots of Divine Intervention could determine next year's outcome. But, I was excited about our upcoming 2003-2004 campaign possibilities. With only one player graduating and him being replaced by two fine players, our future was bright. I looked forward to coaching those coming back and two top freshman recruits, Peter Horstman, and a seasoned transfer golfer, Eric Klinger.

Thanking Nineteen Players For Their Efforts...

This 2002-2003 Liberty Fairway Flames team did great. All nineteen players had a part in our team's success and, therefore, all are listed first by seniority, then alphabetized by their last name. Jonathan Biegle (Sr.), Nick Heyland-Team Captain (Sr.), Denton Lomax (Sr.), Paul Carey (Jr.), James Yoo (Jr.), Jonathan Dickinson (So.), Gary Hui (So.), Joe Norman (So.), Albie Powers (So.), Jackson Battle (Fr.), Anthony Beckles (Fr.), Peter Hong (Fr.), Jordan Mitchell (Fr.), Sam Nelson (Fr.), Zack Phillips (Fr.), Matthew Richards (Fr.), Andrew Turner (Fr.), Trevor Williams (Fr.), and Toni Zanotti (Fr.).

Seventeen team members competed in at least one tournament during the year, on a team or as an individual. It could be an NCAA record for the largest number of players to compete in a given year from any one team.

Let me *thank golf course members and staff* for their support *in the use of their course to benefit college golf.*

Georgia: Savannah's Crosswinds-Lake Park's Francis Lake.

North Carolina: Beacon Ridge, Brierwood, Caverns CC Resort, The Carolina, Magnolia Greens, Nags Head Links, River Landing, Sea Pines Ocean Course, and Woodlake CC.

Sunset Beach, NC: Angels Trace, Bay Tree Plantation, Colonial CC, Pearl Links, Sandpiper Bay, and Sea Trail.

Myrtle Beach, SC: Azalea Sands, Eastport, Falcon, Glen Dornoch Waterway, Grande Dunns, Prestwick, Legends CC, and Wild Wing Plantation. Plus: Litchfield Resort and The Tradition at Pawley's Island.

Virginia (Northern): The Homestead Resort and Conference Center, Pleasant Valley and South Riding Golf Club. *Virginia (Central):* Boonsboro, Country Side, Falling River, The Greenbrier, Hat Creek, Hidden Valley, Ivy Hill, London Downs, Mariners Landing, Oakwood, Poplar Grove, Poplar Forest, Roanoke CC, Stoney Creek at Wintergreen, Water's Edge, Waterfront, Westlake and Winton Golf Club.

Seven Things I Learned From Our First NCAA Trip …

1) Our first East Regional trip was worth the expenses.

2) It is worth the effort to make an NCAA Regional.

3) To prepare better for it, play 7,200 yard courses.

4) Play the NCAA Regional course as often as possible

5)) Work harder on mental preparations "focusing."

6) Enjoy the trip. It may be your last.

7) Thank those who make the event happen every year.

"Thanks" NCAA Division-1 Men's 2003 Golf Committee:

Val Hale, Brigham Young University

Randy Lein, Arizona State University

Gerald Meyers, Texas Tech University

Ron Petro, Rhode Island University

Fred Warren, East Tennessee State

Donnie Wagner, NCAA

"Thanks" Mid Atlantic Region 2003 Advisory Committee:

Scott Allen, George Washington University, Chair

Pat Lyons, Iona University

Francis Vaughan, University of Pennsylvania

Maura Waters, Rutgers University

People serving in their specialized calling who also go the extra round, so to speak, and take a place on some committee or board that keeps college golf on track, deserve our thanks and recognition. They are the reason college golf has risen to the top of intercollegiate sports.

241

EPILOGUE

"Big Shots" Bring You Back...

Golf is a family affair, as I have heard Jack Nicholas say. I've played many times with my four sons-in-law: Troy Rice, Steve Clark, Tom Gaffney, and Bryan Bauer. But, if there is one thing that binds every golfer of the past and future together, it is a thrilling golf shot.

Every coach is thrilled by a great golf shot. I remember my first "big shot" to see from a college player. I witnessed this one during my volunteer semester and it helped encourage me to take the coaching position. Todd Casabella hit a great third shot on a par 5. I enjoyed it immensely and told him.

While standing at the back of the green, I watched his ball land about thirty feet short of the flag. It made its way to the hole, like a snake on a mission, sliding side to side. I could see that it was going to go in, while still twenty feet away from the cup. When it did go in, I jumped and shouted with joy, "Thanks, Todd, for that adrenaline rush." I knew that my competitive spirit was going to be thrilled, time and time again, with the "big shots" my college guys would produce.

Three Eagles, Same Hole: "All-In-A-Row"...

I did not get to see the three best "third shots" to ever happen (that I know of) in the same tournament and on the same hole in college golf. It all happened at Penn State in 2004 during my last college tournament as coach. This is remarkable. My sophomore player, Jordan Mitchell, had an eagle (two under) on the fifth hole, a par 5, one in each of all three tournament rounds. He was six under par on that one hole. It included a driver each time, two two-irons and one three-iron for the second shot and three one putt greens: 5 feet, 20 feet and 40 feet. It is like a hole-in-one three times. I would submit that this feat probably never had been done before in all the years of college golf during the same tournament and on the same hole.

While in a kneeling position, Jordan could hit the driver farther than most college players could in a normal stance. He, by far, turned out to be my best trick shot artist in twelve years. In fact, his artistic talents took him in another direction the year after I retired. With guitar and voice, he left to try his talent in music. Having Jordan back in college golf would be *"nice and good"* as Matt Richards would say.

How About *"Them"* Holes-In-One...

October 10th of our fall 2000 season, Yong Joo aced the longest par 3, approximately 240-yards, I had ever personally witnessed. His brilliant "five wood" took flight in the final day of the Wolf Pack Invitational, landing at the front of the green, winding perfectly up to the cup. My Australian s*harp shooter*, Allen Hill, had his hole-in-one at a Big South Championship. He aced Windamier Country Club's seventeenth in the second round on the seventeenth day of April 2001. Others made holes-in-one while at Liberty. Justin Jennings made his during an ODU practice round at Seascape Golf Course on then, par 3, number thirteen. Mark Setsma's ace came at London Downs, our home course, on the second hole from 220-yards out. Mark Humrichouser added one at the Campbell University event in his senior year. It came on a 185-yard par 3, and he used a four iron.

Some "Big Shots" In My Life...

My own "Big Shots" that I will never forget were made while playing golf with special people. I have made some eagles on par 4s and 5s with no one around to enjoy them, as so many of us have done. Making my only hole-in-one, I played golf with two of my oldest and dearest friends, Mark Michael and Richard Cannon. The thrill still hangs around and sometimes comes up in our conversations. A person I had met for the first time, a new friend, witnessed it, too. His name is John Dunn. I had driven the sixty miles down to Evansville, Indiana, to meet up with my friends for a game of golf. Standing on the par 3 fifteenth tee box at Rolling Hills Country Club, we joked about making a hole-in-one. The tee was elevated, making the 197-yards play ten-yards shorter. I used a four iron. The ball flew like a dart to the green. It landed about ten feet in front of the hole and rolled straight into the cup. Mark said something first. "Hey, that has a chance to go in." Richard Cannon followed up, "Geno, you got yourself a hole-in-one. You are buying." It happened a few days after my thirty-first birthday, on September 30, 1971. However, having gotten saved eight months before, I set the boys up for a good meal instead of alcoholic drinks. It cost me less and I could remember the "special" moment with my friends much easier the next day, and headache free.

My only "double-eagle" occurred while playing with my older brother at Miami Lakes Country Club in Florida. We stood side by side, watching my second shot. Using a four wood, it landed ten feet in front of the 499-yard ninth hole. My brother Richard said, "It is going toward the hole. It has a chance. It went in!" We jumped up and down exchanging high fives.

Another great shot came at my home course, the Vincennes Elks Club on June 2, 1958. We were playing the fourth hole. I hit first and it looked like the ball was going in, but it stopped a foot past the hole. Birdies counted for two skins. With the first two players off the green, I looked like a lock. My older brother, Richard, hit next saying, "I think I'll get inside you, little brother." Hitting a five iron into the sun, he thought his ball went over the green. When I went up to spot my ball, there was his in the hole. I did my best to rejoice with him, realizing my putt for a birdie no longer mattered.

Your Own "Big Shot" To Remember...

Memories stay with you when it comes to a "Big Shot." They include: the course, the hole, par for the hole, the club used, playing partners, and exactly how it happened. Memories are the pictures of my mind. Picture a "Big Shot."

Have you had any "Big Shots" in your life? It will encourage you when a mental check brings back the details.

List One "Big Shot" Of Your Own...

Golf Course_____

Hole_____ Par_____ Club Used_____

Playing Partners_____

_____....._____

How It Happened_____

_____

_____

Frank's *GT* Golf Group   Frank's Indiana Golf Group

Landrey's *1992-2004 *Alphabetical Roster

Jared Albert, Tom Anthony, Jonathan Bathe, Jackson Battles, Anthony Beckles, Jonathan Beigle, Andy Braddock, Paul Carey, Kelly Chambrelain, Andrew Comer, Kyle Cousins, Jamie Coleman, Jonathan Dickinson, Chris Easley, Ryan Ferguson, Tommy Giles, John Hahn, Jason Hailey, Chad Hall, Bryan Hayes, Chad Hendley, Jeromy Henry, Kenny Hobbs, Peter Hong, Peter Horstman, Chad Howell, Todd Humrichouser, Nick Heyland, Allen Hill, Gary Hui, Justin Jennings, Brandon Jutras, Yong Joo, Jason Kincannon, Eric Klinger, Gary Leeds, Denton Lomax, Rob McClellan, Jordan Mitchell, Clint Moon, Mike Morris, Josh Mullins, Chris McTavish, Danny Myers, Sam Nelson, Joseph Norman, Tyler Phillips, Zack Phillips, Albie Powers, Brent Reagan, Matthew Richards, David Roseberry, Mark Setsma, Todd Setsma, Garrick Stiles, John Sorrel, Andrew Stoll, Jeffrey Thomas, Arnold Thompson, Randy Tipmore, Andrew Turner, Jon Wolfe, Dan Willis, Andy Weisinnger, Trevor Williams, Doug Widrig, Jon Wolfe, Dan Willis, James Yoo and Tony Zanotti. Adding three recruits the year I retired, Josh Bain, Parker McCoy and Mike Turner makes seventy-three players. If I've missed someone I am sorry.

Landrey's 11 Year Team Records, 1992-2003

Best team 18-hole score: 279, Penn State, 4/26/2003
Best team 36-hole score: 567, Penn State, 4/26/2003
Best team 54-hole score: 860, Penn State, 4/26-27/2003
Most team members competing: 17, 2002-2003
Most team victories in a year: 3, 2002-2003
NCAA Regional appearances: 1, 2002-2003
Mid Atlantic Coach of the Year: 1, 2002-2003

I truly hope that you enjoyed reading the book.
My prayer is that God will bless you and your family.

Many Great Golfing AWAGA Getaways to You All

ABOUT THE AUTHOR

Coach Landrey and Carol find time to pose together
(After 2004's Spring Season, Coach Landrey Retired)

Frank E. Landrey and his wife Carol reside in Virginia. Married for forty-two years, they have four daughters; four sons-in-law, and thirteen grandchildren.

Education: Lincoln High (1959), Georgia Tech BS (1963), Luther Rice Seminary, MA/Ministry (1986), Liberty University, MA/Counseling (1991), International Baptist Theological College, Honorary Doctor of Divinity (1991).

Athletics: Lincoln High School's Five Sports (1955-1959) plus Georgia Tech's Basketball and Golf (1959-63).

Work: Life of Kentucky (1963-64), Stubnitz (1965), J.R. Landrey, Inc. (1965-96). Pro Golf Ideas, Inc. (1993-2005).

Politics: Candidate Local and State, Committee to Restore the Constitution Lobbyist, Freedom Columns and 1988 New Orleans National Convention (R) Delegate (1978-1988).

Ministry: Christian Business Men's Committee, DeHass Ministries, Fellowship of Christian Athletes, Gideon International, Missions In Action/founder, Stress Seminars, Sword of the Lord Evangelism Subscription Drives, and served on George Dooms' TTT Youth Ministries Board. *"Mentoring these last twelve years on inner city route 3 to Crystal, Courtney, Chris, Destine, Tre-Quan, Tykwon, Neecho, and Toni plus 30 other kids on Jack Gillaspie, Dick Flack, Joe and Jim Shaner's bus has been a real blessing."*

RECOGNITION

The author has endeavored to credit all known persons holding copyright or reproduction rights for passages quoted and for information used in illustrations, or ideas either by personal contacts or by listing their works as follows.

Basic Books/New York, *Letters to a Young Golfer*, Copyright Bob Duval/Carl Vigeland 2002.

Barnes and Noble Books/New York, *Golfers On Golf*, Foreword by Peter Jacobsen, Copyright-Frank Coffey 1997.

Fairway Press/North Carolina, *Golf Can't be this Simple*, Copyright-John Toepel, Jr. 2002.

Simon & Schuster/New York, *The 8 Traits of Champion Golfers*, Copyright-Dr. Deborah Graham/Jon Stadler 1999.

Simon & Schuster/New York, *Golf Is Not A Game Of Perfect*, Copyright-Robert Rotella 1995.

Simon & Schuster/New York, *Golf Is A Game Of Confidence*, Copyright-Robert Rotella 1996.

Simon & Schuster/New York, *And If You Play Golf, You're My Friend*, Copyright-Harvey Penick, Bud Sharke, and Helen Penick 1993.

Spire Books-Fleming H. Revell Company/New Jersey, *Sipping Saints*, Copyright-World Challenge, Inc., and Fleming H. Revell Company, Author David Wilkerson.

Thomas Nelson/Tennessee, *Attitude 101 What Every Leader Needs To Know*, Copyright-Maxwell Motivation, Inc. 2003.

Thomas Nelson/Tennessee, *The Maxwell Leadership Bible*, Copyright-Maxwell Motivation, Inc. 2002.

Zondervan Publishing House/Michigan, *Anger Is A Choice*, Copyright-Zondervan Corp. 1982, Author Tim LaHaye.

Please accept my deepest apology if I have missed listing your book, copyright date and/or publisher. —*Frank Landrey*

Notes From Friends and Players Last Forever...

Dear Coach Landrey:

It seems just yesterday when you picked me up at the train station. At the time I didn't know if Liberty was the place for me, but now I am able to see very clearly that the Lord had his hand on my decision. Thanks for giving me the opportunity to play golf for you. We have shared many mountain tops as well as low valleys. I will treasure the time that I spent with you on and off the golf course.

Your brother in Christ, Kenny Hobbs (Buzz)

COACH!

CONGRATULATIONS ON YOUR SUCCESS!! YOU'RE STILL THE BEST COACH IN THE COUNTRY IN MY OPINION! THANK YOU FOR THE UPDATES..... YOU STILL ENCOURAGE ME!!

I HOPE TO GET YOU THAT ARTICLE ON MY EXPERIENCE LAST SUMMER SOON. I'M TRYING TO MAKE MORE MONEY.... ONCE I MAKE MY FIRST MILLION I'LL HELP GET YOU THAT PRACTICE FACILITY!!

TAKE CARE OF YOURSELF!
-Justin

Hey Coach,
thanks for all your help and hard work,
I'll look forward to next semester. Paul

Hey Coach,
Thanks so much for being a wonderful role-model, friend, and coach. You are a Godly influence in my life and you have
This is how God encouraged me greatly. God showed his love
among us:
He sent his one and only Son
into the world.

1 John 4:9 (NIV)

bless you and Thank You. Rett

Coach, for all
Thank + love you
the time into our team.
Put r the best!
Yours
Andi

Thank you so much for all the support!!
Zach

Coach,
Thanks for all of your hard work, support, and dedication. look forward to the seasons to come.
Patch

Coach,
Thank-you for all of your effort and dedication to the team. May God truly bless you and your family in the year to come and this Christmas season
Eric Klinger

Coach,
Thanks so much for the commitment that you have given the golf team. You are a great example to each one of us
Gordon "Don't steal my dessert"

Coach,
Thanks for all of your determination, thanks for bringing great attitude to the team + game.
"BRBEST"

Coach,
Thanks for all the time and commitment to the team and for all you do for us.
Andre

Coach,
Thanks for all your encouragement and hard work.
JL

As we celebrate
our Savior's birth
at Christmas,
I'm reminded of how
you bring His love to others
in such a special way
all year long.

Wishing You a Blessed
Holiday Season

Coach,
Thank you for all the time reflect you put into the program. Most of all thank you for all the prayers. Coming to LU has been such a blessing, and without you this opportunity, this wouldn't have been possible.

Hey Coach, "SITTAWAGA"
I just want to thank you for giving me the opportunity to come down to Liberty to be a part of a great journey. Thank you for your dedication, inspiration and your encouragement on and off the field. It has been my greatest pleasure to play for Liberty and serving the Lord with you. James

CONCH, SO MUCH THANKS
FOR EVERYTHING. THANKS
FOR THE ENCOURAGEMENT, AND
LEADERSHIP. GOD bless,
Todd

Dear Coach,
Thank you for your support and for fellowship. Keep going strong mate. Your mate Alex

Dear Coach,
Thank you for your support and prayers and I look forward. And I know God has inspired to work for us in the future.
DOVE

Dear Coach,
Thank you for all that full season. Also thank you for always. Merry Christmas

You're always so kind
and thoughtful,
it's difficult to say,
How much appreciation
this 'Thank You'
brings your way.

Merry Christmas

Coach, thanks
for everything
and for a great
opportunity,

Chris R. Harrell   Rob McElhenn

Jeremy

250

Coach,

I want to thank you
for the many things you have
done for me. Because of
you it has ~~time~~ allowed me to experience
so many great things, I
have enjoyed the times with
the golf team, and with
you. You ~~a~~ truly represent
God in all that you do,
something that hasn't gone
unnoticed. Thank you for
everything

Jon Wolfe

Operation Outreach

Thanks to my best Christian friend, Jim Shaner, who has backed me in every kind of golfing venture for my guys to have more of what was needed to make a college Division-1 golf program happen. How could I ever repay him for his friendship over these past twelve years as Liberty's golf coach would be a fitting epitaph from me to him. Now, Jim has helped me put into print these inaugural 3,000 copies of True Tales of College Golf. *E-mail him at ShanerAuto@AOL.com for great car care.*

It is only fitting that I acknowledge a father who gave of his time (traveled with the team for the two years his son played here at Liberty, having arrived by way of transfer) and of his money to support the program long after his son graduated. In fact, he brought friends of his from hundreds of miles just to help establish Liberty as an Intercollegiate Host for tournaments. Now, his fine JAE Company has contributed to the costs of placing my first book's printing into your hands. His web site is www.JAECompany.com

Operation Outreach

My thanks are extended to Dean Phillips for his support in making this book available. Dean was the first quarterback that Liberty University had, serving four years in that position from 1974-1977. He held the total offense record for ten years. My appreciation toward him goes far beyond his long attachment to Liberty. Having two of his sons play golf for me allowed us to become great friends. What a guy...E-mail: DeanHPhillips@Yahoo.com

I want to thank Brakebush Brothers, Inc. for their help to publish my first 3,000 books. Their Christian principled business practices make me proud to be associated with this family business. They not only have integrity; in my opinion, Brakebush Brothers makes the best precooked and breaded chicken in the food service industry. www.Brakebush.com 1-800-933-2121

Golf courses who helped me publish my first 3,000 copies and who will be stocking *True Tales of College Golf* are:

Golf Course	Head Pro/Director of Golf
Thistle Golf Course	*Gene Weldon*
Sunset Beach, NC	*800-571-6710*
Boonsboro Country Club	*John Comninaki*
Lynchburg, VA	*434-384-3411*
Winton Country Club	*Eddie Moran*
Amherst, VA	*434-946-7336*
Hat Creek Golf Club	*Bill Singleton*
Brookneal, VA	*434-376-2292*
Mariners Landing Golf Club	*Todd Hammock*
Huddleston, VA	*540-297-7888*
Southern Woods Golf Club	*Rick Kelso*

Home Course for the World Woods Junior Golf Tour

Ivy Hill Golf Club	*Tracy Newman*
Forest, VA	*434-525-2680*
Poplar Forest Golf Course	*Jeffrey Thomas*
Forest, VA	*434-534-9418*
Oakwood Golf Course	*Jeffrey Thomas*
Lynchburg, VA	*434-384-8777*
The Water's Edge Country Club	*Smith Mountain Lake, VA*
The Waterfront Country Club	*Smith Mountain Lake, VA*
The Westlake Golf and CC	*Smith Mountain Lake, VA*

The following golf and book stores helped me place my first 3,000 books in circulation by advertising in them and by stocking *True Tales of College Golf.*

Martins PGA Tour Superstore	*2310 Highway South*
North Myrtle Beach, SC	*843-272-6030*
Martins PGA Tour Superstore	*1400 29th Avenue*
North Myrtle Beach, SC	*843-839-4653*
PGA Tour Superstore	*1005 Holcomb Woods Pkwy*
Roswell, GA	*770-640-0933*
PGA Tour Superstore	*2911 George Busbee Pkwy*
Kennesaw, GA	*Phone TBD*

TO ORDER WITH VISA, MC, OR DISCOVER CARD
1-877-463-9543 FREE CALL
WEB SITE: WWW.THENEWLIFE.COM
$15.00 each • 2-5 Books LESS 5 % • 6-11 Books LESS 20%
Buy 12 for a team or gift LESS 30%
Plus Sales Tax, Shipping & Handling Costs